THE REALITIES OF REDISTRICTING

2 pages

- redistricting periodically is necessary to prevent skewed elections and maintain representatives

- must watch state constitutions

- senitorial distncts (between each state's 2 appointed senators)

- voting rights matter
  - 9 state governments are notorious for racial discrimination in voting
- data is released this year from census that will

- integrity of the community? state verses local effects? - can you be for both?

THE REALITIES OF REDISTRICTING

Following the Rules and Limiting Gerrymandering in State Legislative Redistricting

Jonathan Winburn

LEXINGTON BOOKS

A Division of
Rowman & Littlefield Publishers, Inc.
Lanham • Boulder • New York • Toronto • Plymouth, UK

LEXINGTON BOOKS

A division of Rowman & Littlefield Publishers, Inc.
A wholly owned subsidiary of The Rowman & Littlefield Publishing Group, Inc.
4501 Forbes Boulevard, Suite 200
Lanham, MD 20706

Estover Road
Plymouth PL6 7PY
United Kingdom

British Library Cataloguing in Publication Information Available

Library of Congress Cataloging-in-Publication Data

Winburn, Jonathan, 1977–
The realities of redistricting : following the rules and limiting gerrymandering in state legislative redistricting / Jonathan Winburn.
p. cm.
Includes bibliographical references and index.
ISBN-13: 978-0-7391-2185-6 (cloth : alk. paper)
ISBN-10: 0-7391-2185-5 (cloth : alk. paper)
1. Gerrymandering—United States. I. Title.
JK1341.W56 2008
328.73′073455—dc22 2007047342

Printed in the United States of America

∞™ The paper used in this publication meets the minimum requirements of American National Standard for Information Sciences—Permanence of Paper for Printed Library Materials, ANSI/NISO Z39.48–1992.

To my parents, Donnie and Sheila;
my lovely wife, Amanda;
and our beautiful daughter, Addison

Contents

Acknowledgments

The idea for this project began with notes doodled during a lecture by Dennis F. Thompson at Indiana University during the fall of 2002. Thompson was discussing fair elections and, particularly, his principle of equal respect in the American electoral arena. One aspect of this is the political process of drawing district boundaries. From this initial lecture, I spent the next several years turning those scribbles into my dissertation and now into this book. Whereas most studies of redistricting look at Congress and then usually only the end results, this book explores the process from 2000 to 2002 across eight states from start to finish. One goal is to better understand how the process actually works, and hopefully this is presented in a way that reaches both academics and non-academics alike. The other primary goal is to set a path for reform that could lead to a better democratic process with less political gamesmanship surrounding, theoretically at least, the fairly simple task of drawing lines on a map.

The completion of this project spanned three universities and leaves me with many people to thank for making this book possible. Lots of thanks goes to the Indiana University political science department for great support and to the members of my dissertation committee: Gerald Wright (chair), Marjorie Hershey, Michael Ensley, and Tom Evans. Jerry Wright deserves special thanks for all that he did to help me in graduate school. His National Science

Foundation grants (SES-0094635 and SES-0242571) provided the support necessary to complete the data collection and his mentoring helped turned this into a theoretically interesting project. My colleagues and friends at Indiana gave much needed advice on many different drafts at many different stages of this project. Brian Schaffner, Tracy Osborn, Michael Wagner, Jessica Gerrity, Eric Zeemering, and Jas Sullivan, to name a few, deserve special thanks for comments along the way. More importantly, to all of our friends at IU, thanks for allowing me to have fun and stay sane through the entire process.

My two years at Western Kentucky University allowed me to pare down the dissertation into a manageable book manuscript and update my findings. I would like to thank the department for my time there with a special thanks to Scott Lasley and my research assistants, Jin Gao and Bethaney Adams. I would also like to thank my colleagues at the University of Mississippi, and specifically Greg Day, for helping on the finishing touches.

I would like to thank Lexington Books and Joseph Parry for seeing this project through from our initial meeting at the American Political Association meeting.

In terms of research, I thank the many people from Atlanta to Olympia that I talked to about their redistricting and electoral processes. In each state, I talked to several people that helped me out greatly. From political pundits to GIS data experts, I thank everyone that gave me their time and knowledge. Particularly, I thank Charles Eckstein (Texas), Deputy Attorney General Dennis R. Dunn (Georgia), Ed Sarpolus (Michigan), Joel Miller (Indiana), and Jamie Franklin (Kentucky) for their help.

Finally, my family has always supported me and this project has been no different. While they often only heard some vague talk of a "book I was close to finishing," they always believed in my work. I cannot even begin to thank my parents for all their support throughout my years as a student and now as a professor. My wife Amanda has had the thankless task of following me throughout this process and luckily (I hope) for Addison and the pups, I can now turn more attention back to them. As always, any mistakes are completely my fault.

1

Introduction

Redistricting and Democratic Concerns

"One of the most important factors in the 2002 elections was redistricting, which probably had more to do with the outcome of the elections than any traditional issue—more than education, roads or health care, and maybe even the economy."[1] Many journalistic accounts of the 2000 round of redistricting repeat this sentiment as politicians, citizen groups, pundits, and journalists stress the crucial role redistricting plays in the political system. Politicians themselves generally acknowledge the importance of redistricting and the potential partisan implications, but rarely as openly as a Democratic chairman preparing the new districting plan for a Democratic-led county board in Illinois, who said, "We are going to shove it [the district map] up your f— ass and you are going to like it, and I'll f— any Republican I can."[2] To many politicians and pundits, the partisan implications of redistricting are one of the most important issues on the political agenda.

For example, Jim Nicholson, former chairman of the Republican National Committee commented, "The winners [those who gain control of redrawing the maps] are going to determine the political landscape in at least the first decade of the next millennium, because they are the people who are going to preside over the process of reapportionment and redistricting of their respective states as a result of the 2000 census."[3] Former Ohio State

Representative Vernon Sykes (D-Akron) commented on a key question between redistricting and representation when he said, "The way you draw district lines . . . really controls or directs the advocacy of the representative."[4] Redistricting is a multi-faceted, complex process that often comes down to the common denominator of who has the power to control the process and how those in control translate their power into favorable electoral outcomes.

In addition to being a question of interest to politicians, redistricting is a fundamentally important question for social scientists. Given the complexity of the process, there are many questions to ask and many ways to study redistricting. For example, questions of the role and influence of racial redistricting dominated much of the courts' dockets and studies throughout the 1990s[5] in a similar way that the effect of reapportionment had a central place in the literature in the 1960s and 1970s.[6] A string of court decisions in the 1990s appeared to set the stage for large-scale partisan redistricting in the 2000s, as one expert suggested, "The 2000 round will be characterized as the rejuvenation of partisanship."[7]

The Self-Interest Problem

The role of redistricting in the American political system has important normative and theoretical implications for the health of the American democratic system. "The character of our democracy is at stake in how we elect our representatives as much as in which representatives we elect and what laws they enact."[8] In fact, democracy does not exist without elections. For a democracy to endure, elections must not only take place, but be held in a free, open, and competitive manner where citizens' voices can be heard. The American electoral system promotes these types of elections with two strong and viable parties competing with candidates able to not only represent their party's message, but their own individual views in hopes of persuading the voting electorate. Voters, in turn, cast their ballots with the hope that their candidate will win, but with the knowledge that their vote will count and they exercised their rightful power in a democracy.

However, some concern exists over the voters' ability to control their democracy. Redistricting presents one concern with the basic fear that elections may be made a process "in which the representatives have selected the people" rather than one "in which the people select their representatives."[9] The judges in *Vera v. Richards* expressed this sentiment in regards to gerrymandering in the 1990s Texas congressional districts, but highlight a broader concern in legislative control over redistricting and one that is a general concern in terms of popular sovereignty over elections. The American electoral system is particularly vulnerable to this concern, as control of redistricting is fundamentally a partisan and political matter.[10]

The idea of legislators having the power to undermine popular sovereignty is not a new concern limited to modern redistricting. James Madison and John Locke are among other philosophers who have struggled with this problem. Locke's concerns center on the ability of citizens to choose their representatives with fair and equal rules. In his Second Treatise, he argues, "People shall choose their representatives based on just and undeniably equal measures."[11] He also places an importance on timely reform to electoral rules to allow for the fairest possible elections. In terms of legislative representation, Locke's view translates into timely redistricting every decade to create equally populated districts drawn under fair and equal rules for all citizens. If the rules are just, then the outcomes are fair.

Perhaps James Madison best espoused the concerns of legislative control over popular sovereignty in his writings and speeches around the time of the Constitutional Convention. Madison trusted the "normal process of representation" in situations where representatives share a common interest with their constituents, not one in which they "have a personal interest distinct from that of their constituents."[12] Madison saw a conflict of interest between representatives and constituents in decisions that involved future membership in the representative institution. Madison recognized when representatives decide questions of their fate or of their party that a potential, while not necessarily definite, conflict exists with their constituents. Madison saw the most danger in the desire for incumbent legislators to protect their institutional practices and arrangements regardless of constituent desires. Dennis Thompson provides an excellent overview of Madison's writings on the topic and produces what he calls the Madison Proviso. The Madison Proviso states "no democratic institution should have the final authority to determine the rules or settle the disputes about its own membership."[13]

Based on the Madison Proviso, redistricting has the potential to undermine popular sovereignty in several important ways. When faced with redrawing their own district boundaries, legislators may favor individual incumbent protection, but they can also attempt to improve the fortunes of their own party or even attempt partisan collusion to protect institutional stability. The most common concerns revolve around a conflict of interest that legislators have in preserving their seats and electoral safety and party leaders have in preserving the majority or attempting to add to the majority in the legislature. Another potential conflict with constituent desires exists when party leaders work together to protect all incumbents against challenges in an attempt to keep their coalitions in place. The most common conflicts in redistricting are incumbent protection and partisan gerrymandering. However, institutional collusion also occurs. In the latest round of redistricting, Tennessee presents a good example of collusion where the controlling Democrats agreed to a bipartisan incumbent protection plan in hopes of gaining concessions from the Republicans on their ongoing budget battle.[14] Regardless of which outcome legislators attempt to protect, this may be taking power away from the voters and their popular sovereignty over elections. This power did not go unnoticed by the editors of the *Chattanooga Times Free Press*:

> It's against the law to steal your vote. For the most part, legislators of honor would not do it just as a matter of conscience, even without law. But strangely, there are many political parti-

> sans who have no hesitation whatsoever about taking action that steals the representation that your vote is supposed to assure you. They do it by rigging election districts to produce predetermined results.[15]

Or by one *St. Petersburg Times* columnist who railed against legislative redistricting:

> There is nothing the Legislature does—except, perhaps, when it is whoring for the telephone companies—for which it is less accountable to the voters. Any other districting method would be an improvement. Even a roomful of chimpanzees with crayons. They, at least, would be innocent of malice and self-interest.[16]

Martin Dyckman summed up quite succinctly the normative threat presented here, "You didn't choose your legislators. They chose you."[17] Legislative control of redistricting presents a frightening normative threat for the health of the American democratic system, but is this a real or perceived threat? Are legislators able to take their control of the redistricting process and manipulate electoral boundaries to essentially gain their desired outcomes, whether it is to protect themselves, create gains for their parties, or keep institutional stability between the parties?

Or, is this democratic threat simply theoretical due to the practical limitations and constraints found within the American system and process of redistricting. Despite these concerns over control of the democratic system, we know very little about how our system of redistricting either exploits or protects the voters. Given the tradition of allowing states to devise their own electoral rules, the country does not have one system of redistricting. Instead, America has fifty distinct systems where each state devises their own rules and methods for handling the decennial undertaking. The purpose of this book is to delve into the varying rules and systems across the country to determine if the states already have constraints in place that limit political manipulation of popular sovereignty.

The Research Questions

Can redistricting determine electoral outcomes? If so, how is this accomplished and what factors make it more likely, and if not, what constrains or limits the influence of redistricting? Also, what difference does it make who controls redistricting? These are the fundamental research questions that I look at in this book. To answer these questions, I examine state legislative redistricting from the period after the release of the 2000 census through the 2002 elections. While much has happened since the 2002 elections, I focus on the two-year period in which most of the redistricting action takes place across the country. Therefore, I address the issue from that time frame and, where appropriate, discuss important developments since 2002. Given the normative problem, I do not address congressional redistricting since members of the House do not have direct control over their district's fate. Further, within this state legislative focus, I do not analyze all fifty states. Instead, I examine eight theoretically appropriate cases to complete an in-depth study of the process rather than a more general analysis across the country. My approach peels back the complexities of redistricting in an attempt to understand not only the final electoral outcomes produced, but also the important steps that led to the outcomes. Overall, my findings, within the context of my theoretical framework, uncover important institutional facets and constraints to consider when discussing the health of the American democratic system and potential reforms to the redistricting process.

A Look Ahead

In chapter 2, I lay out a redistricting theory based on the incentives and constraints built into the process and provide the framework for my research design. In this chapter, I establish this theory by first reviewing the political science research and court rulings on redistricting. Next, I discuss the primary incentives and constraints remappers[18] face. In terms of the incentives,

I argue the partisan composition and electoral competition of a legislature is the primary impetus for the type of redistricting attempted. Based on these factors, I discuss the various gerrymandering strategies remappers may use and the expectations of each of these theories. I then turn my attention to the constraints that may limit remappers from reaching their gerrymandering goals. I emphasize five broad factors in this theory. These are the control of the process, control of government, use of traditional districting principles, potential court involvement, and the use of coterminous districts. After discussing how these incentives and constraints theoretically influence redistricting, I examine how each factor applies throughout all fifty states. This provides an overview of the redistricting environment throughout the country. In terms of the research design, I select my specific cases for analysis and lay out the general hypotheses. I then provide a detailed account of the methodology used for testing the influence of constraints on political gerrymandering. In selecting the cases, I place these states in the context of the theoretical incentives and constraints discussed earlier in the chapter. I choose states that fall into what I call the primary division of redistricting control: who controls the remapping and partisan control of government. This division leads to the four typologies: (1) legislative remapping and unified partisan control of government; (2) legislative remapping and divided partisan control of government; (3) partisan commission remapping; and (4) neutral commission[19] remapping. Within each typology, I select two states based on key theoretical variations for a total of eight states examined in this book. I discuss my general hypotheses for the redistricting outcomes within the context of this typology and the specific constraints within each state selected.

After selecting the cases, the remainder of the chapter provides the framework for how I answer my research questions. I begin by discussing the data used throughout the study. I then focus on the methodology used to answer each of the research questions. In this section, I discuss the various methods used in past studies, how my data collection allows for a more specific analysis, and the specific methods I utilize. This chapter serves as the template for the four empirical chapters. In each of those chapters, I follow the general outline prescribed in this chapter.

Chapters 3 to 6 are the empirical analyses. Each chapter includes two states that fit within the key divisions of redistricting control. Each state provides an interesting historic and current redistricting situation. The first of these chapters looks at redistricting under unified government-legislative control in Georgia and Michigan. The Georgia case shows partisan gerrymandering run amuck. In 2002, the Democrats faced relatively few institutional constraints and were able to manipulate the new maps to their clear advantage. However, other factors in the state, namely population shifts, limited the translation of this partisan gerrymander into electoral gains. The Michigan case shows how constraints can successfully limit partisan gerrymandering. Despite the Republicans' control of the process, the well-defined rules within the state limited their ability to gain a definite advantage.

Chapter 4 is the divided government-legislative control chapter. In this chapter, the remappers in Indiana and Kentucky had similar goals, but faced different constraining environments. In Indiana, the state provides few constraints and the House Democrats were able to successfully draw maps to their advantage. In Kentucky, a specific constitutional rule severely limited the Senate Republicans from implementing a partisan gerrymander. The next two chapters move to commission control. In chapter 5, I examine the partisan commissions in Texas and Ohio. In Texas, the Republicans were able to parlay few constraints and a favorable electoral environment into a successful and far-reaching partisan gerrymander. In Ohio, the specific and well-defined constraints limited the Republicans from reaching all of their specific districting goals. The final empirical chapter looks at the neutral commissions in Washington and Idaho. This chapter highlights the effectiveness of neutral commissions in limiting partisan gerrymandering. I also show these commissions did not necessarily function as expected, and implemented bipartisan plans in spite of the partisan goals of the commissioners. The heavily constrained process limited partisan gerrymandering, but did not remove partisanship from the process.

One finding that emerges from each of these chapters is the important role of constitutional rules, no matter who controls the process and the rather conditional nature of the extra-constitutional constraints. In particular, I show the significant role of traditional districting principles. Specifically, the principle against splitting political subdivisions plays a key function in constraining the remappers from gerrymandering.

Chapter 7 is the concluding chapter. In this chapter, I bring together the results from the four previous chapters and discuss the various redistricting reform movements across the country. Based on my findings, I prescribe a practical path for limiting redistricting abuses. I argue that specific constitutional rules are the key to limiting partisan gerrymandering and discuss the pros and cons of commission redistricting. I conclude by returning to the normative problem. I argue redistricting may hinder popular sovereignty, but the conditions must be ripe for this to occur. Overall, remappers do not have the freedom to hinder popular sovereignty that many people assume, but at the same time, in many states, the potential for using partisan gerrymandering to limit the electorate's power over the system remains.

Notes

1. Tim Storey, "2002 State Legislative Elections," *Spectrum: The Journal of State Government* 76 (2003): 7–11.

2. Richard L. Engstrom, "The Post-2000 Round of Redistricting: An Entangled Thicket within the Federal System," *Publius: The Journal of Federalism* 32 (2002): 51–70. Note: Dashed included in the original.

3. Center for Voting and Democracy, "Revealing Quotes about Redistricting," 2001, http://www.fairvote.org/op_eds/revealquotredist.htm#litigation (accessed 19 Jun. 2005).

4. Center for Voting and Democracy, "Revealing Quotes."

5. See, for example, David Epstein and Sharyn O'Halloran, "Measuring the Electoral and Policy Impact of Majority-Minority Voting Districts: Candidates of Choice, Equal Opportunity, and Representation," *American Journal of Political Science* 43 (1999): 367–95; and Carol Swain, *Black Faces, Black Interests: The Representation of African-Americans in Congress* (Cambridge, Mass.: Harvard University Press, 1993).

6. See, for example, Gordon Baker, *The Reapportionment Revolution* (New York: Random House, 1967); and Robert Erikson, "Malapportionment, Gerrymandering, and Party Fortunes," *American Political Science Review* 66 (1972): 1234–45.

7. Ronald Weber, "Emerging Trends in State Legislative Redistricting," *Spectrum: The Journal of State Government* 75 (2002): 13–15.

8. Dennis Thompson, *Just Elections: Creating a Fair Electoral Process in the United States* (Chicago: University of Chicago Press, 2002).

9. *Vera v. Richards*, 861 F. Supp. 1304 (S.D. Tex.) (1994).

10. David Butler and Bruce Cain, *Congressional Redistricting: Comparative and Theoretical Perspectives* (New York: MacMillan, 1992).

11. John Locke, *The Second Treatise of Government*, ed. Thomas P. Peardon (New York: Macmillan, [1690] 1952), 91.

12. Thompson, *Just Elections*. See also: Max Farrand, *The Records of the Federal Convention of 1787* (New Haven, Conn.: Yale University Press, 1966).

13. Thompson, *Just Elections*, 134.

14. Duren Cheek and Bonna de la Cruz, "Passed House Remap Plan Easier on GOP," *Nashville Tennessean*, 11 January 2002.

15. "Stealing Your Representation," *Chattanooga Times Free Press*, 3 January 2002.

16. Martin Dyckman, "In Florida, We Don't Choose Our Legislators, They Choose Us," *St. Petersburg (Florida) Times*, 12 October 2003.

17. Dyckman, "In Florida."

18. Throughout this book, I use the term remappers to refer to those in control of redistricting. I use this as a general term to refer to those in control regardless of institutional or partisan affiliation.

19. Throughout the book, I refer to neutral commissions and bipartisan commissions interchangeably.

2

An Incentive and Constraint Approach to Understanding Redistricting

This chapter discusses the theory and methods involved in this book. For readers only interested in the outcomes, chapters 3 to 6 provide those. In this chapter, I set up a theory of redistricting that examines the common strategies involved in the process and then focus on the potential constraints that may limit or help the successful implementation of these strategies. I then provide an overview of the legislative redistricting following the 2000 Census and conclude with a discussion of the methods used to answer the theoretical questions.

The partisan success legislators generate during redistricting is mixed and studies have yet to identify clearly under what circumstances remappers can be successful in either implementing their preferred plans and then when these plans accomplish the desired outcomes.[1] Many factors go into redistricting, making it a complex process to study effectively. Before I jump into the complexities of the process in individual states, I need to address the theoretically most important factors that are applicable, at least to some degree, to all states. The simplest version of this model breaks down into two key components: incentives to gerrymander and obstacles toward gerrymandering.

The Incentives

Every legislator must deal with the two primary factors of their individual reelection goals and the partisan goal of maximizing seats. Ideally, an individual legislator wants to have an individually safe district and have their party hold a majority of the seats as each of these have important consequences for the ability of a legislator to pursue their agenda within the institution. David Mayhew's seminal work *Congress: The Electoral Connection* assumes reelection is the primary goal of all legislators and this assumption continues to be a dominant standard in work on legislative behavior.[2] For the reelection seeking legislator redistricting presents an opportunity to increase their chances by improving their district to match their electoral needs. In this manner, legislators should seek the protection of an incumbent gerrymander to the extent possible. However, legislators are also partisans and must pursue partisan goals as well. The dominant goal of partisans during redistricting is to gain seats to become the majority, increase the number of seats they hold, or after some point of safety, simply maintain their advantage.[3]

However, the ideal situation discussed above does not usually play out in reality, and the two goals may present a conflict on the legislator's incentives to either protect themselves or help the party.[4] To determine how legislators should balance these goals, I look at the party balance in a state. Simply, in competitive states where the majority party could change with the loss of a few seats, legislators should pursue a partisan gerrymander and in those noncompetitive states where a partisan shift is unrealistic, legislators can be more concerned with self-preservation than the goals of the party. The key feature in the model is interparty competition within a state. V. O. Key in his description of the democratic ills of the one-party South paints interparty competition as the driving force behind a healthy representative system.[5]

The redistricting literature clearly demonstrates the importance of competition in the strategies of remappers during the redistricting process.[6] In competitive states, the partisans in control are more likely to develop a plan that helps their party stay in the majority, a partisan gerrymander, and, when one party dominates a legislature, redistricting is less likely to produce a partisan dispute or drastic changes in the district boundaries and is more likely to produce a plan that protects incumbents.[7] Partisan gerrymandering is more likely in competitive states with more cohesive parties fighting for majority control. While incumbent gerrymandering will be more likely in noncompetitive states where the party structure tends to break down and the utility is lessened for the party to fight for new seats. These two factors are both important for legislators controlling their own electoral districts and what types of plans they should attempt to implement.

While the general goals of gerrymandering focus on the overall changes generated by new maps, the strategic focus is on how to shift individual districts to achieve these goals. The dominant theory of gerrymandering that emerges in the redistricting literature focuses on the incentives and strategies for states to "pack and crack" to achieve partisan goals or protect incumbents.[8] The third primary strategy is one of a neutral strategy that is most likely employed in states with bipartisan commissions. This strategy does not attempt to partisan gerrymander or protect incumbents, but redistricts on some other criteria.[9] From these three situations, I examine three "pure" strategies (partisan, incumbent/institutional protection, and neutral), or strategies which focus on only one goal of gerrymandering.

Individual districts fall into four theoretical categories: (1) electorally safe, majority party controlled districts (Type 1 districts); (2) electorally competitive, majority party districts (Type 2 districts); (3) competitive, minority party districts (Type 3 districts); and (4) safe, minority party districts (Type 4 districts).[10] Figure 2.1 highlights the ideal changes remappers would implement under various gerrymandering strategies.[11]

The first strategy is the partisan gerrymander. Under partisan gerrymandering, the party in control of the process, whether it be the legislature or a partisan commission, attempts to redraw the maps to maximize the seats gained by their party. Under this condition, the remappers should shift supporters in their safe districts (Type 1) into competitive districts. Type 1 districts will become less safe, but will keep enough partisan supporters to avoid electoral defeat. The competitive districts controlled by the majority party (Type 2) should become safer by most likely gaining partisan support from Type 1 districts or supporters from the minority-controlled districts, where possible. The goal is to secure the partisan control of these districts. Safe minority districts (Type 4) should become safer as the majority party recognizes these districts as ones they cannot win and concede them to the out party. The controlling party should attempt to waste minority party votes by packing them into as safe districts as possible.

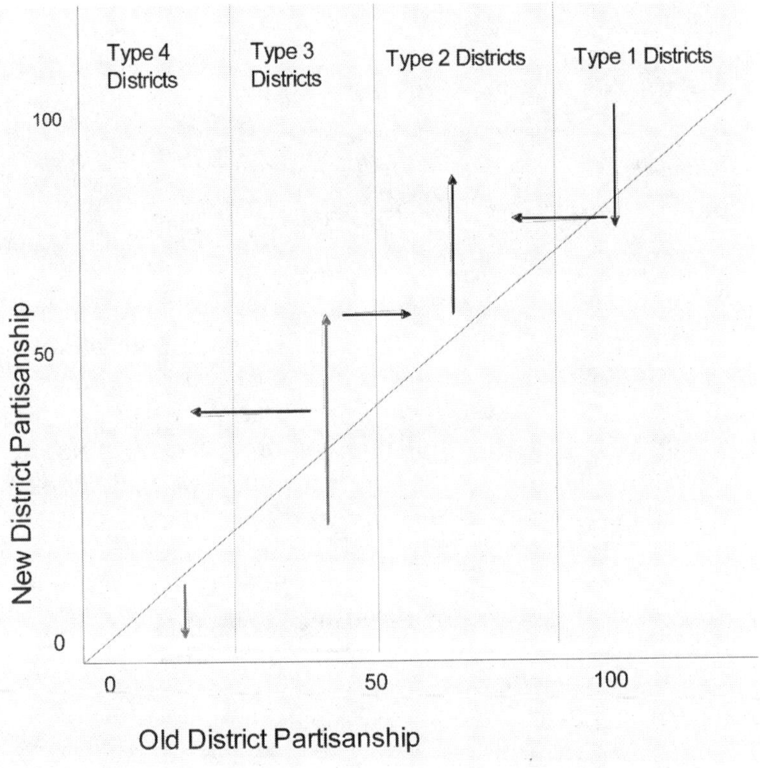

Figure 2.1a. Ideal Partisan Gerrymandering Strategy
District partisanship represents the base district vote for the controlling party. Horizontal line represents the "no change" line between old and new districts.

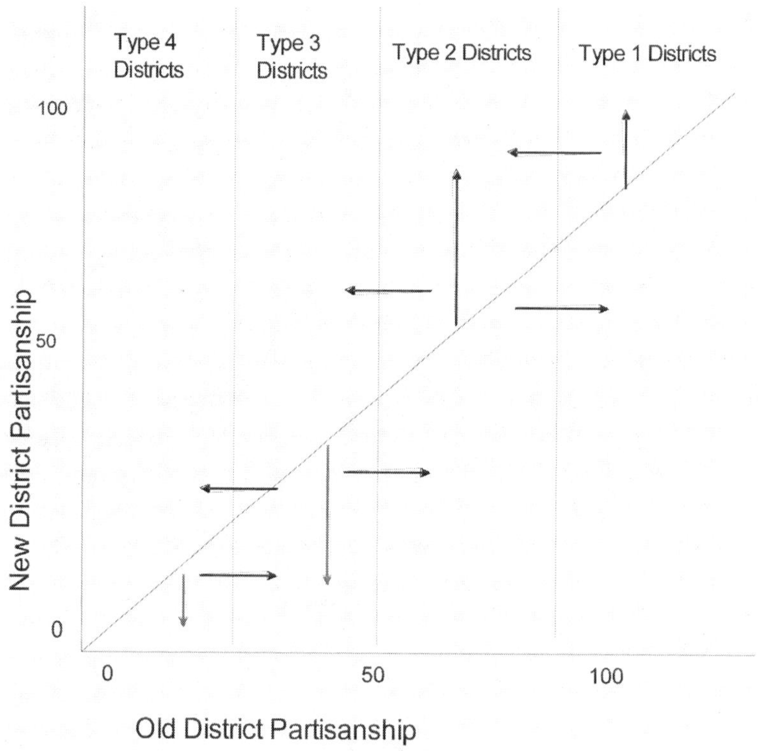

Figure 2.1b. Ideal Incumbent Gerrymandering Strategy
District partisanship represents the base district vote for the controlling party. Horizontal line represents the "no change" line between old and new districts.

The focus for the controlling party should be on the competitive-minority party districts (Type 3). There are two main strategies when deciding what to do with these districts. The first would be to systematically make each of these districts a little safer for the controlling party with the hope that the additional partisan support is enough to pick up some of these seats. The other strategy would be to target a few select districts and pack them full of partisan supporters. In this case, the remaining Type 3 districts will either stay relatively unchanged or a few may even become packed with minority party supporters pushing them into the Type 4 category. The overall goal is for the controlling party to gain seats. Thus, they should attempt to maneuver the Type 3 districts in a manner most conducive for seat maximization.

Overall, under a partisan gerrymander the controlling party should expect to win all Type 1 and Type 2 districts (given they were able to increase their partisan safety) and lose all Type 4 districts. Type 3 districts are the toss-ups under this strategy as the controlling party should improve their chances either in small increments in as many of these districts as possible or greatly increase their chances in a few targeted seats.

The second "pure" strategy is a plan of incumbent/institutional protection. I am including the institutional term because this strategy focuses on protecting the status quo by helping all incumbents regardless of party. This strategy most likely occurs under legislative control with divided government. Individual legislators have the most to gain from incumbent protection and may favor this strategy to partisan gerrymandering under certain conditions. One such example of legislative collusion comes from Tennessee where the Democrats who controlled redistricting made a deal with the Republicans to put forth a plan to protect all incumbents, to the extent possible, in exchange for concessions on the ongoing budget battle.[12]

With this strategy, all district types should generally see changes that make them safer. The most competitive districts (Type 2 and Type 3) should see the most changes with Type 1 and Type 4 districts undergoing less change. There are a couple of scenarios for how each district type could become safer. The first involves Type 1 and Type 4 districts giving up some safety to help their partisan counterparts in Type 2 and Type 3 districts, respectively. However, in most cases, incumbents do not like losing partisans regardless of their electoral safety and may be reluctant to provide much help. The other scenario for promoting institutional stability is for the competitive districts to trade partisan safety. In this case, the Type 1 and Type 4 districts should undergo few changes and Type 2 and Type 3 districts should swap partisan support where possible. In either case, the purpose is to create safe seats held by incumbents from both parties, with the aim being uncompetitive elections where few incumbents face the possibility of defeat at the polls.

The final "pure" strategy is that of neutral redistricting which is most likely under bipartisan commissions. In this strategy, there should be no systematic pattern of change based on district types, as the focus is not on partisan gain or incumbent protection. Rather, the commissions should, theoretically at least, consider neutral factors such as population change and traditional districting principles. Rules, in most bipartisan commissions, prohibit the consideration of incumbent protection and partisan factors, and hence constitute another safeguard against gerrymandering. District changes should occur irrespective of district type as the emphasis is not on partisan control, but rather on other factors that either apply to both parties (or incumbents) equally or, most likely, do not even consider partisanship (or incumbent standing).

While the three "pure" strategies lay the foundation for gerrymandering theory and allow for a clear understanding of the motives behind the process, it is also important to consider the most common "mixed" strategies that emerge from these. These mixed strategies add a layer of complexity to the theory, but at the same time bring us a step closer to the reality of redistricting. Very few cases ever fall into a situation where achieving the goals of a "pure" strategy is feasible. There are many derivations of how these strategies can mix, but I will focus on the most common of these strategies and provide more details on the derivations in the following chapters. Most important for my theoretical focus of how effectively constraints can limit gerrymandering is how the neutral strategies mix, or most often, work against the goals of both the partisan and incumbent strategies.

Perhaps the most common of these "mixed" strategies is a combination of partisan gerrymandering and incumbent protection. In many cases, the controlling party has to walk a fine line between trying to maximize their partisan goals while keeping not only their incumbents happy, but also producing plans agreeable enough that the minority party will not obstruct the process. In this situation, the controlling party should focus on improving their competitive districts (Type 2) with partisan help from their safe districts (Type 1), however, they may not be able to borrow as much electoral support from their safe districts as most incumbents are risk averse and do not like to lose any support, no matter their safety.[13] Given the minority party has the ability to obstruct the plans in some manner, the controlling party should be careful not to greatly upset the minority party incumbents. As such, they may only target a few select Type 3 districts (minority controlled competitive districts), perhaps ones where they know ahead of time the incumbent is not running for reelection or by making a deal with the minority leadership. The controlling party is forced to make strategic considerations between electoral security, attempting to gain seats, and packing minority party districts.[14]

Within the partisan gerrymandering strategy is a special and important place for the strategies of racial gerrymandering.[15] During the 1990s racial redistricting emerged as one of the most important redistricting issues, especially in the South. As such, the role that majority-minority districts play has become a key factor remappers must consider. The partisan impact of majority-minority districts has received much attention over the past decade with two primary schools of thought emerging. The first is that racial gerrymandering is generally an indirect cause of Democratic losses and that Republican gains have occurred independent of redistricting.[16] The second, and more compelling finding, is that by packing black voters into majority-minority districts more minorities benefit to the detriment of the overall success of the Democrats.[17] In this scenario, the Republicans benefit greatly from majority-minority districting as the packing of minority voters, who traditionally are strong Democratic voters, into a few concentrated districts allows Republicans to gain more seats overall.

During the 2000 round of redistricting, Republicans pushed the strategy of maximizing majority-minority districts in several states in hopes of gaining more seats overall. For example, in Arkansas, the NAACP supported Republican Governor Mike Huckabee's proposal to add additional majority-minority districts; while the state's Legislative Black Caucus argued against the NAACP. The Democratically controlled redistricting commission passed a plan with fewer majority-minority districts then Huckabee's plan and immediately faced legal challenges from the NAACP.[18]

Racial gerrymandering has a direct influence on the strategies and goals of partisan gerrymandering, and puts Democratic remappers into an interesting situation. Under Democratic control, majority-minority districts will increase the number of Type 1 districts by packing black voters into as many districts as possible and "wasting" partisan support that the remappers could spread among competitive districts. The "bleaching" of the surrounding districts often leads to increase Republican support and an overall increase in both Type 3 and Type 4 districts. Overall, a focus on majority-minority districts should guarantee a specific amount of safe Democratic districts and may hinder the remapper's ability to support their competitive districts (Type 2) and/or target competitive Republican districts (Type 3). Under Republican control, the strategy of racial gerrymander plays into the remapper's partisan goals. Republicans should attempt to pack as many Type 4 districts (safe-Democratic) into majority black districts as they can to increase their overall chances in both the marginal Type 2 and Type 3 districts. In states with large minority populations, a Republican partisan gerrymander may resemble a racial gerrymander without necessarily focusing on improving minority representation. Overall, racial gerrymandering adds an interesting variable to the mix of partisan redistricting strategies.

The final "mixed" strategy is one that combines the neutral strategy with the desired strategies of the remappers. In most cases, remappers who desire either a partisan or an incumbent gerrymander do not want to combine the constraints of neutral strategies into their plans. However, these are factors they must consider, to some degree, in every state. A "pure" neutral strategy does not favor one party or allow for preferential treatment to incumbents and should not produce any systematic effects for the different district types. When remappers must incorporate neutral factors into their strategies, be it pure partisan or incumbent or some combination of the two, these factors should mitigate the outcomes. The new maps should not produce as strong of changes to the district types as the "pure" strategies suggest.

This goes directly to the heart of this study. Do the constraints in place in a state influence the outcomes of the plans and limit the ability of the remappers to implement their partisan goals? If so, I should find evidence of the constraints working throughout the states. This evidence will vary depending on the state and the constraints in place, but the outcomes should be similar. The district changes should reflect these constraints, whether it be to promote competition, uphold political subdivisions, and/or accommodate population shifts, across the district types and not have outcomes dictated by the theories of partisan and/or incumbent gerrymandering.

These strategies assume various incentive structures for those in control of the process. The key factor is the competitiveness or party balance under most conditions with the exception of when a bipartisan commission is in control. Under this condition, some other neutral criteria replace the partisan and/or incumbent goals produced by the party balance in a state. This discussion looks at the strategies remappers may pursue under the assumption they can achieve what they want free from constraints. However, the constraints in the process are the key theoretical limitation to the successful achievement of these goals.

The Constraints

Competition may structure the goals of legislator's during the redistricting process, but legislators must contend with several important obstacles in attempting to turn those goals into reality. State legislative redistricting has two important factors that separate it from congressional redistricting. The courts general allowance of deviation from absolute population equality and a greater emphasis on traditional districting principles provide state legislative remappers with an interesting set of obstacles to maneuver when redrawing district boundaries.

Essentially, redistricting is fifty separate processes with no two exactly the same; however, several key factors run through all of these processes and how legislators attempt to reach their incentives. I focus on five broad factors that reach across all fifty states:

- Control of the process
- Control of government
- Institutional factors
- Past court rulings and the likelihood of court involvement
- Use of traditional districting principles

Control of the Process

The traditional American method of redistricting vests the legislature with the authority to redraw legislative boundaries. Throughout history, most states treated redistricting as any other type of legislation with gubernatorial veto power being the main outside check on the legislature. This method builds an inherently political bias into the process.[19] Most other countries that use "first past the post" electoral systems have recognized this bias and have switched away from legislative or political control to a commission format. The driving reason behind these switches was to take the direct power of redistricting out of the legislators' hands by vesting it into a body designed to be free of the conflicts of interests inherent with legislative redistricting.[20]

Back in the states, commissions are the most common and seemingly practical alternative to legislative redistricting.[21] While supporters of commissions admit it is not a perfect solution and one that is open to many of the dangers of legislative redistricting, it should at the very least mitigate the power of the legislature in the process. Theoretically, at least, the hope is that commissions will be fair and neutral bodies that do not draw lines for partisan gain but rather produce maps that are fair toward both parties and, more importantly, take better account of constituency sovereignty.

The use of commissions throughout the states varies. Currently, twenty-two states use commissions in some form during state legislative redistricting, and of those twenty-two, twelve enacted the plans used in the 2002 elections. States use commissions in three main capacities: as the main body in charge of the process, as advisory bodies to the legislature, and as backups in case the legislature fails to complete the process. Twelve states put the initial authority in the hands of a commission (nine of the twelve enacted plans) while four states use them in an advisory manner and six are used as backups (half of which enacted plans). There are also three main forms of membership used for the commissions: the bipartisan tiebreak method, general partisan methods, and the statewide official method. Ten of the states use a bipartisan tiebreak method in which the parties appoint an even number of members and those members then select a chair of the committee. Six of the states use the general partisan method in which there are either an odd number of members appointed from various offices or an even number without the appointment of a chair. Colorado is a good example of a partisan commission in which of the eleven members appointed, two each come from the party leaders in the legislature, three from the executive, and four from the judiciary. The partisan split could be 9–2 if the executive and the judiciary appoint clearly partisan members to side with two of the members from the legislature. Finally, six states use the statewide official method in which the members come from various elected statewide offices. The most common being the governor, secretary of state, and attorney general. Oregon is an interesting case since it does not have an official commission, but if the legislature fails to act as it did in 2002, then the process falls completely to the secretary of state's office. Of these methods, the bipartisan tiebreak appointment method is closest to a neutral commission as both the statewide and partisan appointment methods can easily give one party control over redistricting.

Clearly, there is no one set method to the use of commissions across the states. In all cases, legislators are losing power over redistricting to a third party; however, not all commissions necessarily take away the partisanship from the process. While each commission format takes away direct legislative control over the process, it does not necessarily eliminate partisan influence. The commissions made of statewide officials or members appointed by the leadership give one party the majority of the members. Only the bipartisan commission format takes both the direct influence of legislators out of the process and neutralizes party control.

Control of Government

Determining who controls government is a good "first cut at the question of partisan effects of redistricting,"[22] and has received much attention by political scientists. Under divided government, gaining agreement on a redistricting plan should take more compromise between the parties and thus lessen the ability of one party to produce a plan that produces many electoral gains. Under unified government, legislators have an easier time pursuing their strategies as the minority party has no direct control over the process. Studies show that under unified government control of redistricting there is a bias favoring the controlling party.[23]

While partisan control of government does not necessarily guarantee redistricting success it is reasonable to assume that majority party legislators would prefer to work under conditions of unified government in attempts to implement their plans. Divided government is clearly more of a constraint on the process than unified government. While under unified government, there may still be disagreements between party leaders and incumbents over the best type of gerrymander to pursue or over individual district changes, the ability to compromise should be greater with one party in control.

Institutional Factors

Many institutional factors are idiosyncratic to the individual states and as a result, the way in which redistricting law deals with these issues is highly variable across the country. I will address the particular institutional rules of each state in detail in the empirical chapters, but broadly, I consider the potential constraints of using coterminous districts and a single redistricting plan for both chambers within a state.

We usually think of legislative redistricting producing separate maps for a state's upper and lower chambers. However, many states have coterminous boundaries or maps where the house districts are embedded within the senate districts. Commonly, in states without embedded districts the legislature allows each chamber to draw their own plans. For example, in Indiana a longstanding tradition allows each chamber, regardless of partisan control, to draw their plans with little or no interference from the other chamber. However, in states where senators and representatives share a district this forces at least three incumbents (and in some cases more) in each district and leaders from both chambers to become involved in approving one plan for the entire state and not separate plans that can accommodate differing partisan and incumbent needs.

The Legal Environment and the Likelihood of Court Involvement

The courts[24] have set the standards for what states can and cannot do in the redistricting process. As court decisions have evolved over the years, the rulings have left an ambiguous, at best, and sometimes contradictory judicial entanglement for the states to follow when implementing redistricting plans.[25] While the states have primary control over their own redistricting plans, most of the legal constraints placed upon them come from the federal courts. In 1962 when the Supreme Court ruled in *Baker v. Carr*[26] that redistricting was indeed justiciable this opened the proverbial floodgates to judicial intervention and the courts have continually played a major role in establishing redistricting rules ever since. The major requirement established by the Supreme Court in an early line of cases following *Baker* was the basic "one person, one vote" rule that requires strict district population equality on the basis of the U.S. Constitution and equal representation. In a line of cases through the 1980s, the courts firmly established strict population equality as the dominant and overriding factor in congressional redistricting and that no level of population inequality is too small to ignore.[27] However, the courts have not taken such a strict interpretation of population equality with state legislative redistricting. While population equality remains the leading principle, the courts have established a 10 percent standard for population deviation without the states having to defend the constitutionality of the plans.[28] Additionally, the courts have occasionally ruled plans with greater than a 10 percent deviation constitutional if the states justified a rational policy for the deviations.[29]

The courts have also spent time reviewing racial districting mainly in congressional plans. However, the Voting Rights Act (VRA) designed to implement the Fourteenth Amendment by prohibiting district lines that "dilute the vote of protected minorities" or have a "retrogressive" impact on the ability of minority groups to elect candidates of their choice is generally more important than the courts.[30] Section 5 of the Voting Rights Act currently takes on particular importance for nineteen states, as they must present their plan in either whole or part to the Department of Justice for preclearance based on the plans effect on minority voting strength.[31] At the congressional level, cases involving racial interests are subjected to strict scrutiny and the courts generally held in favor of plans involving majority minority districts until the 1993 decision in *Shaw v. Reno*.[32] The *Shaw* decision involving congressional plans in North Carolina was the first time the court struck down a plan on the basis of race being the predominant factor and ruled the state could not make race the only districting factor while ignoring other traditional principles such as compactness and communities of interest in either congressional or state legislative districting.

While the courts have taken an active role in questions of racial districting, they have, for the most part, sidestepped any involvement with partisan gerrymandering. The courts avoided the issue by ruling it was not justiciable until a 1986 case involving Indiana legislative districts. In *Davis v. Bandemer*,[33] the courts finally took up partisan gerrymandering as a justiciable issue by overturning a lower court ruling that the plan was an unfair partisan gerrymander against the Democrats. The Supreme Court ruled the plan was not unconstitutional based on their criteria for a partisan gerrymander. However, they set the criteria so abstract and vague that no plan has ever been ruled a partisan gerrymander under the standard. In a set of cases during the 1990s, the courts sanctioned the use of partisanship as a predominant factor while ruling race could not be used as a predominant factor. From these cases in the 1990s, remappers in 2000 could assume that districting plans "will be safe from invalidation under the standard adopted in *Davis v. Bandemer*" and appear free to assume the courts will not stop them from engaging in complete partisan gerrymandering.[34]

Beyond questions of partisan and racial gerrymandering, recent court rulings have muddied the waters in other important ways. In 1993, the Supreme Court ruled "federal courts are to defer not only to state legislatures, but also to state courts, when those bodies have acted in a timely fashion to consider redistricting."[35] This ruling is important for several reasons. First, it puts the state supreme courts back in the redistricting mix as an important player. Second, it has produced venue battles among litigants that can now decide between federal and state courts when challenging a plan. Third, the ruling puts renewed importance on state and local redistricting policies found in state constitutions and statutes along with past practices built around traditional redistricting principles.

Going into the 2000 round of redistricting, state legislative line drawers had a generally well-established 10 percent population deviation range from which to construct district boundaries. States that fall under section 5 of the Voting Rights Act faced stricter racial requirements than other states, but also had the knowledge that the courts established that race could not be the predominant factor in drawing lines at the expense of other traditional principles. However, the courts have not consistently upheld this position. The remappers also knew the federal courts were unlikely to overturn any plans based on partisan gerrymandering, and they faced the uncertainty of what role state courts would play given the Supreme Court's deference to them in the 1993 *Growe v. Emison* decision.[36] The courts appeared ready to recognize a greater role for traditional districting principles; although some doubt the court's willingness to enforce those principles, or to interpret them in a manner consistent with the principles' formal applications.[37]

Beyond the implications of their rulings, judges are also political actors who have their own incentives and goals involved with the redistricting process as "judges care about the partisan electoral consequences of their decisions and about the jurisprudential consequences."[38] While it may be advantageous for legislators to prefer court involvement if they know for certain the courts would produce a map that helps either their partisan or personal fate, legislators can receive no guarantees of these outcomes. Legislators could possibly win big with the right judicial involvement, but they may also lose big if the court making the final decision favors the other party.

North Carolina presents an excellent example of this from the 2000 redistricting. Early in 2002, the Democratically controlled legislature implemented new plans that appeared to be a partisan gerrymander that would allow them to keep control of the legislature. The Republicans, unhappy with the plans, filed suit in Johnston County Superior Court where Judge Knox v. Jenkins Jr. ruled the Democrats' plan unconstitutional and implemented, with the help of the Republicans, his own maps. The State Supreme Court then stepped in and declared Jenkins' maps to be used for the 2002 elections only, and ordered the legislature to redraw their own maps for the rest of the decade.[39]

Potential court involvement may force legislators to follow the law or the traditional districting principles in a state more so than they otherwise would have. If legislators know the courts may become involved they are more likely to draw constitutionally acceptable plans because, while it will not necessarily lessen the chances of a plan being challenged, it should lessen the chances of it being overturned. The role of the courts is one of the most unknown factors legislators face heading into redistricting. However, one indicator of potential court involvement is how active the courts were in a state from the previous decade. In states where the courts struck down plans or drew plans, legislators know the courts are willing and able participants in the process. On the other hand, in states where there was little judicial activity, legislators may feel as if they have more freedom in drawing the lines.

The Use of Traditional Districting Principles

The term "traditional districting principles" is the judicially recognized term for seven policies or goals that states have used over the years in drawing district boundaries in addition to population equality. While the courts officially recognized these principles in the *Shaw*[40] decisions of the 1990s as race-neutral criteria, line drawers have worked with these, in some form, throughout the history of redistricting.[41] These broadly fit into two categories: geographic and political or legal. They are

- Geographic Principles
  - Compactness
  - Contiguity
  - Preservation of Counties and Political Subdivisions
- Political or Legal Principles
  - Preservation of Communities of Interest
  - Preservation of Prior District Core
  - Protection of Incumbents
  - Compliance with the Voting Rights Act

Compactness is the most discussed of the traditional principles by both the courts and scholars. The courts have recognized that appearances do matter in redistricting and have held that geographic compactness is a guard against all types of gerrymandering. In the 1994 *DeWitt v. Wilson* decision, a federal district court in California found that compactness must serve a "functional" component and that it does not necessarily refer to geometric shapes but to the ability of citizens to relate to each other and their representatives to relate effectively to their constituency.[42] Throughout the years, the courts have relied on a variety of measures from the "eyeball approach" of picking out bizarre districts on the map to some of the two dozen measures developed by social scientists.[43] Neither the courts nor scholars have declared one measure the "best" for judging the compactness of districts. Recent decisions have held only that compactness is an important principle, but have not established a definition for measurement purposes.

The courts have weighed in less on the principles of protecting political subdivisions and communities of interest. Often considered together, political subdivisions are only one of several definitions of communities of interest that may include geographic features, media markets, economic markets, and racial and ethnic neighborhoods.[44] A set standard remains ambiguous, as the courts have not established a concrete definition for what constitutes a community of interest. The courts first recognized this problem in *Carstens v. Lamm*, a challenge to the 1980 Colorado congressional districts, in which the court ruled protecting communities of interest, in whatever appropriate form, was important to consider when equal population was not an issue, but did not provide a definition as they based their ruling in the case on equal population grounds.[45] Recent decisions suggest the courts are not likely to define this criterion either. The Pennsylvania Supreme Court dismissed this principle as too elastic and the Wisconsin Supreme Court acknowledged the importance of considering communities of interest but stated that the court dangerously made decisions based on subjective choices.[46]

The courts have relied on political subdivisions as a more concrete principle in cases over the years, but have not explicitly ruled political units as the only standard for defining a community of interest. While there are various types of local government units from counties and towns to school and special districts, the courts have generally accepted counties (or their equivalent in a few New England states) as an appropriate measure. For state legislative plans only, the courts have ruled on several occasions that population deviations of 10 percent or more are acceptable if these deviations are a necessity to avoid subdividing counties between districts. In the most recent decisions, the courts have upheld not splitting county boundaries in Colorado, but some courts are using loopholes, such as constitutions that say county boundaries can be split only when "absolutely necessary" to not enforce this standard.[47]

The remaining standards appear less controversial and open to challenges. The contiguity of districts has a court accepted definition of being one in which "a person can go from any point within a district to any other point without leaving the district."[48]

The adherence to the Voting Rights Act is well established in terms of racial districting, and the principles of incumbent protection and maintaining district cores have not been prominent in courts decisions up to this point.

With the courts recent decisions in *Shaw v. Reno* and *Growe v. Emison*,[49] the use of traditional districting principles may take on a new importance in redistricting practice. The statutory or constitutional requirement to make districts compact or not to split county subdivisions or communities of interests should serve as a constraint on the remappers. In states with multiple principles either written into the constitution or codified, legislators should find it even more difficult. Overall, the use of these principles should take away some of the uncertainty as to what constitutes acceptable district boundaries and what does not. At the same time, they also decrease the ability of legislators to manipulate maps for partisan gain as specific rules limit the ability to weave district lines throughout the state in attempts to gain a partisan advantage.

However, while the courts appear more willing to enforce the use of these principles, some doubt if this will actually hinder partisan gerrymandering as the courts only vaguely or abstractly refer to implementing these principles without suggesting any substantial measurement criteria. Richard L. Engstrom argues the court rulings from the 1990s may actually backfire and lead to more partisan gerrymandering as "[t]he legal constraints on how districts may be drawn became more ambiguous as a result of these decisions. This ambiguity creates opportunities to try, at least, to manipulate district boundaries for political purposes."[50] In addition, Richard N. Engstrom argues the relationship between geography and voters is a subtle one in which, based on voting turnout, "existing political boundaries are not, perhaps, as essential to the healthy functioning of democracy as some claim."[51]

Having these principles may not necessarily translate into much of a constraint; however, the courts can only apply them in states in which they are actually law. Therefore, the potential constraint only exists in states with these principles in place, and as such, remappers must factor in this potential constraint when drawing their maps. In states without any such laws, remappers are free to pursue plans irrespective of these principles and should be less constrained in drawing the districts.

A Statewide View of the 2000 Redistricting Cycle

Examining each of the individual obstacles legislators face in redistricting provides an initial look at the complexities of the process; however, this does not say much about the overall atmosphere within the states. To do this, in figure 2.2, I combine each of the five obstacles with the main incentive of competition to generalize about the ability of the legislators in each state to control their own electoral fate. The purpose of figure 2.2 is not to provide a hard and fast empirical measure for each of these states but rather to provide a comparative placement

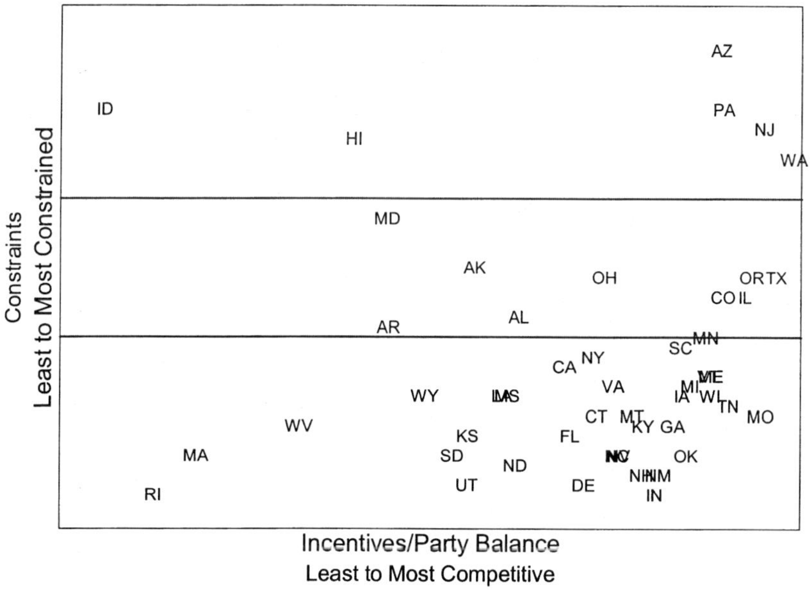

Figure 2.2. Legislative Redistricting Incentives and Constraints

States above the top line all use neutral commissions. States between the top and bottom line use some form of partisan commissions with the exception of Alaska (neutral commission) and Alabama (legislature). In the states below the bottom line, the legislature has primary control of redistricting. Constraints are based on a weighed formula using the five factors discussed in the text.

of the states based on the competition levels of the legislature and the potential constraints against legislative power in redistricting.

The horizontal axis represents the partisan balance in each state, going from left to right from the least to most competitive states. The least competitive states are those with almost complete one party control with the most competitive states being those with an even partisan split (50 percent party balance). My theory predicts that states along the right hand side are more likely to want a partisan gerrymander as majority control is up for grabs. The least competitive states should not be concerned with partisan balance, but are more likely to focus on individual incumbent or institutional goals for the new districts. It is hard to define where the focus on partisan gerrymandering stops and incumbency gerrymandering begins. There is probably no set standard as this line probably shifts depending upon the state and the legislators involved. Most states fall in this gray area, between 55 percent and 65 percent majority control.

The vertical axis represents the combination of the five factors discussed above in how much of a constraint these factors place on legislative control of redistricting. The scale moves from the least constrained at the bottom to the most constrained at the top. Once again, this measure is not designed as an empirical measure, but for use as a comparative ranking. I ranked the constraints in this order of theoretical constraining power: control of process, control of government, likelihood of court involvement, use of traditional principles, and institutional factors. The use of commissions receives the most weight and the horizontal lines represent the distinction between those states above the top line which use bipartisan commissions, and those below the bottom line are all states in which the legislature redrew the maps for 2000. The middle group is mostly states that use a partisan commission format although a few are legislative controlled states. Within these three groups is a variation of the remaining four factors on how constrained the remappers were during the process.

The most constrained states are those that use bipartisan commissions. These states are found along the top of the chart with the more potentially partisan commissions slightly less constrained. Among the legislative states, there is a nice variation with some states found near the line dividing the commission states and some states showing relatively few constraints, such as Indiana and Rhode Island. Overall, this chart suggests that not all attempts at legislative gerrymanders have the same likelihood of success given built-in institutional or potential extra-institutional constraints on the process. If this theory of incentives and obstacles holds then the legislators in highly competitive states like Arizona and Washington did not have much of a chance to enhance their electoral chances while those legislators in the apparently less scrutinized worlds of Indiana and Delaware had much greater opportunities to draw lines to fit their partisan needs. On the other hand, in noncompetitive states such as Idaho and Hawaii sitting incumbents had little influence over their own districts as bipartisan commissions had the duties of redrawing the lines. However, those sitting incumbents in Rhode Island, Massachusetts, and West Virginia appear to have had a much easier time setting themselves up for reelection. Most states do not fit these extremes and fall somewhere in the middle of the obstacle-laden path of redistricting.

The Eight States

Control of redistricting and partisan division within a state provides four theoretical subgroups to select states from: unified legislative control, divided legislative control, partisan commission control, and neutral commission control. In states with traditional legislative control, I select the unified states of Georgia with Democratic control and Michigan with Republican control and the divided states of Indiana and Kentucky. From the commission states, I use the bipartisan states of Washington and Idaho and the partisan states of Texas and Ohio where the Republicans controlled the commissions in both states.

General Expectations

The least constrained situations are where the legislature controls the process in a unified government and the most constrained is when the legislature loses control of the process to a neutral commission designed to disregard partisan and incumbent strategies. The other two categories are not as clear; however, for my normative focus the theoretical distinction works quite nicely. In the divided government case, legislators maintain control of the process but have the roadblock of both parties having control of some part of the process. In this situation, partisan gerrymandering appears more constrained than incumbent gerrymandering. This may actually be the most ideal situation for bipartisan incumbent protection as the parties may prefer the compromise of protecting themselves to pushing partisan agendas. Under partisan commissions, the opposite would appear to be true as the commissioners from outside the legislature should be more concerned with the party's agenda than that of the incumbents. In these situations, partisan gerrymandering could flourish to the detriment of incumbent protection. The power of the constraints in these categories is conditional upon the preferred strategies of the remappers.

My general hypotheses are the states that fall into the unified legislative group will have the fewest constraints to implement the legislature's preferred strategy. States in the divided legislative group will have more constraints than the unified states, but fewer than the commission states. The constraints become more stringent in states with neutral commission control, with these putting the most constraints on legislative strategies. Partisan commissions mitigate direct legislative control of the process but leave partisanship built into the process. In these cases, institutional or incumbent protection plans appear more constrained but partisan strategies may actually flourish.

Examining the specific expectations for the states within each group is a two-step process. First, I discuss the strategic incentives within each state and lay out hypotheses for what type of gerrymander those in control should attempt. Second, I examine the constraints in each state and formulate hypotheses regarding the likelihood of successful implementation of the strategies within each state.

Incentives

Party balance gauges the immediate and primary goals of both the parties and the legislators for maintaining, increasing, or possibly gaining control in the competitive chambers, and in the safe chambers shifting focus away from partisan control to either maintaining the status quo or incumbent protection. Majority control over the past decade provides another way of understanding competition in the legislatures. For the chambers that have switched control, the parties should be much more aware of the potential for either gaining or losing power, while states with one party dominance do not have the need to worry about partisan gerrymandering.

Idaho represents the state with the least competition. The Idaho Republicans held the safest of majorities with 87 percent of the House seats and 91 percent of the Senate seats. Competition for the majority was clearly not a factor in Idaho and represented quite a drastic change from only ten years before where the Democrats and Republicans were tied in the Senate. In the House, the Republicans enjoyed much safer control during the same time period, although, the Democrats held between 35 and 40 percent of the seats before 1994. The other Republican states had greater levels of competition than Idaho. In Ohio, the Republicans held fairly safe majorities in both chambers with just under 60 percent of the seats in the House and 63 percent of the seats in the Senate. After the Democrats lost control of the House in the 1994 Republican Revolution, the Republicans have held steady control. The Republicans held control in Michigan, but in a more competitive environment with only a two-seat advantage in the House and a four-seat advantage in the Senate. Over the previous decade, the Republicans held control of the Senate for the entire time, but did not gain the majority in the House until 1994 after which the Democrats gained power back in 1996 before falling into the minority for the remainder of the decade.

The Democrats enjoyed the majority in both Georgia and Washington. In Georgia, the Democrats were adjusting to life in a competitive environment. In the Senate, they held a tenuous four-seat majority and in the House, the majority appeared safer with a fifteen-seat advantage over the Republicans. However, over the previous decade the Democrats saw a steady decline of their majority in both chambers from over 80 percent in 1988 to their 2000 level of below 60 percent. In both chambers, the Democrats held the majority, but their control was slipping away. The Republicans only needed to gain four seats for the majority in the upper chamber, and needed a fifteen-seat swing (but only 8 percent of the total races) to gain control in the House. In Washington, the competition could not be any closer. The Democrats held the bare thin majority of one seat in both chambers. Throughout the 1990s, the power switched hands on several occasions with even a couple of ties in the House.

Divided government was present in Indiana, Kentucky, and Texas. In Indiana, the Republicans controlled the Senate while the Democrats were holding on to a bare majority in the House. The decade of the 1990s brought a steady increase in Republican safety in the Senate as they gained six seats from 1990 through 2000 to hold thirty-two of the fifty seats. The party balance in the House looked a bit different as the majority changed control twice along with a tie during the decade. Going into redistricting the Democrats held a small three-seat majority. In Kentucky, the Senate is the competitive chamber with the House still being safely Democratic. The Republicans held a one-seat majority in the Senate, the first time the Republicans controlled a chamber in the history of the state. The path to power was similar to many other southern states in the 1990s as the Democrats went from being safely in control in 1990 to being out of power in 2000. In the House, the Democrats held steady control with around 65 percent of the seats throughout the 1990s. Texas showed a similar pattern to most southern states as the legislature went from one-party in 1990 to highly competitive in 2000. The Republicans gained a one-seat majority in the Senate in 1996 and held that slim margin through 2000. In the House, the Democrats saw their power slowly erode throughout the decade until they held a bare three-seat majority in 2000.

Based on partisan competition, redistricting strategies emerge for the eight states. The two unified legislative states both are in a position to attempt partisan gerrymanders. The divided legislative states are in the interesting positions of wanting partisan gerrymanders in one chamber and in more of an incumbent protection situation in the other. The partisan commission states appear split with the Texas Republicans in position to push for a partisan gerrymander while the Ohio Republicans are in a safer position to help their own incumbents while also trying to increase the size of their majority. In the neutral commission states, the Idaho Republicans are clearly safe and have no need for a partisan gerrymander while the Washington Democrats clearly have the need for a partisan gerrymander.

Constraints

Control of the Process

For the ability of the legislators themselves to control their own redistricting destinies, at the very least, they need to draw the new maps. This is the traditional method of redistricting in America and four of the cases still use this method. Georgia, Indiana, Kentucky, and Michigan all use this traditional model and place constitutional and statutory responsibility for redistricting in the hands of the legislature with the governor retaining veto power over the plans, in the same manner of all other legislation in these states.

The other four states use commissions. These states at various points in the process take the power from the legislature and give control to a commission to remap the states' legislative boundaries. While all commissions take the physical control away from the legislature, the potential for partisan influence varies depending upon the type of commission used. These commissions also vary on how the membership is selected, who serves on the commission, and whether or not these bodies have primary responsibility for redistricting or take over after the legislature fails to implement new maps. Each of these factors is state specific and do not necessarily change the theoretical expectations, and I will address these in detail in the later chapters. For now, it is most important to recognize the important theoretical difference between the partisan and bipartisan formats. The states with partisan commissions, Ohio and Texas, set up a process where partisan plans and strategies may thrive. It takes away the direct power for legislators to control their own destinies, but it keeps open the door for legislative influence, especially for the legislators from the party that controls the commission. Partisan commissions should limit bipartisan incumbent protection plans of the sort where the parties agree to protect themselves and essentially protect the status quo. However, these commissions may be more likely to pursue pure partisan gerrymanders as the outside members have little incentive to protect institutional arrangements between the parties.

The legislators from Washington and Idaho are least likely to have influence over the outcomes as these states employ neutral commissions with the specific purposes of limiting both incumbent and partisan influences over the process. In terms of constraints against the ability of legislators to pursue their desired strategies, neutral commissions clearly stand out as the most limiting.

Control of Government

The key division for the legislative states is whether or not the state has unified or divided government. In each of the four legislative states, each chamber produces their own plans drawn by the majority party of the chamber. The chambers then put their plans together as a package for approval by the governor. The divided government implications are clear. In states with unified control, the Democrats in Georgia and the Republicans in Michigan, the majority party should have the clearest path to implementing their preferred strategy. The minority party has little room for influence as the majority should have the votes to pass their plans in both chambers and the likely approval of the governor. The majority should have the relative freedom to pursue any strategy they want, partisan, incumbent, or some mix thereof. The divided states (Indiana and Kentucky) are constrained by the need to work in a bipartisan manner to reach a mutually satisfying plan. In both states, the Democrats should be in a slightly better position as both states had a Democrat in the governor's mansion. However, the Republicans in both states were in a situation to influence the process as they put together the map in the chamber they controlled and approved the other chamber's plan. Under divided government, the ability to pursue a statewide partisan gerrymander appears quite limited while the pursuit of an incumbent gerrymander or a chamber specific partisan gerrymander seems more viable.

The Role of Traditional Districting Principles

The importance traditional districting principles play in legislative redistricting is not all together clear. The courts have not established an unequivocal standard for when these principles must be upheld and when they can be ignored. Theoretically, they should limit the ability to gerrymander, but how much so is hard to quantify. Additionally, we do not know if some principles are more important than others, and if they carry the same weight throughout the country. For purposes of establishing the hypothetical ability for gerrymandering in each state, the more principles a state has in place the more the remappers should be constrained. The analysis in each state examines these constraints closer and provides more details for how and when these principles influence or do not influence the production of new districting plans.

Table 2.1 shows the traditional districting principles in place for the eight states. Each state has a requirement that districts must be contiguous and this factor rarely causes any controversy or discussion as it is well established when drawing districts. Only Washington and Michigan really address this issue in dealing with what constitutes contiguous districts in the Puget Sound area of Washington and the connection between the Upper and Lower Peninsulas in Michigan. Indiana has the fewest requirements with only a principle for contiguous districts. Kentucky

Table 2.1. Traditional Districting Principles in the Eight States

State	*Total*	*Principles in Place*
Unified Legislative		
Georgia	5	Contiguity, VRA, Subdivisions (Counties)*, Protect District Core*, CAN Protect Incumbents*
Michigan	3	Contiguity, Compactness, Subdivisions (Counties, City, and Townships)
Divided Legislative		
Indiana	1	Contiguity
Kentucky	2	Contiguity, Subdivisions (Counties)
Partisan Commission		
Ohio	3	Contiguity, Compactness, Subdivisions (Counties, Townships, Municipalities, City Wards)
Texas	4	Contiguity, Compactness, Subdivisions (Counties), VRA
Neutral Commission		
Idaho	5	Contiguity, Compactness, Subdivisions (Counties), Communities, CANNOT Protect Incumbents
Washington	5	Contiguity, Compactness, Subdivisions (Local Boundaries), Communities, CANNOT Protect Incumbents

Notes: Units in parentheses for the political subdivisions principles refer to the rank order for how remappers are to protect the political units.
* = Conditional based upon whether the first two principles are met.
VRA = States fall under the Voting Rights Act
Source: NCSL and compiled by author

only has two principles in place with a requirement against splitting counties in addition to contiguous districts. Michigan and Ohio both add a compactness requirement to these two principles. Michigan also specifies that counties should not be split, first and foremost, but if that is necessary due to population then both cities and township boundaries are not to be split where population allows. Ohio goes a step further by specifically specifying down to the city ward level what political boundaries cannot be split. Texas adds a fourth requirement that the Justice Department must preclear all plans for racial fairness under conditions of the Voting Rights Act (VRA). Georgia, Idaho, and Washington all have five principles in place. Georgia emphasizes contiguity and VRA status as primary principles with secondary concern for protecting county boundaries, the previous district core, and incumbents. The VRA is not applicable in either Idaho or Washington, but both states' constitutions add that communities of interest in addition to political subdivisions should not be split. Both states also specifically prohibit the protection of incumbents or even considering where incumbents live in drawing the new maps.

Overall, these states provide a nice variation for the use of traditional districting principles both in terms of the total numbers used in each state and the different principles used within the states. Seven of the eight states employ the principle against splitting political subdivisions, but the differences in how each state defines the requirement adds an interesting and complex layer to how these principles serve as constraints. For purposes of generating hypotheses, Indiana clearly has the fewest constraints against gerrymandering while both Idaho and Washington appear to be the strictest against both potential partisan and incumbent gerrymandering.

Likelihood of Court Involvement

Another important potential constraint against legislative success in redistricting is the courts. When the courts get involved in the process, legislators lose control. Heading into a new round of redistricting, legislators (or commissioners) do not know with certainty whether the courts will be involved (or at what level), but can have a good idea from the previous court involvement in a state. The courts did not take any action in three states with neither Indiana nor Washington having any suits filed against the 1990 plans. The Georgia courts took no action in the four suits brought throughout the decade. In the remaining five states, the courts were involved to some degree in the 1990s. In Idaho, two suits were filed and the courts simply approved the legislature's plans with no changes. In Kentucky and Ohio, the courts rejected the first plans implemented by the remappers and ordered the maps redrawn. The second set of plans met the courts approval in both states. In Texas, the courts considered sixteen lawsuits and made minor corrections to the legislative plans. Finally, in Michigan, the courts completely threw out the legislature's original plans and implemented their own maps.

Institutional Constraints

The final constraint I consider is the role of institutional rules and design. To do this, I look at the use of coterminous districts or shared boundaries between house and senate districts. For the states that use coterminous districts, boundary sharing should limit the legislator's abilities to implement their strategy of choice. This boundary sharing should force more compromise across chambers as the remappers only produce one plan instead of two. Three states use coterminous districts: Idaho, Ohio, and Washington. Both Idaho and Washington use "pure" coterminous districts where one senator and two house members share the same district. In the house, candidates apply to run for either seat A or B although there is no geographic distinction between the two. Ohio uses a slightly different form; within each of the thirty-three senate districts is three house districts. Each of the ninety-nine house districts has its own boundary, but it must conform to the senate districts in sets of three. This set up should serve as less of a constraint than the "pure" version, but more of one than the dominant method of having independent house and senate districts. The variation is not the best on this constraint as the three states that use coterminous districts all use commissions; however, this still allows some empirical testing of the theoretical dimension.

Overall Expectations

After looking at each of the constraints individually, table 2.2 summarizes the incentives and strategies for each state broken down by the four primary groups. The table shows the expected

Table 2.2. Expectations for Redistricting Strategies and Likelihood of Successful Implementation

State	*Expected Strategy*	*Key Advantages*	*Key Constraints*
Unified Legislative			
Georgia	Partisan–D	Unified political control, prior Democratic plans	VRA Preclearance, GOP population shifts
Michigan	Partisan–R	Unified political control, favorable GOP population shifts	Strict statutory requirements, prior court involvement
Divided Legislative			
Indiana	Compromised incumbent and/or partisan	Virtually no constraints	Divided political control
Kentucky	Compromised incumbent and/or partisan	Legislative control	Constitutional requirements, prior court involvement, divided political control
Partisan Commission			
Ohio	Partisan and incumbent–R	political control of commission and legislature	Strict constitutional requirements, prior court involvement, coterminous districts

(*continued*)

Table 2.2. (*continued*)

State	*Expected Strategy*	*Key Advantages*	*Key Constraints*
Texas	Partisan–R	political control of commission, favorable GOP population shifts	Prior court involvement, VRA preclearance
Neutral Commission			
Idaho	Neutral—geographic fairness	Bipartisan commission strict constitutional requirements	Commission used for first time, prior GOP plans
Washington	Neutral—competitive	Bipartisan commission with past success, strict constitutional requirements	No obvious constraints

redistricting strategy, and the key advantages and constraints for successful implementation of these strategies. Once again, the unified legislative states should have the easiest time. Within the unified group, neither Georgia nor Michigan stands out as having a clear advantage for implementing their strategies. Both have unified control with a history of court involvement and have similar traditional districting principles in place.

In the divided states, Indiana clearly stands out as having fewer constraints. The legislators have no traditional principles to work with, little previous court involvement, and independent districting plans. Only divided government appears to constrain the Indiana legislature, which is in a situation to push for both partisan and incumbent protection plans. Kentucky, strategically, is in a similar situation but must deal with the potential for court involvement. Additionally, the legislators must take into account the constitutional requirement against splitting counties.

In the partisan commission states, both Texas and Ohio have advantages and disadvantages for implementing the goals of the commission. In Ohio, the commission removes the legislators directly from the process, but the Republicans controlled both the commission and the legislature. With solid Republican control of the legislature, the commission did not have a clear need to partisan gerrymander, and without direct legislative control, legislators were not in a position to compromise for incumbent protection. Overall, the commission should worry more about partisan than incumbent concerns. In Texas, the Republicans also controlled the commission and had a clear strategy to partisan gerrymander to gain control of the House and strengthen their tenuous majority in the Senate. The Texas commission had to also account for Justice Department involvement and a history of court involvement. The Ohio commission was working under strict, and quite specific, constitutional requirements along with coterminous districts and with the knowledge of past court involvement. Overall, the constraints appear less in Texas as the commission was in a more favorable position to implement their preferred plans.

Finally, in the neutral commission states, the commissioners in both Idaho and Washington have detailed guidelines for avoiding both partisan and incumbent gerrymandering. In both cases, the legislator's preference for incumbent protection in Idaho and partisan gerrymandering in Washington appeared safely locked out of the process. However, the Washington legislators appeared to have the biggest disadvantage as the commission had a successful history of implementing plans according to the constitutional requirements. The Idaho legislators appeared to have a slightly better chance for influencing the outcomes because 2000 was the first year for the commission to complete redistricting and in previous decades the legislature controlled the process.

Scope and Data

The final section of this chapter discusses the data and methodological approach used in the next four chapters. At this point, readers more interested in the results rather than the process may want to skip ahead to chapter 3. I introduce each of the primary methods used and for readers interested in details pertaining to each type of analysis I provide further explanation in the appendixes.

Data

To analyze my questions information from both pre- and post-redistricting plans is necessary. For this purpose, I rely on precinct level data as the primary data source for the analysis. The precinct data comes from my work on Gerald Wright's Representation in America's Legislatures (RAL) project.[52] For the eight cases selected, for the old plans, I gathered the 2000 presidential vote (and in most cases more electoral data) for every precinct and matched those precincts with their appropriate state legislative districts. After the implementation of the new plans, I again matched precincts with districts and then merged this with the presidential vote and district information from the old plans. In each of these eight cases, the 2002 and 2000 precinct information merged successfully, with only a few minor problems. In areas of large growth, new precincts were created to accommodate this growth and even out precinct population. Often these overpopulated precincts were split into sections, such as Precinct 1A and Precinct 1B, to accommodate these changes. In a few cases, a county completely renamed and redrew their precincts. For the eight states selected, this occurred in Louisville-Jefferson County, Kentucky and Webb County (Laredo), Texas. Luckily, in both cases, I was able to obtain the city clerks conversion sheets that provided a method to track the changes. In all eight states, the 2000 and 2002 data merged successfully at over 90 percent precinct matches, including newly created precincts.[53]

From the precinct level data, I aggregate to the district level for both the 2002 and 2000 plans to account for the physical change the districts undergo as well as the partisan change in the districts. The ability to aggregate provides important analytical advantages for comparing specific district level changes that is missing from most redistricting studies. Most studies are restricted to district level data, whether it is demographics, electoral outcomes, or a base partisanship measure. This additional level of data provides greater detail to understand the changes between redistricting plans.

In addition to the precinct level data, I collected information regarding who controlled the process, their motives, the redistricting rules governing each state, candidate information from both the 2002 and the last election prior to the redistricting.[54] I relied on information from the National Conference of State Legislatures (NCSL) and FairVote.org for who controls redistricting and the rules governing the process. In addition, Fair Vote.org collected redistricting related newspaper stories from every state that allowed me to study the remappers' intentions. As for the election data, this is all easily available from each state's website and provides the necessary district level returns from both the pre- and post-redistricting elections as well as information on incumbents and challengers in each district. Population and demographic data available from the Census Bureau is the final component of the data collection. For each state, I collect district and precinct (where available) information on the population of the districts before and after redistricting along with the racial composition of the old and new districts.[55]

As with most redistricting studies, I develop a base measure of partisanship to serve as the primary indicator of district opinion and change between plans. The need here is to tap into the underlying public opinion in a district. In this study, I rely on the 2000 presidential vote as this base vote. Most studies employ either registration data or some down ballot executive races within a state to capture the underlying partisanship of a district. Registration data or vote-based measures for district partisanship appears virtually interchangeable.[56]

I use presidential vote rather than either registration data or down ballot races for several reasons. First, not all states compile and make available registration data at the precinct level. Second, I need a measure that is comparable across all states and not idiosyncratic within a state. Presidential elections provide a national scope where all voters across the country are voting for the same candidates. The 2000 election is a particularly good election to use because not only did Al Gore and George W. Bush present a clear distinction for the voters, but the electorate was nearly evenly split across the country. In addition, the presidential vote captures the same underlying partisanship as other down ballot races.[57] Finally, the presidential vote is recent, while voter registration records are often outdated. While individual's partisan affiliation may change over time, their voter registration does not necessarily reflect this change, especially in the South. Throughout the book, I measure the base vote as the two-party percentage of the presidential vote usually in terms of the Gore vote, unless otherwise noted.[58] Overall, the presidential vote serves as a good indicator of district preference and allows for comparability across the states.

Methodology

In each of the next four chapters, I present an analysis of gerrymandering and redistricting constraints using a two-step approach: first, I examine the politics in each state, and then I focus on the changes between the old and new maps. The analysis of the changes in the plans provides evidence of gerrymandering and the influence of the constraints in each state. I then analyze the electoral outcomes of these new maps using data from the 2002 elections. Each of the four case study chapters follow a similar analytical approach with slight variations based on interesting facets of each case and, in a few minor places, data availability.

I begin the analysis by studying the actors, their strategies, and the politics involved with redistricting from the time of the release of the 2000 Census data to the implementation of the 2002 plans. Then I examine the district level changes produced in the 2002 plans as compared to the plans in place during the 2000 elections.[59] The detailed examination of the plans provides the most appropriate area for understanding the goals and strategies used by the remappers along with the effectiveness of the constraints in the process. This is also one of the most understudied areas in redistricting research. I finish by analyzing the more traditional questions of redistricting studies by examining the electoral outcomes immediately following the implementation of new legislative maps.

Redistricting Methodology and Measurement

The vast majority of studies into partisan redistricting start with the assumption of a gerrymander commonly based on control of government, and then proceeds to look at the effects of redistricting on aggregate electoral outcomes. These studies are usually framed in terms of district competitiveness, the seats-votes relationship, or partisan seat gains or losses. Other studies examine these questions in more detail on select cases. These studies represent the common approach to studying redistricting.[60]

Although the methods and findings may differ, the one common denominator of these studies is the focus on the outcomes produced by the plans at the state, chamber, or district level. By focusing on outcomes, most scholars either assume or theorize about the strategies employed and the changes individual districts underwent during the remapping and do not actually test for these changes. This book digs deeper by examining the entire redistricting process from the district level, and thereby linking strategies to outcomes.

Other aspects of redistricting have received some scholarly attention. The most common of these studies tries to explain the types of gerrymanders produced or the strategies that go into redistricting. The first group examines what conditions produce certain types of gerrymanders. The second set of studies looks at the strategies and motives that go into redistricting and the success of the implementation of these motives. Both of these types of studies provide greater detail into the redistricting process by examining not only the electoral outcomes, but the process that led to those outcomes as well.[61]

For my analysis, I need components of each of these types of studies. However, most of these studies do not provide much guidance into how to study this from a district level perspective. This seems primarily due to the focus of most studies on the electoral outcomes and the lack of data availability at the subdistrict level. However, John Cranor, Gary Crawley, and Raymond Scheele's 1989 study and Scott W. Desposato and John R. Petrocik's 2003 article overcome this data problem and I rely on much of their methodology, as discussed below.[62]

To examine the question of the actors, strategies, and politics involved in the process, I conduct a thorough analysis of the redistricting process in each state. I start with newspaper articles in each state from the time period of January 2000 to January 2003. I collected these by searching both LexisNexis and the database provided by FairVote.org. This provides for a plethora of information from all eight states as the media supplied in-depth coverage to redistricting throughout this period. While the newspaper coverage alone provided more than enough insight into the strategies, goals, and politics in each state, I supplemented these articles by contacting experts in each state to confirm these findings and answer any lingering or unclear questions into each state's redistricting. In addition, I researched both the current state laws and constitutional provisions covering redistricting and the history of redistricting in each state. I accomplished this by reading through the constitutions and relevant statutes of each state. For the historical data Leroy Hardy, Alan Heslop, and Stuart Anderson's 1981 volume into the history of redistricting in the fifty states provided an excellent resource.[63] All of this information gave plenty of background information needed to understand more fully the outcomes of the current redistricting. From this, the first section of each substantive chapter gives an account of the laws and history in each state along with what happened during the current redistricting. These sections provide interesting details that answer the first question and inform and modify the theoretical expectations for the empirical outcomes the plans produced.

Given the precinct data I have collected for pre- and post-redistricting, I am in an excellent position to study district level changes that most previous studies have not been able to examine. To determine what type of gerrymander, if any, was implemented I conduct a series of tests at the district level to see what changes the individual districts underwent and if these changes point to a partisan or incumbent advantage or if the plans appear to be neutral. Furthermore, by examining the district changes I should find evidence for whether or not the constraints in place in a state actually limited the ability of the remappers to reach their goals. District specific changes provide much greater detail and explanatory information about the nature of a redistricting plan and show the changes intended by the remappers before the elections took place.[64] I focus on district specific changes by looking for evidence of gerrymandering. This evidence includes the partisan displacement in each plan, core retention of the old districts, and predicting the partisanship of the new districts.[65]

The key to understanding the changes between plans is examining the partisan and geographic shifts between old and new districts. To show the extent of changes between the old and new plans, I aggregate the precinct data to the district level. This aggregation provides the power to examine subdistrict changes that most studies cannot capture, and allows for a comparison of pre- and post-redistricting to assess the degree of partisan shifts and boundary changing.

Determining the Parent District

The first step in comparing district level changes is determining which new districts to compare with the old districts. The initial inclination is to match districts by number. In this situation, the partisanship of new district number 1 would be compared with the partisanship of old district number 1. For studies that only focus on electoral outcomes or other details of the plans' outcomes, this type of method may work without any problems. However, for an analysis of district level changes this simple assumption does not work. The more appropriate way to compare district changes is to determine a "parent" district. A parent district is the single largest contributor of population to a new district.[66] If for example, district 1 did not change during redistricting and the numbering scheme stayed the same (some states completely changed their numbering scheme) then its parent is the old district 1. However, most new districts derive from multiple districts with the parent district making up the majority of the new district. However, in a small number of cases, a new district comes from only small proportions of many districts and determining a "parent" district becomes problematic. I address these specific concerns within each individual chapter. Throughout the analysis, I compare new districts with its parent district, unless otherwise noted.

It is also important to note that not all old districts serve as parent districts in the new plans and that some old districts serve as the parent district for multiple new districts. This usually occurs for a couple of reasons. The first is gerrymandering. Thc controlling party may want to eliminate specific districts and they do this by splitting the old district into many fragments within the new plans. The other is for population reasons. Underpopulated districts may not become parent districts since population changes may dictate the shifting of the number of districts within an area. This can also lead to overpopulated districts being carved into multiple parent districts in the new plans.

To determine partisan control of each district, I code for controlling party or out party based on the partisanship of the member in that district prior to redistricting. For the old maps, this is simply the party of the legislator holding the district after the 2000 elections, and for the 2002 plans, I code the controlling party based on the partisanship of the incumbent from the parent district. The controlling party is measured based on which party is in control of the process for a given chamber.[67] Therefore, the Democrats were the controlling party in Georgia, the Indiana House, and the Kentucky House, and the Republicans in Michigan, Ohio, Texas, the Indiana Senate, and the Kentucky Senate. I then code each district as either competitive or safe based on the folded 2000 presidential vote. Safe districts are those with a Gore base vote above 60 percent or below 40 percent, and competitive districts are those that fall in between 40 and 60 percent.[68]

I combine these two measures to form the district typology variable consisting of controlling party-safe districts, controlling party-competitive districts, out party-safe districts, and out party-competitive districts, or the district typologies discussed earlier in the chapter.[69] This district typology variable provides an almost evenly distributed sample with the controlling party/safe districts and controlling party/competitive districts each making up 29 percent of the districts, and both categories of the out party districts making up 21 percent of the sample.

Measures of Gerrymandering

Unfortunately, there is not one clear test for the level of gerrymandering in a redistricting plan. Therefore, I use several different measures to determine the type and extent of gerrymandering implemented. I introduce those measures here and provide more complete details in appendix 1.

Partisan Displacement

The first analysis presents the partisan displacement found in each of the plans. Partisan displacement looks for evidence that districts underwent systematic change based on the district typologies, and to what extent these changes meet the remapper's gerrymandering expectations. I trace the composition of each new district by breaking down the proportion of the base vote that was added, subtracted, and stayed the same. If there is no systematic change, then either the plans were neutral or the remappers were unable to implement their strategies based on some constraining factors.

Next, I test for gerrymandering by examining the district changes and modeling the partisanship of the 2002 districts. For each plan, I present a scatter plot showing the partisan shifts between the old and new districts. The scatter plots capture the fundamental changes in the districts and allows for a nice test of the theoretical outcomes predicted under different gerrymanders, as shown in figure 2.1. Another way to show these changes is to model the partisanship of the new districts as a function of key variables in the redistricting process. If the remappers implemented a gerrymander, then I should find evidence that matches expectations of the gerrymandering theories discussed earlier in this chapter. For each chamber, I test three models of district partisanship with the 2002 district partisanship being the dependent variable in each. See appendix 1 for more details on model specification.

District Intactness

The amount of change each district undergoes is not only important in terms of partisan displacement, but also in terms of physical change or intactness of the district's constituency. I refer to this as district intactness or the core retention of a district. The core retention of a district is important for the continuity of representation by allowing incumbents to represent the majority of the same constituents from the old to new plans.[70] There are two primary reasons for a lack of district intactness between plans. The first is to move constituents between districts to account for population shifts within a state. For most districts, this involves shuffling a minority of constituents, by either adding or subtracting population, but allows for the majority of the district to remain intact between plans. However, some districts must undergo either complete or almost complete boundary shifts to accommodate either concentrated population losses or gains in a state. The most common scenario involves the areas of population decline, the inner cities and/or rural areas, losing entire districts to the faster growing suburban areas.

The second reason for small core retention of constituents is gerrymandering. In either a partisan gerrymander or controlling party incumbent gerrymander, the majority party will attempt to keep their incumbents' districts intact while splitting the core districts of the out party incumbents. The reason is simple. Incumbents like to represent constituencies with which they are familiar. New constituents bring in more uncertainty for the incumbents personal vote.[71] Under a bipartisan incumbent gerrymander, the remappers will try to keep all incumbents' districts as intact as possible while using open seats to equalize population. In most situations, a neutral plan will focus on population shifts and protecting the needs of incumbents.[72] Once again, see appendix 1 for more details.

Other Measures of Gerrymandering Intent

Strategic gerrymanders can also manipulate other aspects of redistricting to gain their desired advantage. One way is to pair incumbents together to create open seats. Remappers may combine this strategy with partisan displacement techniques particularly when creating open seats that the controlling party believes they can win.

Another method, specific to state legislative redistricting, is the manipulation of district populations. The standard for congressional districting is absolute population equality; however, for legislative districts the generally accepted standard is a 10 percent population deviation. Within this, partisan gerrymanders may attempt to place their districts in underpopulated districts while putting the out party into overpopulated districts.[73] This effectively wastes unfavorable partisans while maximizing the controlling party's partisan supporters. This represents population packing as the out party's partisans are packed into as few districts as possible by maximizing the population in these districts. Where pertinent, I show the incumbent pairings and district population bias and discuss how these findings fit into the gerrymandering strategy in each state.

Electoral Outcomes

The remainder of the analysis in each chapter turns to the more traditional area of redistricting studies: electoral outcomes. This completes the analysis where most studies begin. This analysis examines the influence of redistricting on Election Day by doing a descriptive analysis of the results followed by a multivariate analysis with a vote-share model. I take the estimates from the vote-share model to predict the partisan winners in each district and compare these to the actual outcomes. I conclude with a look at the seats-votes relationship from the 2002 elections.

In the multivariate analysis, I use a variant of the popular linear seat-vote share techniques to estimate the vote shares for the controlling party in a chamber. The results of this model allow for a check on the influence of redistricting by comparing the actual outcomes with predicted outcomes under both the 2002 elections setting and interesting counterfactuals, such as the elections being held with the 2000 districts or without the influence of incumbency. The general purpose is to test for whether the strategy implemented translated into actual seat gains.[74]

The final piece of the analysis is the seats-votes relationship. While there are many techniques for examining this relationship, conceptually, these studies all focus on the same underlying factor of the swing ratio. Commonly referred to as responsiveness, the swing ratio is the percentage change in legislative seats associated with a 1 percent change in legislative votes. The two distinct operationalizations of this ratio are the historical swing ratio and the hypothetical or single year swing ratio. Since I am only looking at one election period, the hypothetical or single year swing ratio is the appropriate measure, and for more details see appendix 3.[75]

A plan's effect may be different from its intent. With the electoral analysis, I am able to compare the effects of redistricting with the intent of the changes made during redistricting. By combining the intentions of the remappers, the constraints during the process, and the effects of the plans on the electoral outcomes, I answer the main questions of this study. I also provide a more detailed analysis into the entire process that other studies cannot capture.

Conclusion

In this chapter, I have discussed the guiding theory and methods used in each of the next four chapters. The next four chapters delve into redistricting in each of the eight states. In each of these chapters, I refer back to this chapter as the guide for my analysis and provide specific details in the context of each case. One broad theme in each chapter is the importance of the constraints within each state. No single test or measure can accurately capture the effect of these constraints, as such, I study both what happens during the remapping stage and the electoral outcomes to examine both the incentives and constraints of redistricting. This provides an answer to both the intent and effect of redistricting for how both the process and outcomes influence the fairness of our democratic process. The detailed analysis that follows reveals the realities of redistricting throughout the states.

Notes

1 For examples, please see Bruce Cain, "Assessing the Partisan Effects of Redistricting," *American Political Science Review* 79 (1985): 320–33; Gary W. Cox and Jonathan N. Katz, *Elbridge Gerry's Salamander: The Electoral Consequences of the Reapportionment Revolution* (Cambridge: Cambridge University Press, 2002); Guillermo Owen and Bernard Grofman, "Optimal Partisan Gerrymandering," *Political Geography Quarterly* 7 (1988): 5–22; and Edward Tufte, "The Relationship

between Seats and Votes in Two-Party Systems," *American Political Science Review* 67 (1973): 540–54.

2. David Mayhew, *Congress: The Electoral Connection* (New Haven, Conn.: Yale University Press, 1974).

3. Bruce Cain and Janet Campagna, "Predicting Partisan Redistricting Disputes," *Legislative Studies Quarterly* 12 (1987): 265–74.

4. Owen and Grofman, "Optimal Partisan Gerrymandering."

5. V. O. Key, *Southern Politics in State and Nation* (New York: Vintage Books, 1949).

6. For examples, please see Harry Basehart and John Comer, "Partisan and Incumbent Effects in State Legislative Redistricting," *Legislative Studies Quarterly* 16 (1991): 65–79; and Cox and Katz, *Electoral Consequences*.

7. Cain and Campagna, "Predicting Partisan Redistricting Disputes."

8. Many articles deal with this issue. For examples, please see Cox and Katz, *Electoral Consequences*; Cain, "Assessing the Partisan Effects"; and John Cranor, Gary Crawley, and Raymond Scheele, "The Anatomy of a Gerrymander," *American Journal of Political Science* 33 (1989): 222–39.

9. Jeffrey C. Kubin, "The Case for Redistricting Commissions," *Texas Law Review* 75 (1997): 837–72.

10. This district typology follows from the analysis in Donald Ostdiek, "Congressional Redistricting and District Typologies," *Journal of Politics* 57 (1995): 533–43. This district typology allows "for more precise statements of redistricting effects" (535) based on the specific expectations of different gerrymandering strategies.

11. I discuss the "pure" strategies under the assumptions that (a) the remappers are only attempting to implement one goal without considering the other factors and (b) they are able to attempt these strategies without worry of the constraints on the process.

12. Duren Cheek and Bonna de la Cruz, "Passed House Remap Plan Easier on GOP," *Nashville Tennessean*, 11 January 2002.

13. For more details, please see Cox and Katz, *Electoral Consequences*, and Brian F. Schaffner, Michael W. Wagner, and Jonathan Winburn, "Incumbents Out, Party In? Term Limits and Partisan Redistricting in State Legislatures," *State Politics and Policy Quarterly* 4 (2004): 396–414.

14. David J. Gopoian and Darrell M. West, "Trading Security for Seats: Strategic Considerations in the Redistricting Process," *Journal of Politics* 46 (1984): 1080–96.

15. Most racial redistricting studies have focused on the African American community. The general strategy holds for the growing Latino communities as well. Although, research has yet to determine the effects of Latino majority-minority districts given the more geographic dispersion of the Hispanic population and the not as strong identification with one party.

16. For examples, please see Bernard Grofman and Lisa Handley, "Estimating the Impact of Voting-Rights-Act-Related Districting on Democratic

Strength in the U.S. House of Representatives," in *Race and Redistricting in the 1990s*, ed. Bernard Grofman (New York: Agathon Press, 1998), 51–66; and John R. Petrocik and Scott W. Desposato, "The Partisan Effects of Majority Minority Districting, 1992–1994," *Journal of Politics* 66 (1998): 613–33.

17. For examples, please see David Lublin, *The Paradox of Representation* (Princeton, N.J.: Princeton University Press, 1997); David Lublin and D. Stephen Voss, "Racial Redistricting and Realignment in Southern State Legislatures," *American Journal of Political Science* 44 (2000): 792–810; and Carol Swain, *Black Faces, Black Interests: The Representation of African-Americans in Congress* (Cambridge, Mass.: Harvard University Press, 1993).

18. Seth Blomeley, "Black Groups at Odds on Redistricting," *Little Rock Arkansas Democrat-Gazette*, 23 September 2001; Seth Blomeley, "Board Still at Odds over Redistricting," *Little Rock Arkansas Democrat-Gazette*, 25 September 2001; and James Jefferson, "NAACP Suit Challenges Ark. Redistricting Plan," *Memphis Commercial Appeal*, 24 May 2002.

19. For a detailed discussion, please see Mark Monmonier, *Bushmanders and Bullwinkles: How Politicians Manipulate Electronic Maps and Census Data to Win Elections* (Chicago: University of Chicago Press, 2001).

20. David Butler and Bruce Cain, *Congressional Redistricting: Comparative and Theoretical Perspectives* (New York: MacMillan, 1992).

21. Jeffrey C. Kubin, "The Case for Redistricting Commissions," *Texas Law Review* 75 (1997): 837–72 presents a detailed comparison of the potential advantages and disadvantages of commission use and the various formats.

22. Richard Niemi and Simon Jackman, "Bias and Responsiveness in State Legislative Districting," *Legislative Studies Quarterly* 16 (1991): 184.

23. For examples, please see Basehart and Comer, "Partisan and Incumbent Effects"; Cain, "Assessing the Partisan Effects"; John W. Swain, Stephen A. Borrelli, and Brian C. Reed, "Partisan Consequences of the Post-1990 Redistricting for the U.S. House of Representatives," *Political Research Quarterly* 51 (1998): 945–67; Amihai Glazer, Bernard Grofman, and Marc Robbins, "Partisan and Incumbency Effects of 1970s Congressional Redistricting," *American Journal of Political Science* 31 (1987): 680–707; Richard Born, "Partisan Intentions and Election Day Realities in the Congressional Redistricting Process," *American Political Science Review* 79 (1985): 305–19; and Gary King, "Representation Through Legislative Redistricting: A Stochastic Model," *American Journal of Political Science* 33 (1989): 787–824.

24. I refer to the "courts" generally for both the federal and state level. I try to note when specifically discussing the Supreme Court or a specific state or federal court.

25. Nathaniel Persily, "Forty Years in the Political Thicket: Judicial Review of the Redistricting Process since *Reynolds v. Sims*," in *Party Lines: Competition, Partisanship, and Congressional Redistricting*, eds. Thomas E. Mann and Bruce E. Cain (Washington, D.C.: Brookings Institution Press, 2005), 67–91, provides a good review of the courts involvement in redistricting.

26. 369 U.S. 186.

27. These cases include *Reynolds v. Sims*, 377 U.S. 533 (1964); *Wesberry v. Sanders*, 376 U.S. 1 (1964); *Kirkpatrick v. Preisler*, 394 U.S. 526 (1969); *White v. Weiser*, 412 U.S. 783 (1973); and *Karcher v. Daggett*, 462 U.S. 725 (1983).

28. In the 2004 ruling in *Cox v. Larios*, 124 S. Ct. 1503, the Supreme Court found plans unconstitutional that fell beneath the 10 percent deviation threshold. This may signal a change to the presumed constitutionality of plans within this limit, but did not affect the time period under study throughout the book. The *Cox* case involved Georgia redistricting and I will return to it in the next chapter.

29. National Conference of State Legislatures, *Redistricting Law 2000*. (Prepared by the Redistricting Task Force for the NCSL's National Redistricting Seminar, Denver, March 1999.)

30. Richard Engstrom, "The Post-2000 Round of Redistricting: An Entangled Thicket within the Federal System," *Publius: The Journal of Federalism* 32 (2002): 56.

31. NCSL, *Redistricting Law*.

32. 509 U.S. 630.

33. 478 U.S. 109.

34. Engstrom, "Post-2000 Round," 61. See also Ronald Weber, "Emerging Trends in State Legislative Redistricting," *Spectrum: The Journal of State Government* 75 (2002): 13–15.

35. Engstrom, "Post-2000 Round," 57.

36. 507 U.S. 25.

37. Please see Engstrom, "Post-2000 Round"; and Micah Altman, "Districting Principles and Democratic Representation" (Ph.D. diss., California Institute of Technology, 1998).

38. Cox and Katz, *Electoral Consequences*, 68.

39. Lynn Bonner, "Suit Seeks New Maps," *Raleigh News and Observer*, 4 September 2002.

40. *Shaw v. Hunt*, 116 S. Ct. 1894 (1996) and *Shaw v. Reno*, 509 U.S. 630 (1993).

41. NCSL, *Redistricting Law*. Butler and Cain, *Congressional Redistricting* and Bernard Grofman, "Criteria for Districting: A Social Science Perspective," *UCLA Law Review* 33 (1985): 77–185, give excellent in-depth discussions of these principles and their interaction with the goals of partisan gerrymandering, and I draw on their findings in presenting my synopsis.

42. 856 F. Supp. 1409 (ED Cal). See also NCSL, *Redistricting Law*.

43. Monmonier, *Bushmanders*.

44. Butler and Cain, *Congressional Redistricting*.

45. 543 F. Supp. 68 (D. Colo) (1982).

46. Engstrom, "Post-2000 Round."

47. These decisions include *Brown v. Thompson*, 462 U.S. 835 (1983); *Mahan v. Howell*, 410 US 315 (1973); and *Quilter v. Voinovich*, 794 F. Supp. 695 (N.D. Ohio) (1992). See also Engstrom, "Post-2000 Round." To measure the influence of tra-

ditional districting principles I focus on the principle of upholding political boundaries, specifically county boundaries. I do this for several reasons. First, in recent years, both the courts and redistricting reform groups have focused on this principle as important to limiting gerrymandering and as a neutral criterion for redistricting. Second, the measurement presents straightforward interpretation. Other options include the communities of interest and compactness standards. However, communities of interest is a vague notion that without a clear definition is hard to accurately formulate, and with compactness no one measure is accepted as a standard and the courts have gone away from enforcing this standard in recent years (Monmonier, *Bushmanders*). In addition to the empirical tests of upholding political boundaries, within each chapter, I use the data from the process and background of each to focus on what role the specific principles in each state play to develop a more complete understanding of how closely the remappers followed these principles or how successful they were at implementing their plans around these factors. See appendix 2 for more details on this analysis.

48. Engstrom, "Post-2000 Round," 67.

49. 507 U.S. 25 (1993).

50. Engstrom, "Post-2000 Round," 55.

51. Richard N. Engstrom, "District Geography and Voters," in *Redistricting in the New Millennium*, ed. Peter F. Galderisi (Lanham, Md.: Lexington Books, 2005).

52. For more details on the RAL project, see http://www.indiana.edu/~ral.

53. For those precincts that did not merge successfully, the data was not included in the aggregated base partisanship measures.

54. For most chambers this was the 2000 elections. Due to staggered senatorial elections, 1998 was the last election for half of the Indiana, Kentucky, Ohio, and Washington Senates.

55. The Census Bureau began a program during the 2000 Census to match all state voting precincts with the Bureau's Voting Districts. The states had the option to participate during the 2000 data collection. Some states participated fully, others partly, and a few not at all.

56. For examples of registration data studies, please see Cain, "Assessing the Partisan Effects" and Scott W. Desposato and John R. Petrocik, "The Variable Incumbency Advantage: New Voters, Redistricting, and the Personal Vote," *American Journal of Political Science* 47 (2003): 18–32. For examples of down ballot studies, please see Cranor et al., "Anatomy" and Ronald Keith Gaddie and Charles S. Bullock III, "The Political Consequences of an Uncontrolled Redistricting" (paper presented at the annual meeting of the Southern Political Science Association, New Orleans, January 2005). J. Morgan Kousser, "Estimating the Partisan Consequences of Redistricting Plans-Simply," *Legislative Studies Quarterly* 21 (1996): 521–41 finds both methods produce similar results.

57. For more details, please see Gerald Wright, Tracy Osborn, and Jon Winburn, "Parties and Representation in the American Legislatures" (paper

presented at the annual meeting of the Midwest Political Science Association, Chicago, April 2004) and Gerald Wright and Jon Winburn, "The Effects of Size and Party on the Dimensionality of Roll Calls" (paper presented at the annual conference on State Politics and Policy, Tucson, Ariz., March 2003). In the 2003 paper, we show that presidential vote and down ballot races load onto one factor at above .90.

58. I do not use a Left (Gore plus Nader)-Right (Bush plus Buchanan) measure because not all states in the sample reported the Nader and/or Buchanan vote and I want the measure as comparable as possible across states. Additionally, for all legislative electoral returns, I also use a two-party measure and exclude all third party totals. I report these in terms of the Democratic vote share unless otherwise noted.

59. I limit my comparison to the last plans put into place from the 1990 round of redistricting. In each of the eight states, these plans were in place for the majority of elections during the 1990s and the 2000 election.

60. This literature spans decades and covers many different questions. For representative examples of the literature, please see Cox and Katz, *Electoral Consequences*; John Ferejohn, "On the Decline of Competition in Congressional Elections," *American Political Science Review* 71 (1977): 166–76; King, "Representation Through Legislative Redistricting"; Kousser, "Estimating the Partisan Consequences"; Cain, "Assessing the Partisan Effects"; and Paul Gronke and J. Matthew Wilson, "Competing Redistricting Plans as Evidence of Political Motives: The North Carolina Case," *American Politics Quarterly* 27 (1999): 147–76.

61. For examples, please see Cain and Campagna, "Predicting Partisan Redistricting Disputes"; and Michael P. McDonald, "A Comparative Analysis of Redistricting Institutions in the United States, 2001–2002," *State Politics and Policy Quarterly* 4 (2004): 371–95.

62. Cranor et al., "Anatomy" and Desposato and Petrocik, "The Variable Incumbency Advantage."

63. Leroy Hardy, Alan Heslop, and Stuart Anderson, eds. *Reapportionment Politics: The History of Redistricting in the 50 States* (Beverly Hills, Calif.: Sage Publications, 1981).

64. Ostdiek, "Congressional Redistricting."

65. Cain, "Assessing the Partisan Effects" deals with partisan displacement; Gaddie and Bullock, "Political Consequences" addresses the core retention issue; and Cranor et al., "Anatomy" examines predicting the partisanship of new districts.

66. Cox and Katz, *Electoral Consequences*.

67. Given the neutral commissions and coterminous districts in use in Idaho and Washington, I use a modified typology based on how many seats a party holds in a district. I discuss the specifics in chapter 7.

68. This +/-10 percent designation for competitive and safe districts is common throughout the literature. See Emily Van Dunk and Ronald E. Weber, "Constituency-Level Competition in the U.S. States, 1968–1988: A Pooled

Analysis," *Legislative Studies Quarterly* 22 (1987): 141–59 and Gary Jacobson, "The Marginals Never Vanished: Incumbency and Competition in Elections to the U.S. House of Representatives, 1952–1982," *American Journal of Political Science* 31 (1987): 126–41 for a detailed discussion of measuring safe and marginal seats. See the earlier discussion on the use of presidential vote as the standard base vote for each district.

69. I recode those safe districts to competitive districts in cases where the partisanship of the incumbent does not match the partisanship of the district. A good example is Rep. Jerry Denbo, an Indiana House Democrat from the heavily Republican 62nd district made up of the French Lick area. In this case, Denbo's district is one of the controlling party's and a safe district. However, the controlling party is the Democrats and the electoral safety favors the Republicans. In these cases, I consider the districts competitive as, in Denbo's case, the Democrats' ability to win in the 62nd is not due to the underlying partisanship of the constituents, but rather Denbo's personal characteristics and decade-long representation of the district. This is the case in fewer than 100 of the over 1,200 districts included.

70. Gaddie and Bullock, "Political Consequences."

71. Desposato and Petrocik, "The Variable Incumbency Advantage."

72. However, this is not always the case as some states specify core retention as a guiding redistricting principle and specifically prohibit the use of incumbent information.

73. Gaddie and Bullock, "Political Consequences."

74. For good explanations and examples of the linear seat-vote share technique, please see Andrew Gelman and Gary King, "Enhancing Democracy through Legislative Redistricting," *American Political Science Review* 88 (1994): 541–59; Ronald Keith Gaddie and Charles S. Bullock III, *Elections to Open Seats in the U.S. House: Where the Action Is* (Lanham, Md.: Rowman and Littlefield, 2000); and Kousser, "Estimating the Partisan Consequences." The primary alternative to the vote shares linear regression model is an MLE model with a dichotomous seat won or loss dependent variable;w see Cain, "Assessing the Partisan Effects." I used both models throughout the analysis and found the substantive results changed little in each of the cases. See appendix 3 for more details.

75. For good discussions of the conceptualization and operationalization of the swing ratio and the seats-vote relationship, please see Richard Niemi and Patrick Fett, "The Swing Ratio: An Explanation and an Assessment," *Legislative Studies Quarterly* 11 (1986): 75–90; Gelman and King, "Enhancing Democracy"; and Andrew Gelman and Gary King, "A Unified Method of Evaluating Electoral Systems and Redistricting Plans," *American Journal of Political Science* 38 (1994): 514–54.

3

Unified Legislative Control

Georgia and Michigan

It's not realistic to take the politics out of the process. This is Politics 101. No map is adopted without political considerations on the part of one party or the other.

—Georgia State Democratic Chairman
David Worley[1]

A plan complying with the rules is not a gerrymandered plan.

—Michigan Senate Reapportionment Committee
Chairman Bill Schuette[2]

For both the Republicans in Michigan and the Democrats in Georgia, the 2000 redistricting presented the parties with an excellent opportunity for partisan gerrymandering. Theoretically, the redistricting climate in both states fit into the least constrained, and most open for a partisan gerrymander, typology of redistricting control: a unified government with legislative authority over the maps. However, the world for remapping was not that simple in both cases.

The Georgia political landscape heading into the new millennium looked similar to many southern states as it was transforming from a traditional one-party Democratic state to the new reality of not only competitive two-parties, but also Republican majorities in many areas. In terms of redistricting, the Democrats were attempting to maintain control in the legislature despite statewide partisan and population shifts toward the Republicans. However, in their favor, they faced few constitutional constraints that facilitated their partisan gerrymandering strategy. In Michigan, the Republicans were hoping to build upon their relatively new majority status in a state that was highly competitive and often divided throughout the 1990s. Despite their majority status, the Republicans had to overcome a history of court involvement and deal with a strict set of statutory rules to achieve a partisan gerrymander. These two states provide an interesting comparison of when a party may successfully gerrymander and when constraints can even limit legislators under the most favorable of conditions.

Redistricting Law and History

Georgia

Over the past forty years the dominate forces behind Georgia redistricting have shifted from malapportionment and rural dominance in the 1960s and 1970s to fair racial representation in the 1980s and 1990s to most recently partisan gerrymandering. Heading into the 1960s, the Georgia legislature had some of the worst malapportionment in the nation. This was due to the Georgia constitution of 1877 which provided a county-unit formula for seat distribution.[3] In 1963, at the beginning of the reapportionment revolution, the courts ruled this county-unit system unconstitutional in *Gray v. Sanders*,[4] a ruling that affected the apportionment model in many states. With the county-unit system ruled unconstitutional, the Georgia legislature had to redistrict based on equal population. The rurally dominated legislature, who reaped the benefits of the county-unit system, was quite resistant to this fundamental change. This led to a decade long battle between the legislature and the courts as Georgia passed seventeen major redistricting plans between 1961 and 1974.[5]

In 1971, the legislature attempted to deal with malapportionment directly as the General Assembly entered into an agreement with the University of Georgia to handle the technical aspects of redistricting. The legislature retained complete political control, but allowed the university task force to put together the technical components of the plan to meet constitutional and court standards as well as the legislature's goals.[6] The Democratic leadership instructed the university task force to prepare reports with only total population figures without any mention of racial data. The legislature completed new generally equally apportioned plans in November of 1971. However, the Justice Department did not preclear the plans on grounds of minority vote dilution. This led to a court battle as the General Assembly decided to hold its ground and not meet the Justice Department's recommendations. As a result, the U.S. Supreme Court ruled in favor of the Justice Department's right to force district changes and through extensive informal negotiations the General Assembly finally adopted approved plans in 1974.[7]

Heading into the 1980s, the legislature appeared to learn the lesson of adjusting for minority voting strength. The House and Senate plans received Justice Department preclearance and did not face any significant litigation throughout the decade.[8] The one-party Democratic legislature adapted to both a shift in urban and minority representation. In the 1990s, the legislature went too far in the other direction and introduced plans with too many majority-minority districts. In *Johnson v. Miller*, the congressional plan was declared unconstitutional on the grounds that race was the predominant factor in one district.[9] As a result, the legislature voluntarily redrew the House and Senate plans for fear the courts would make the same ruling in future litigation.[10] The resulting plans in 1995 received both Justice Department preclearance and court approval.

The state constitution grants the legislature control of redistricting in Article III, Section II. While the governor has veto power over the plans, traditionally, given the Democratic dominance in the state, the executive has allowed the legislature to handle the process without interference. Also, over the years, the chambers adopted an informal rule of not altering each others plans and approving them without debate.[11] The constitution also provides that senate districts must be single member and contiguous. The General Assembly assigns primary redistricting authority to two committees, the House Legislative and Congressional Reapportionment Committee and the Senate Reapportionment and Redistricting Committee. Traditionally, the committees then form a joint committee to adopt the exact guidelines each must follow and then the House committee produces the House and congressional plans while the Senate committee handles the Senate map. In 2001, the joint committee adopted the following general guidelines:

a. Each district should be drawn to reach substantial population equality with an overall population deviation of less than 10 percent.
b. All plans must comply with the Voting Rights Act and the United States and Georgia Constitutions.
c. All districts shall be contiguous.
d. Where the above-stated criteria are met, efforts may be made to maintain the integrity of political subdivisions as well as recognizing other established redistricting principles.[12]

In particular, these other established redistricting principles are a reference to keeping counties intact, protecting the previous district core, and that the committees may consider where incumbents reside while redrawing the districts. Overall, the most important factors for the remappers are adherence to the 10 percent population standard and meeting VRA requirements. The other guidelines are much more flexible and not strict constitutional rules. Overall, the legislators appeared to have a relatively free rein over the process. The constitutional rules are not very specific and the committees' self-imposed guidelines full of loopholes.

The Georgia Democrats had both the most pressing need for a partisan gerrymander and the least constrained path to accomplish it. Heading into 2002, for the first time in the last hundred years, the Democrats faced losing power in the legislature. During the 1990s, the Republicans gained forty seats in the House and thirteen in the Senate to make the legislature not only competitive but put the GOP within striking distance of a majority. The need for a partisan gerrymander was clear as the Democrats attempted to hold on to their majority status. The relative lack of constraints in the state favored the Democrats in their quest for a partisan gerrymander. Constitutionally, the primary constraint was equal population that applies to all state legislative redistricting while providing a relatively lax set of rules for the implementation of traditional districting principles. Outside of the constitution, all Georgia redistricting plans fall under VRA requirements to gain Justice Department preclearance. Additionally, the Democrats faced the potential for court involvement in a growing Republican state. Overall, I expect to find evidence of partisan gerrymander that helps the Democrats hang on to their majority.

Michigan

The redistricting history in Michigan involves a complex mix of geographic, partisan, racial, ethnic, and judicial interests. The state's first constitution in 1837 instructed the legislature to draw multi-member districts based on equal population. However, this changed in the 1850 constitution as new settlers in rural areas led the call for a new districting system. The new constitution directed the legislature to use a formula of county-based representation that provided a set number of districts for the Upper Peninsula. The third constitution, adopted in 1908, tinkered with this formula by dropping the special provisions for the Upper Peninsula and extending the small town advantage throughout the state.[13] Malapportionment became widespread as the rural majority from outside Detroit did not redistrict in either 1930 or 1940.

The most sweeping changes to the process came in the 1960s with both federal court rulings and another state constitution. In 1961, a voter-approved constitutional convention established a bipartisan apportionment commission that appointed an equal number of Democrats and Republicans from designated regions throughout the state. The new rules also established single member districts for both chambers and an 80 percent population-20 percent geographic apportionment formula. This formula was quickly overturned by the federal courts and forced the commissioners to adopt new plans in 1964 based on equal population standards.[14]

The most significant change in the 1963 constitution was the switch from legislative to commission control of redistricting. In the 1970s, the apportionment commission struggled to implement new plans as partisan, ethnic, and racial tensions flared. The commission publicly declared they wanted to uphold African American representation in the Detroit area, and this upset several ethnic groups, particularly several Polish legislators, who called for a seat on the commission.[15] The result was a deadlock. The commission on straight party line votes failed to produce new plans. The Michigan Supreme Court then implemented a Democratic plan in 1972, and the remainder of the decade was filled with litigation over the plans and the role of the commission.

Heading into 1980, most people expected another deadlocked commission and the courts to redraw the lines.[16] This is exactly what happened, and the state Supreme Court went a step further declaring the 1963 rules governing redistricting unconstitutional. This ended the unsuccessful run of the apportionment commission and gave the legislature responsibility of the process again. It also left the state without any valid redistricting guidelines.[17] However, the courts did suggest standards for use in redistricting. Commonly known as the APOL criteria, named after a special master the courts consulted in the 1970s and 1980s, the rules laid out step-by-step guidelines for remappers to follow with a special focus on population equality and protecting political subdivisions.[18]

In the 1990s, the legislature regained control of the process for the first time in thirty years. However, the divided legislature was unable to produce any new maps as neither party's plans moved out of committee. This forced the courts once again to draw new plans just as they had done since the mid-1960s.[19] In

1996, the Republicans, who had recently gained control of the legislature, codified the APOL criteria in attempt to limit future court challenges.[20]

In 2000, the legislature had control of the process with newly codified, not constitutional, guidelines. These rules laid out specific criteria for the legislature to follow and stressed the following:

a. single member districts
b. contiguous districts
c. an allowable 10 percent population deviation
d. preserve county boundaries
e. if necessary to split county boundaries, then the fewest whole cities or whole townships necessary shall be shifted
f. uphold city and township boundaries within counties that must be split
g. specific definition for compact districts
h. specific guidelines for dealing with districts that include island communities and cut across the Great Lakes
i. must uphold the Voting Rights Act
j. provides the state supreme court with original jurisdiction in state court litigation.

Additionally, the statute declares the legislature must rank each plan introduced on how closely it follows the criteria.[21] The legislature is supposed to pick the plan that most closely follows the guidelines. Overall, the APOL criteria provide specific, systematic, and potentially constraining rules for the legislature to follow.

The Michigan Republicans faced a slightly different road than the Democrats in Georgia. The Republicans held a relatively small but apparently safer majority in both chambers and were in a position to push for a gerrymander to help build their majorities. Despite the unified Republican control, the path to a partisan gerrymander appeared quite constrained. Specifically, the APOL criteria laid out clear rules for the remappers to follow. Additionally, the courts used these criteria in the past by implementing every plan since the 1970s. One factor the Republicans had in their favor was term limits, particularly in the Senate. With nearly three-fourths of the Senate incumbents forced out, the party had more of an opportunity to manipulate these districts without accounting for incumbent concerns. Overall, I expect to find evidence of a Republican attempt at partisan gerrymandering. I also expect the constraints in place to prevent a widespread pro-Republican plan, but for the GOP to draw favorable districts to the extent possible.

The 2000 Redistricting: Context and Perception of the Plans

Georgia

The 2000 redistricting turned into one of the most partisan, confusing, and litigation-filled battles in the country. For my purposes, I am examining only what happened to the maps for the 2002 elections. During this initial remapping, the Democrats controlled the process in both chambers. After the 2002 elections, the courts ordered new plans drawn by the Republicans that drastically altered the 2002 maps, I will return to these events later in the chapter and then again in chapter 7.

When the legislature completed the initial maps in a special session in the late summer of 2001, the Democrats openly admitted their objective "was to craft new districts to elect more Democrats and fewer Republicans."[22] The maps still needed gubernatorial approval and in a surprise move, Democratic Governor Roy Barnes broke with the tradition of simply approving the Democratic plans by urging the legislature to reconsider some aspects of the plans during the upcoming special congressional redistricting session.[23] During the congressional session, the Democratic leaders worked with Barnes to satisfy his objections and by so doing left individual Democratic incumbents little input into the process.[24]

The amended plans then went to the Justice Department for preclearance under the Voting Rights Act. In April 2002, a three-judge panel of the U.S. District Court in Washington, D.C., granted preclearance to the House and Congressional maps, but not the Senate maps. The legislature then reconvened to adopt a new Senate map that accounted for the Justice Department's recommendations. In early June, the district court granted the updated Senate plan preclearance. This ended the process for the 2002 election cycle, but the door remained open for more lawsuits after the election due to a pending lawsuit the courts postponed until after the elections.[25]

During the process, the majority Democrats argued redistricting is always political and they were simply doing what they were allowed while the minority Republicans argued for transparency and fairness in the process. State Democratic Chairman David Worley expressed the Democratic view, "It's not realistic to take the politics out of the process. This is Politics 101. No map is adopted without political considerations on the part of one party or the other."[26] Senate Republican Leader Eric Johnson argued the Republican stance, "Democrats have become too focused on what is in their own best interests and not what is in the best interests of the people of Georgia. Redistricting should not be about political power or party control or revenge. It should be about creating fair districts using an open process."[27]

In putting together the new plans, the House and Senate Democrats worked together but had to use slightly different strategies based on chamber rules and conditions. The Democrats knew both plans faced Justice Department preclearance on the issue of minority voting strength. To face this issue the Democratic leadership worked exclusively with the Black Caucus to protect majority-minority districts while cracking some districts with suburban white voters to protect the overall strength of the Democrats. This was a reversal of the 1990s where the biggest disagreements were between the Black Caucus and Democratic leadership over adding more majority-minority districts.[28]

The primary difference in the rules for the two chambers was the allowed use of multi-member districts (MMDs). The constitution forbids MMDs in the Senate but allows them in the House. Traditionally, the Democrats used MMDs in the House to dilute minority voting power. In the 1990s, they used all single member districts to avoid this issue, but decided to bring back MMDs in 2000 as a partisan tool.[29] The Democrats faced few other formal constraints. The constitution says remappers may uphold political subdivisions and protect the previous core, but only if the remappers first meet the population and VRA standards. The Democrats appeared to ignore these provisions completely as they believed the courts would find their plans constitutional as long as the districts fit into the 10 percent population standard and supported minority voting rights.[30] The Democrats had the legal ability to gerrymander, but given the recent growth in Republican strength, they needed some creativity to build or even maintain their majority. Going into the 2002 elections, most observers believed the Democrats were successful in their gerrymandering and the new districts should have allowed them to maintain their majorities and possibly add a couple of seats in each chamber.[31]

Michigan

With majorities in both chambers and a friendly governor, the Republicans took complete control of the 2000 redistricting process. For the first time in over forty years, the Democrats did not have any institutional control of the remapping. However, this did not necessarily guarantee Republican success as the legislature had not successfully implemented a redistricting plan since the 1920s. From the beginning, the process took on a bitter and acrimonious tone as both parties saw the opportunity for Republican dominance in the process. The Democrats decried the ability of the Republicans to abuse their power as Michigan Democratic Party chairman Mark Brewer said, "Voters be damned, that's what this process is all about."[32] The Republicans argued they were not abusing their power, but simply following the rules to complete fair and legal plans. Al Mann, House Republican Caucus liaison, argued the rules in place constrained their ability to partisan gerrymander and the Republicans did not have the free rein the Democrats suggested.[33] Senate Reapportionment Committee chairman Bill Schuette summed up the Republican stance, "A plan complying with the rules is not a gerrymandered plan."[34] Craig Ruff, a consultant with a Lansing think tank, summed up the partisan posturing, "If the shoes were on the other feet, reapportionment would be done the same way, there would just be a different set of amputees."[35]

In the House, the Republicans kept their plans a secret as long as possible and relied on some political trickery to limit debate on the plans. In committee, the Democrats introduced their plan with the expectation the Republicans would introduce their own followed by an open committee hearing debating the plans with the Republicans eventually voting their plan out of committee with a recommendation the full floor adopt the plan. However, this was not to be. Instead, the Republicans did not introduce their plans and simply passed the Democratic plan to the floor without recommendation.[36] Once on the floor, the Republicans amended the Democratic plan by replacing it with their plan. This served an important purpose within the APOL rules adopted by the legislature in 1996. The APOL rules state the legislature has to rank all introduced plans based on how well the plans follow traditional districting principles and population equality and then select the highest ranked plan. By not introducing their plan in committee, the Republicans were able to use the Democratic plan as the only official plan introduced; although they gutted the bill and replaced it with their own version. The Republicans, in an even further move of secrecy, forced a conference committee and implemented the final changes to their plan behind closed doors.[37] Ed Sarpolus, a Michigan redistricting expert who helped develop the APOL criteria, suggested the House Democrats used a poor strategy of not being more vocal about their plan early in the process. This allowed the Republicans to control the process and limited the Democrats to complaining spectators.

In the Senate, the Democrats introduced their plans early in the process and took their cause to the media forcing the Republicans to deal directly with them.[38] The Senate Democrats were careful not to draw a plan that maximized their seat gains, but instead introduced a compromise plan that strictly followed the APOL criteria. Specifically, their plan drew two districts out of Detroit, their stronghold. This forced the Republicans to compromise with the Democrats throughout the process. In the end, the GOP implemented a plan that was close to the Democrats' original plan.[39]

Overall, the Republicans were very successful in drawing a favorable plan in the House and less successful in the Senate. Most experts predicted the House could produce up to a six seat swing for the Republicans with the Senate producing anywhere from a three seat swing to the Democrats to a three seat gain for the Republicans. Both plans appeared to concentrate Republican strength and spread Democratic support more thinly. The APOL criteria played an important role during the process as the Senate Democrats forced the Republicans to compromise on their plans. In the House, the Republicans were able to manipulate the process and shut the Democrats out of the process. Term limits also played a factor. With one-third of all legislators termed out in 2002, the Republicans were able to concentrate more on partisan than incumbent needs. Despite Democrats' threats of court action, neither plan faced any litigation before the 2002 elections as both parties agreed the plans fairly faithfully followed the APOL rules and the Democrats instead focused on overturning the congressional plan.[40]

The Role of Traditional Districting Principles

These two states present an interesting contrast for the potentially constraining role of traditional districting principles, specifically the place of upholding political subdivisions. While the Georgia constitution mentions protecting political subdivisions, the remappers did not place an emphasis on this during the process. On the other hand, the principle played an important role in Michigan as the Senate Democrats forced the controlling Republicans to compromise with them after they introduced a plan that kept more counties intact than the original Republican plan.

As shown in appendix 2, in Georgia, both chambers show an increase in split counties from the 1990 plans. The House plan went from splitting a third of the 159 counties to just over half and from splitting 13 percent of the counties below the ideal population size for a district, or counties that are small enough to fit into one district, to 36 percent. The increase is even more drastic in the Senate. In 1990, the Democrats only split 16 percent of the total counties and just 11 percent of the counties below the ideal size. In 2000, the Democrats split 57 more counties or 52 percent of all counties and 49 percent of the counties below the ideal size. Clearly, the Democrats were not constrained by the principle to protect political subdivisions. Interestingly, the Democrats split more total counties in the Senate than the House despite the fact that only nine counties were above the ideal senate district size. This suggests a greater level of the gerrymandering in the Senate plan as well as a reliance on a different strategy in the House. I will return to that shortly. In 1990, the Democrats paid much more respect to this principle by only splitting 13 percent of the counties below the ideal size in the House and 11 percent in the Senate. In 1990, the Democrats were not in jeopardy of losing their majority and had the luxury of following the constitution. In 2000, this luxury was gone and the Democrats disregarded this principle.

In Michigan, the constraint worked. The remappers split an almost equal number of counties between the 1990 and 2000 plans with the House plans splitting around a third of all counties and the Senate plans only splitting around 12 percent of all counties. More importantly, the House plan only split 10 percent of the counties below the ideal district size, and of these seven counties, the Republicans only split across township boundaries in one county. This prevented the remappers from slicing through counties and splitting the voters in a county into several districts solely for a political advantage. In the Senate, the Republicans only split two counties below the ideal size and did not split across townships in either county. The APOL criteria with specific rules for when a county may be split appeared to limit the Republicans ability to slice up political subdivisions and the principle received public attention when the Senate Democrats introduced a plan that split fewer counties than the original Republican plan. Overall, the Republicans were limited in their attempts to partisan gerrymander as the rules forced them to uphold county boundaries.

District Changes and the Search for Gerrymandering

In this section, to test for partisan gerrymandering, I turn my attention to the district level changes brought about by the new plans. The Georgia House plan needs special attention as the Democrats strategically used multi-member districts and district population deviation to their advantage. In Michigan, I look for differences between the House and Senate plans given the Democrats' lack of input in the House plan.

Parent Districts

The first step in examining district changes is to determine the parent districts in each plan as this gives an indication of the change between the old and new maps. In plans that change little, there is stability between the new and old districts. In particular, the new districts should share the same number as its parent districts and each old district should become one parent district. In plans with a lot of change, few districts will share the same number as its parent district and some old districts will become the parent for multiple new districts while others will be eliminated and not form a parent district.

In Michigan, the determination of parent districts shows some change. In the Senate, only twelve of the thirty-eight districts kept the same number as its parent district. Four old districts became the parent for two new districts while four old districts were eliminated by not forming a parent district. Of the four eliminated districts, three were term-limited districts and the fourth was a Democratic district. The Republicans did not eliminate any of their incumbents' districts. In the House, 71 of the 110 districts kept the same number while 8 districts did not form a parent district and 8 districts became the parent for 2 districts. Once again, the Republicans arranged the districts in their favor. The eight eliminated districts were Democratic districts with an overall base partisanship of 60 percent Democratic while the eight districts that became multiple parents were Republican districts with an average partisanship of 43 percent Democratic.

The Georgia Senate plan kept forty-four of fifty-six districts with the same number while eliminating six districts. To make up for the eliminated districts, the Democrats made four old districts the parent for two new districts and one old district the parent for three new districts. However, there was not a definite pro-Democratic pattern to these changes. Of the six eliminated districts, Republicans held four and Democrats two districts. The average partisanship between the eliminated districts and multiple parent districts was the same at 40 percent Democratic.

The Georgia House underwent the most changes and added an extra layer of complexity for comparisons. The Georgia constitution calls for 180 seats in the House, but does not specify single member districts as it does for the Senate. As a result, over the years the House traditionally used some combination of multi-member and single member districts. The 1990 plans marked the first time in the past half century the remappers used exclusively single member districts. In 2000, the House Democrats went back to a mix of single and multi-member districts. The 2002 districts included 124 single member districts, 15 districts with two seats, 6 districts with three seats, and 2 districts with four seats.[41] In so doing, only thirteen districts kept the same number and forty-eight districts were eliminated. In terms of multiple parents, twelve old districts became the parent for two districts while one old district became the parent district for three new districts. In the most drastic change, the remappers carved district 137 out of 9 old districts with no more than three precincts coming from any one old district. I will return to the strategy for the MMDs later, but for now, it is clear the old and new maps looked almost completely different.

Physical Change

An important part of any districting plan is the amount of geographic change between the new district and its parent. To test for a partisan gerrymander, I examine both the overall change in the new plans and then the amount of change by partisan control of the districts. If a partisan gerrymander is in place, then the controlling party's districts should remain more intact as incumbents like to keep constituents they already know. One way to force an incumbent out of office is to redraw their district with many new constituents.

As shown in appendix 1, the Georgia plans underwent more physical change than the Michigan plans. In both Georgia chambers, the average district only kept 57 percent of their old precincts, while in the Michigan House the average district kept 71 percent of its old territory and in the Senate the average district kept 64 percent of its old territory. Looking at the partisan breakdown reveals the Georgia Democrats kept their districts significantly more intact than the Republican districts. The Democrats left their districts 62 percent intact in both chambers while the Republican districts only remained 52 percent intact in the House and 49 percent in the Senate. In both chambers, the Republican districts gained over 10 percent new constituents than the Democratic districts. In Michigan, the House shows a slight, but not statistically significant, Republican advantage as the Republican districts remained just over 4 percent more intact, but there is no partisan difference in the Senate. Overall, the Georgia plans demonstrate a clear partisan distinction while there are fewer partisan advantages in the changes to the Michigan plans.

Partisan Reconstruction

For a better understanding of partisan gerrymandering, I examine the partisan change in the plans. If a partisan gerrymander is present, this section should reflect the theoretical goals of the strategy. Under a partisan gerrymander, I expect to find four types of activities: (1) safe districts from the in-party losing partisans, (2) competitive districts from the in-party gaining partisans, (3) competitive districts from the out-party losing partisans, and (4) safe districts from the out-party packed with more partisans.

For a detailed understanding of the district changes, table 3.1 presents the partisan reconstruction in each plan. In this table, the "BV Kept" column represents the Democratic vote of the constituents carried over between the parent and the new district, the "BV Added" column shows the Democratic vote of the new constituents added in the district. The key categories are the "2002 BV" that shows the overall partisanship of the district and the "Parent BV" that indicates the overall Democratic vote of the parent district.

The results in table 3.1 highlight the partisan gerrymandering in the Georgia plans. In the House, the Democrats followed the classic partisan gerrymandering pattern. They cracked their safe districts by removing over 7 percent of the Democratic

Table 3.1. Partisan Reconstruction by District Typology

District Type	*BV Kept*	*BV Added*	*2002 BV*	*Parent BV*	*N*
Georgia House					
Control/Safe	81.68	65.33	72.34	79.97	27
Control/Competitive	44.34	41.78	43.19*	44.02	59
Out/Safe	29.65	30.62	29.89*	30.58	49
Out/Competitive	49.53	52.20	53.02	41.27	11
Georgia Senate					
Control/Safe	81.73	53.66	69.80	79.28	12
Control/Competitive	47.84	42.96	45.07	47.17	20
Out/Safe	28.91	29.72	29.39	30.75	18
Out/Competitive	42.66	53.58	48.37	37.51	6
Michigan House					
Control/Safe	34.65	37.29	34.90*	35.39	14
Control/Competitive	45.86	46.93	45.98*	46.09	46
Out/Safe	78.48	75.07	77.88*	77.45	30
Out/Competitive	52.87	52.07	51.92*	53.74	20
Michigan Senate					
Control/Safe	27.62	34.65	30.72	32.79	2
Control/Competitive	47.79	46.39	47.11*	47.22	23
Out/Safe	80.85	65.43	73.62	76.41	10
Out/Competitive	54.46	48.63	52.63	54.39	3

Notes: BV Kept: Percent Democratic vote of those precincts from the parent district. BV Added: Percent Democratic vote of those precincts from outside the parent district 2002. BV: Percent Democratic vote in the 2002 district. Parent BV: Percent Democratic vote of the parent district.

*The 2002 base vote falls outside of the range between the Democratic base vote kept and Democratic base vote added because in each case some of the districts within the typology did not gain any new precincts. Therefore, the Democratic base vote added is calculated only with those districts that gained precincts. Due to this, the average base vote for all districts within these typologies falls outside of the range.

supporters, but these districts remained heavily Democratic at over 72 percent. They did not make their competitive districts safer, but shifted most of the partisan support into the competitive Republican districts. These eleven districts went from 41 percent Democratic to 53 percent Democratic becoming slight-majority Democratic districts. These districts were also 10 percent more Democratic than the competitive Democratic districts. This mostly reflects the strength of incumbency as the controlling party believed their incumbents could win in slightly less Democratic districts. The Senate plan shows the same pattern as the safe-Democratic districts lost nearly 10 percent support and this shifted into the competitive-Republican districts. The Michigan plans do not show high levels of partisan gerrymandering. There is no more than a 3 percent shift in base partisanship in either plan. The Republicans did make the competitive Democratic districts slightly more Republican, but overall did not demonstrate an effective partisan gerrymander.

Multi-Member Districts and Population Deviation: The Georgia Strategy

A closer look at Georgia provides a better understanding of the strategies the remappers used. In Georgia, the Democrats faced relatively lenient rules for gerrymandering, especially with the Black Caucus' approval of the Democratic leadership strategy focused on protecting the party. This approval presumably made the issue of VRA adherence easier to accomplish as the African American leaders worked in tandem with and not against the leadership as in the 1990s. In both chambers, the Democrats had to keep district population within the 10 percent deviation for the plans to reach prima facie constitutionality. The Democrats carefully constructed the maps to fit within the range with both chambers having districts both 5 percent above and below the ideal size. The key to their strategy was to overpopulate Republican districts and underpopulate Democratic districts. This allowed them to pack Republican supporters into as few districts as possible while spreading their own partisans as wide as possible. Their need was evident as the population shifts within the state heavily favored the Republicans.

Due to their inability to use MMDs in the Senate, the Democrats used the population deviation strategy more heavily in the upper chamber. In the Senate, Republican controlled districts were, on average, 3.45 percent overpopulated while the Democratic districts were 2.59 percent underpopulated. This equates to nearly 5,000 more constituents per Republican district than the ideal size of 146,187 and over 3,500 fewer constituents in the Democratic districts.

In the House, the strategy is even more complex as the Democrats combined population with the placement of MMDs to implement a decisive partisan gerrymander. First, in terms of population deviation, Republican districts were 2.06 percent more than the ideal district size while Democratic districts were 1.28 percent underpopulated. Moving to the use of MMDs, the Democrats combined districts together to enlarge the ideal district size to include more territory in these districts. This allowed them to take a core of old Democratic districts and extend the boundaries into predominately old Republican districts keeping the entire district more Democratic. Overall, the twenty-three MMDs were over 5 percent more Democratic than the single member districts.

Another result of the Democratic strategy was paired incumbents. The 2002 plan pitted twenty-eight incumbents into fourteen single member districts. Of these, nine districts had two Republicans with one more having a Republican and an independent incumbent. The remaining four districts had one Democrat and one Republican. In the multi-member districts, four of the two post districts had three Republican incumbents. The Democrats were strategic by pairing thirty Republicans together without pairing any Democrats in the same districts, and making the four districts with both a Democratic and Republican incumbent over 53 percent Democratic. The Senate featured six districts with incumbent pairings; four districts had two Republicans each while the other two included a Democratic and a Republican. By comparison, the Michigan plans did not pair any incumbents together, although term limits made this easier by forcing out 27 of 38 Senate incumbents and 22 of 110 House incumbents. Overall, the use of paired incumbents supports the partisan gerrymander in Georgia while the lack of paired incumbents suggests more constrained plans in Michigan, albeit with the caveat for term limits.

An example from each chamber illustrates the Democratic strategy. Map 3.1 shows two-term Republican Senator Bill Stephens' 51st district.[42] His old district was safely Republican (29 percent Democratic base vote) and stretched from his residence in the northern edge of the Atlanta suburbs northward toward Chattanooga touching the Tennessee border. The district included five counties and was the only district in four of those counties. His new district actually became slightly more Republican (28 percent Democratic), but lost 50 percent of his old constituents and was 4.99 percent overpopulated. The district stretched from his residence and moved in a northeastern direction through the Appalachians to the Tennessee border then moved along the Tennessee border through two counties, in some areas only as wide as a footpath, before moving southward along the South Carolina border. His new district included parts of seven counties and three full counties. By car it covered 199 miles, took over eight hours to drive, and was nicknamed the "elephant ear" district.[43]

In the House, the 60th district and the fate of Republican incumbent Steven Cash is a good example of Democratic targeting. The 60th district was one of the new MMDs in suburban Atlanta. The district was over 64 percent Democratic with most of this support coming from the heavily Democratic DeKalb County. The 60th picked up nearly 75 percent new precincts and became 33 percent more Democratic than its parent, the old 108th, and was 4.7 percent underpopulated. The Democrats used the heavily African American areas of DeKalb County to create a majority-minority district and a safe Democratic district that included parts of predominantly Republican and white Henry and Rockdale counties. As for Cash, he represented the old 108th that was safely Republican (32.26 percent Democratic

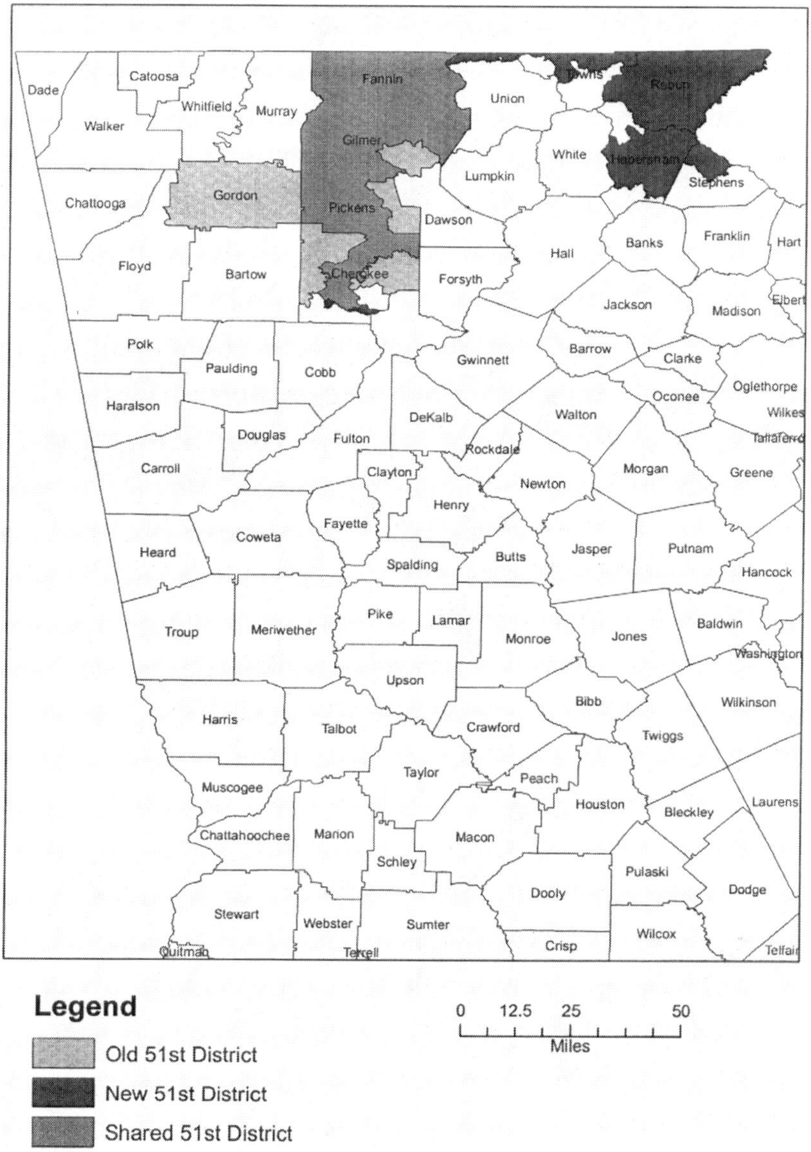

Map 3.1. 51st Georgia Senate District

base vote) and fell completely within Henry County. Instead of facing reelection with 75 percent new constituents in a district nearly 33 percent more Democratic, Cash choose not to run. Upon announcing his withdrawal from the race, Cash commented, "I deeply regret having to make this decision. But the Democrats have effectively shut my voters out of the process."[44]

The Democratic strategy of partisan population deviation worked in the short term, but backfired in the end. After the 2002 elections, the Republicans challenged the Democratic maps on grounds of a violation of the one-person, one-vote requirement. In *Larios v. Cox*, the Republicans claimed an unconstitutional partisan gerrymander due to these population deviations.[45] In March 2003, a federal district court ruled, with the Supreme Court later upholding the decision, the plans unconstitutional, but not directly on grounds of a partisan gerrymander. Rather, the court ruled the state did not uphold a legitimate state goal, such as upholding county boundaries, compactness, or avoiding incumbent pairings, in creating such population deviations. While the Democrats thought they were safe by staying within the 10 percent threshold, the federal court went against precedent and found the plans unconstitutional and ordered new maps.[46]

District Partisanship Influences

To test for evidence of systematic gerrymandering, I examine the changes to district partisanship and model the factors that contributed to these changes. Figures 3.1 and 3.2 plot the 2002 district partisanship and parent base partisanship. In these figures, a key indication of a gerrymander is a pattern to the district shifts. For example, theoretically, in a Democratic partisan gerrymander, I expect out-party (Republican) competitive districts to be safer for the Democrats and vice versa for a Republican gerrymander. If the plans are not a partisan gerrymander, then there should not be a pattern to the districts or they should all fall close to the "no-change" line.

Figure 3.1 highlights the gerrymandering in Georgia. In the House, most of the safest Democratic districts lost some partisan

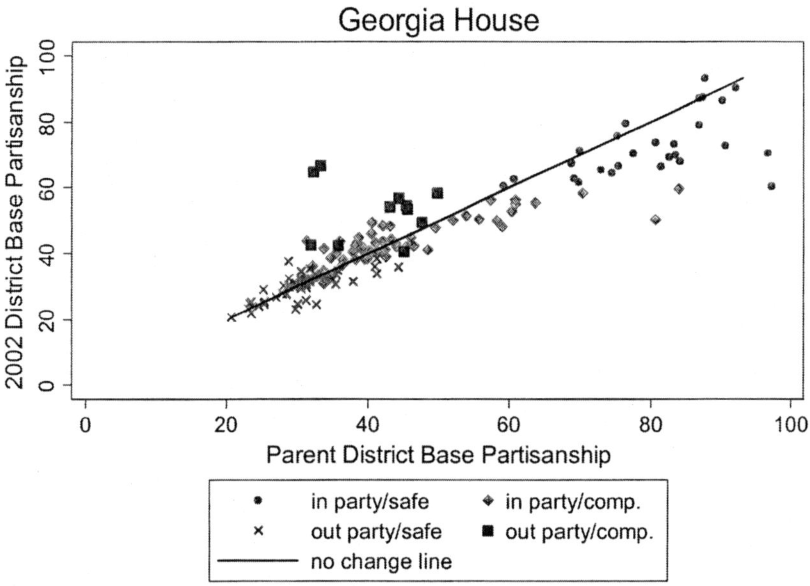

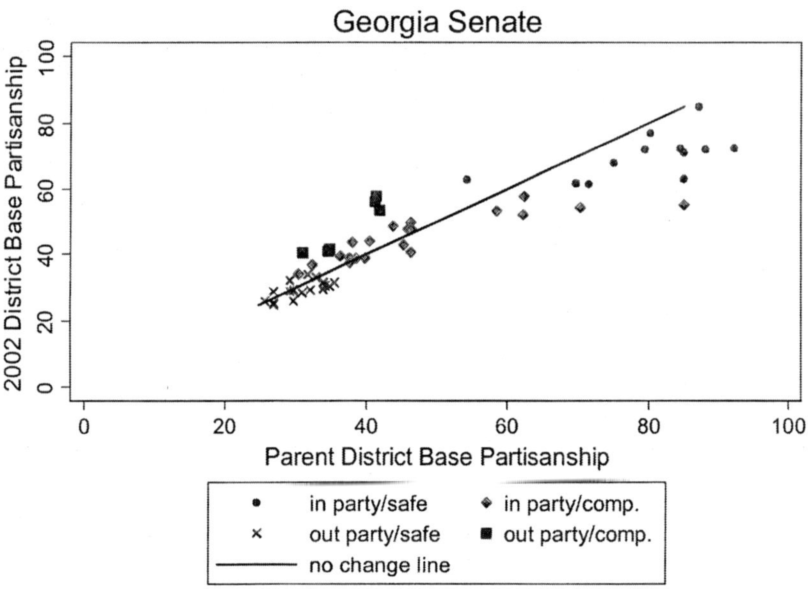

Figure 3.1. Georgia: Comparison of 2002 and Parent District Partisanship by District Typology

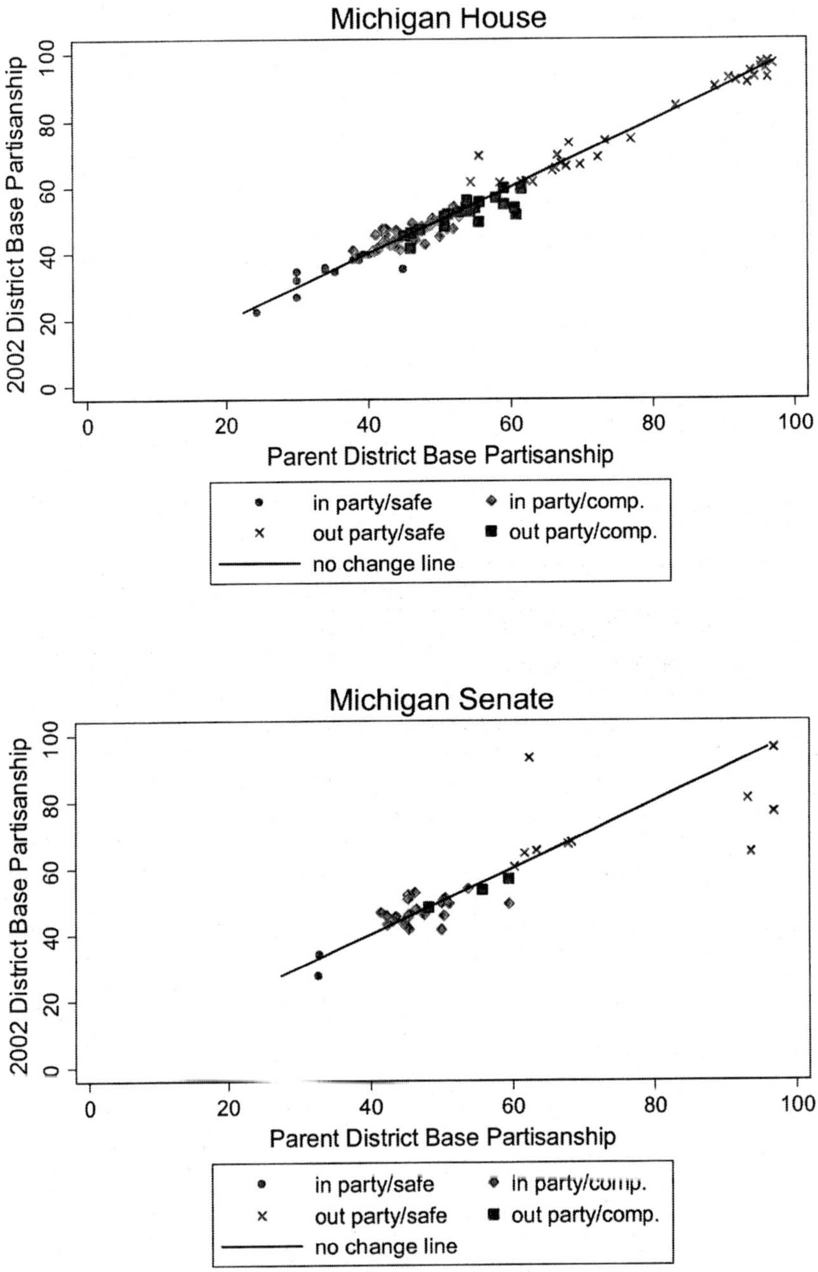

Figure 3.2. Michigan: Comparison of 2002 and Parent District Partisanship by District Typology

support between 2000 and 2002 while a group of competitive Republican districts all gained Democratic partisans along with the most competitive Democratically held districts. In the Senate, a similar pattern emerges with the clear distinction between the safest Democratic districts that fall above 60 percent Democratic and the remaining districts that are around 45 percent and below. This shows the gap between the most Democratic districts and the rest of the state. In figure 3.2, as expected, the Michigan plans do not demonstrate any traits of a partisan gerrymander. In the House, most districts fall near the fitted line showing little change in the new plan. One interesting finding is the large number of moderate districts, which highlights the partisan competitiveness in Michigan. This also suggests the Republicans were not able to implement a partisan gerrymander given their apparent need. The Senate shows more change, but fitting with the previous findings this is not in any systematic manner.

Another test for partisan gerrymandering is to examine the factors that influence the partisanship of the new districts. The regression results in appendix 1 confirm the findings of partisan gerrymandering in Georgia and little support in Michigan. In both the Georgia House and Senate, competitive districts along with underpopulated districts are more Democratic matching with both the partisan gerrymandering theory and the observed strategy used by the remappers. The Michigan House plan demonstrates some factors of a partisan gerrymander as competitive districts were slightly more Republican than safe districts. However, the parent district partisanship was the primary determinant of the 2002 district partisanship as it provided most of the fit to the data (adjusted R^2 of .97). The Michigan Senate does not show any clear pattern of gerrymandering, and the relatively low R^2's suggest some missing factors helped to shape the 2002 partisanship.

Two possible alternatives could be some type of gerrymandering based on a Detroit versus the rest of the state divide or racial districting. However, these variables add little to the model fit. Instead, I argue the plan was simply a compromise plan between the parties that included elements that pleased both parties and did not reflect any one gerrymandering strategy.

Recap of District Changes

The Georgia plans demonstrate a clear partisan gerrymander. The controlling Democrats did not adhere to traditional districting principles and used the population deviation standard to their advantage. The additional use of MMDs in the House shows how the remappers were able to gerrymander within the rules. Overall, the Georgia rules were not overly constraining and the Democrats were able to implement their desired strategy. However, the population shifts within the state made this a more difficult task, but through creative and precise mapping, they were able to implement a plan that should have helped them hang on to their waning majority.

In Michigan, the constraining APOL criteria limited the Republicans ability to advance their cause. The Senate Democrats were effectively able to have a voice by utilizing the rules about ranking competing plans. This led to a compromise between the parties that did not demonstrate any clear patterns of gerrymandering. In the House, the Republicans were able to shut the Democrats out of the process, but the rules still prevented them from implementing an overwhelming pro-GOP plan. Particularly important were the rules against splitting political subdivisions. This limited the Republicans ability to cut across boundaries for their own gain.

Electoral Outcomes

After determining the types of plans implemented, the next step is to examine how these plans translated into electoral outcomes. In this section, I look at who won on Election Day by describing the outcomes from the 2002 elections and then testing for the influence of redistricting by predicting seat gains or losses under various conditions. Finally, I examine the responsiveness found in the plans using the hypothetical seats-votes relationship. In

Georgia, the Democrats appeared poised to keep control and perhaps pick a few seats in each chamber under the new maps. In Michigan, the House Republicans appeared to be in position to gain between three and five seats, while the Senate plan appeared to be a toss-up with predictions ranging from a one- to two-seat pickup for either party.

First looking at the actual seat changes, table 3.2 shows the outcomes of the 2002 elections. The results show mixed success for the controlling parties. In Georgia, the Democrats gained one seat in the House and lost two seats in the Senate. Despite the widespread partisan gerrymander, the Democrats did not make significant gains; however, given their steady decline in the 1990s, the party achieved their primary goal of keeping the majority in a year of sweeping Republican gains in the statewide races. However, the success was short lived. With Sonny Perdue's victory in the governor's race, the Republicans controlled the governor's mansion for the first time in 130 years. Immediately after his victory, Perdue set out to gain control of part of the legislature by lobbying Senate Democrats to switch parties. His tactic was successful as in the next month four Democrats changed parties to give the Republicans a majority.[47] In Michigan, the Republicans picked up five seats in the House, but lost one seat in the Senate. This matched with Michigan redistricting expert Ed Sarpolus' predictions that the Republicans gained an advantage in the House plan, and the Senate Democrats were able to force a compromise plan that slightly advantaged them.[48]

Table 3.2. 2002 Seat Changes

Chamber	*Pre-Election*		*2002 Election*		*Net Change*
	D	R	D	R	
Georgia House*	105	74	106	73	+1 D
Georgia Senate	32	24	30	26	+2 R
Michigan House	52	58	47	63	+5 R
Michigan Senate	15	23	16	22	+1 D

Notes: *One independent not included in both years

Moving to the predicative analysis, table 3.3 provides the seat predictions based on the regression results found in appendix 3. The first column is the number of seats the Democrats held prior to the 2002 elections, the second column is the number of seats they actually won, followed by the predictions using the 2002 districts, the 2000 districts, and assuming all open seats. The percentage of races predicted correctly under each condition is in parentheses.

Overall, the model is quite reliable in its predictions with only the open seat conditions in Georgia predicting less than 80 percent of the outcomes correctly. This shows a high level of confidence in predicting the seats based simply on district level partisanship and incumbency. In the Georgia House, the Democrats actually won three fewer seats than the 2002 model predicted, but won five more seats than under the 2000 districts. While the Democrats gerrymandered the districts in their favor, they could not match these expectations. The key finding is the poor showing of the Democrats in the open seat condition. The Democrats appear to be hanging onto the majority due to the power of incumbency. The Democrats were able to use this factor successfully while redistricting, but, like most southern states, this finding suggests poor prospects for the party after the current set of incumbents leave office. In the

Table 3.3. Seat Predictions

			Predictions		
Chamber	*Previous Seats*	*Seats Won*	*2002 Districts*	*2000 Districts*	*No Incumbents*
Georgia House	105	106	109 (92.18)	101 (87.71)	50 (67.04)
Georgia Senate	32	30	35 (87.5)	30 (82.14)	17 (73.21)
Michigan House	52	47	44 (95.45)	48 (93.64)	45 (90.91)
Michigan Senate	15	16	13 (86.84)	13 (86.84)	14 (84.21)

Notes: Seats won represent total number of Democratic seats won. "Seats won" equals the number of seats won by the Democrats in the 2002 elections. Predictions based on varying district conditions and computed from the regression results in appendix 1. "2002 districts" are the districts used in the elections, "2000 districts" assumes 2002 elections held under the old maps, and "No incumbents" assumes all open seats in the 2002 districts. Percent of total races predicted correctly is in parentheses.

Georgia Senate, the gerrymander did not appear as effective as the party won five fewer seats than the 2002 condition predicted. The 2000 districts predicted the same number of seats as the Democrats actually won showing that the district changes did not translate into the wins the party anticipated. Once again, without the power of incumbency the Republicans would gain a safe majority. In Michigan, redistricting did not help the majority Republicans much. In the House, the GOP captured three fewer seats than predicted under the 2002 districts. However, they did better than the 2000 districts predicted. While they added to their majority, they were not able to capitalize as much as predicted. In the Senate, the Democrats fared better than the model predicted and actually gained a seat. Taking away incumbency in Michigan did not change the results much as the term limits had already limited the influence of incumbency. Overall, given the results from the open seat model, the Georgia Democrats were successful in protecting their majorities through redistricting, while the Michigan Republicans had mixed success with their plans.

Turning to the seats-votes relationship, I examine the responsiveness in each plan. Responsive plans usually show a corresponding shift between the votes a party wins in an election and the seats won. Plans that do not exhibit responsiveness can usually be characterized as having very safe districts with few competitive races. Appendix 3 shows fairly responsive plans in both House chambers. In Georgia, a 5 percent Democratic vote swing would result in an additional three seats for the Democrats while a 5 percent Republican swing would have meant a six-seat loss. In Michigan, the Democrats would gain an additional three seats with a 5 percent pro-Democratic swing and lose five seats with a 5 percent GOP vote swing. In the Georgia Senate, the Democrats would have picked up an additional six seats with a 5 percent Democratic vote swing and would have only lost two seats with a 5 percent GOP swing. This suggests the partisan gerrymander was in place, but the voters did not respond with the votes the party expected. Finally, the Michigan Senate plan showed little change with the Democrats only picking up two seats with a 5 percent Democratic swing with no seat changes with more Republican votes. This suggests the parties were generally safe in the districts they controlled.

Conclusion

The Georgia Democrats won the battle but lost the war. They were able to use the system with few specific constitutional constraints to implement a partisan gerrymander, despite the disadvantages they faced with population shifts and electoral tides in the state. This put them in place to keep the majority in 2002. However, they manipulated the maps in such a way the external constraint of the courts stepped in after the elections and ruled the plans unconstitutional. By so doing, the courts established a new precedent that plans within the established 10 percent population deviation might still be illegal. The Georgia Democrats used the advancements in redistricting technology to use population deviation as a partisan strategy and stay within the established court guidelines, only to have the strategy backfire.

As a postlude to the 2002 Democratic redistricting, with the election of Republican Governor Sonny Perdue the Democrats underwent a quick fall from power. The next two years saw the Democrats lose power in the Senate after the party switching; the courts rule their partisan gerrymander unconstitutional; the Republicans, with a Republican governor and majority control in the Senate, implement their own partisan gerrymander. This fall from power culminated with the 2004 elections where the Democrats lost over twenty seats and the majority in the House.

In comparison, the Michigan case seems relatively uneventful. However, it demonstrates the power of constraints in limiting partisan gerrymandering even under unified government with legislative control.[49] The House Republicans were able to work the system to their advantage, but still did not implement a far-reaching partisan gerrymander. The Senate plan highlights the unique rules within Michigan that allowed the minority Democrats to force the Republicans to implement a compromised plan. Perhaps the one weak link in the Michigan rules is how they are currently established. The legislature codified the rules and has the power to change them at any time unlike most states where the constitution, and its more rigorous amendment process, contains the rules.

The Georgia case represents a cautionary tale of unfettered redistricting in which the legislators manipulated the system to their clear advantage. The voters, not in terms of partisan loyalties but in terms of their control over the democratic process, were hurt as they went to the polls in three straight elections from 2000–2004 with district boundaries drastically different from the previous election and little time to figure out which district they lived in and who represented them. On the other hand, the Michigan case illustrates the effective use of rules and constraints to limit the deleterious effects of partisan gerrymandering on the democratic process. The specific rules in place forced the legislators to follow set criteria that did not completely remove partisan elements from the new plans, but did severely limit them in a state with competitive parties fighting for control of the government.

Notes

1. As quoted in Rhonda Cook and James Salzer, "Redistricting Debate Bare-Knuckle Politics; Parties Fight to Save, Gain Assembly Seats," *Atlanta Journal-Constitution*, 29 July 2001.

2. As quoted in Malcolm Johnson, "Senate OK's Plans for Redistricting," *South Bend Tribune*, 27 June 2001, Michigan edition.

3. According to Keith R. Billingsley, "Georgia," in *Reapportionment Politics: The History of Redistricting in the 50 States*, ed. Leroy Hardy, Alan Heslop, and Stuart Anderson (Beverly Hills, Calif.: Sage Publications, 1981), 82–85, under this system, the most populous 8 counties each received three members, the 30 next largest counties each received two representatives, and the remaining 121 counties each received a representative.

4. 372 U.S. 368.

5. Billingsley, "Georgia." The Georgia Senate went through six plans, the House seven, and the congressional districts four.

6. Billingsley, "Georgia." This contract led to the creation of the Legislative Reapportionment Service Office within the university's Carl Vinson Institute of Government. The Legislative Reapportionment Service Office serves the same role today as it did with its creation in 1971.

7. Billingsley, "Georgia."

8. Deputy Georgia Attorney General Dennis R. Dunn, telephone conversation with author, 16 May 2005.

9. 864 F. Supp. 1354 (S.D. Ga.) (1994). See also National Conference of State Legislatures, *Redistricting Case Summaries from the '90s* (Denver: National Conference of State Legislatures, 1998).

10. Dunn, telephone conversation.

11. James Salzer, "New State Senate Map Approved," *Atlanta Journal-Constitution*, 11 April 2002.

12. Legislative Reapportionment Services Office, "2001–2002 Guidelines for the House/Senate Committee on Congressional and Legislative Reapportionment and Redistricting," 2001, http://georgiareapportionment.uga.edu/fguide.htm (15 May 2005).

13. Kathleen L. Barber, "Michigan," in *Reapportionment Politics: The History of Redistricting in the 50 States*, ed. Leroy Hardy, Alan Heslop, and Stuart Anderson (Beverly Hills, Calif.: Sage Publications, 1981), 161–70.

14. Barber, "Michigan."

15. Barber, "Michigan."

16. Barber, "Michigan."

17. Frederick Headen, "Where Reapportionment Stands Today" (remarks before the American Society for Public Administration, Lansing, Mich., 17 March 1992).

18. Ed Sarpolus, email correspondence with author, 19 December 2004.

19. Headen, "Where Reapportionment Stands."

20. Sarpolus, email correspondence.

21. Michigan Compiled Laws, Act 463 of 1996, http://www.legislature.mi.gov (9 May 2005).

22. "Senate Map Passes Muster," *Macon (Georgia) Telegraph*, 4 June 2002.

23. James Salzer and Rhonda Cook, "House Says It'll Decide Redistricting, not Barnes," *Atlanta Journal-Constitution*, 23 August 2001.

24. Ronald Keith Gaddie and Charles S. Bullock III, "The Political Consequences of an Uncontrolled Redistricting" (paper presented at the annual meeting of the Southern Political Science Association, New Orleans, January 2005).

25. Melanie Eversley, "Redistricting Map for Georgia Goes to Court in D.C.," *Atlanta Journal-Constitution*, 4 February 2002.

26. Cook and Salzer, "Redistricting Debate Bare-Knuckle Politics."

27. Cook and Salzer, "Redistricting Debate Bare-Knuckle Politics."

28. Jim Galloway, "Redistricting Expands White Base; Racial Strategy Key to Democrats' Push to Retain Capitol," *Atlanta Journal-Constitution*, 16 August 2001.

29. Rhonda Cook, "Governor's Part in Redistricting Upsets GOP," *Atlanta Journal-Constitution*, 3 August 2001.

30. Jim Galloway, "Redistricting Expands White Base; Racial Strategy Key to Democrats' Push to Retain Capitol," *Atlanta Journal-Constitution*, 16 August 2001.

31. Bill Torpy, "Election 2002: State Races: General Assembly: Parties Jockey for Legislative Edge," *Atlanta Journal-Constitution*, 6 November 2002, Home edition and Dave Williams, "Districts Still Favor Democrats," *Augusta (Georgia) Chronicle*, 3 November 2002.

32. Kathy Barks Hoffman, "State Democrats Raise Objections on Redistricting," *South Bend Tribune*, 19 June 2001, Michigan edition.

33. Kathy Barks Hoffman, "Politics Could Shape Redistricting Plan More than in Past," *South Bend Tribune*, 15 February 2001, Michigan edition.

34. Johnson, "Senate OK's Plans."

35. Hoffman, "State Democrats Raise Objections."

36. Amy Franklin, "Demos Hit GOP Push on Redistricting," *South Bend Tribune*, 20 June 2001, Michigan edition.

37. Franklin, "Demos Hit GOP."

38. Sarpolus, email correspondence.

39. Chris Christoff, "Districts for State Look Less Partisan," *Detroit Free Press*, 13 July 2001.

40. Sarpolus, email correspondence. Also see Malcolm Johnson, "Redistricting Plans Could Keep GOP in Control," *South Bend Tribune*, 28 June 2001, Michigan edition; Christoff, "Districts for Safe"; and Hoffman, "Politics Could Shape Redistricting."

41. The MMDs used a post designation so that each candidate filed for one post and ran district wide.

42. Stephens kept the same number from 2000 to 2002.

43. Jim Galloway, "Redrawn District Takes All Day to Tour; Doubled Area Creates Challenges," *Atlanta Journal-Constitution*, 11 August 2001.

44. Kevin Duffy, "District 60, State House: Redistricting Blamed in Decision to Quit Race," *Atlanta Journal-Constitution*, 2 August 2002.

45. 300 F. Supp. 2d 1320 (N.D. Ga.) (2004).

46. Gaddie and Bullock, "Political Consequences." Traditionally, plans within the 10 percent range were assumed constitutional without state justification. This case marked a significant shift in the courts decisions. It now appears states may still deviate population within this range, but must provide a rational for the deviations.

47. Dick Pettys, "Republicans See Excitement, Heavy Burden in New Government," *Associated Press State and Local Wire*, 11 January 2003.

48. Sarpolus, email correspondence.

49. For a slightly different view of the Michigan plans, see John R. Chamberlin, "The Republicans Take Control: The 2001 Redistricting in Michigan," in *Redistricting in the New Millennium*, ed. Peter F. Galderisi (Lanham, Md.: Lexington Books, 2005), 201–16. Chamberlin suggests the Michigan plans, particularly the congressional map, represented one of the most successful partisan gerrymanders throughout the country.

4

Divided Legislative Control

Indiana and Kentucky

> I am not under the illusion the public cares about this. It is an insider game, important to the 100 (representatives).
>
> —Indiana State Representative Ed Mahern[1]

> Redistricting is not the most political thing up here. It's the most personal thing up here.
>
> —Kentucky State Representative Joe Barrows[2]

Under divided government, the legislators conducting the remapping are fundamentally more constrained than those legislators from unified states. Divided government allows both parties to have an institutional role in the process and forces both parties to agree on any new plans. During redistricting before the 2002 elections, both states had a Democratic governor and a Democratic majority in the lower chamber. The Republicans controlled the Senate in both states. In Indiana, the House Democrats held a bare majority of only three seats and hoped to implement a partisan gerrymander to help them maintain this majority. In the Senate, the Republicans were safely in the majority and did not attempt a partisan gerrymander. In Kentucky, the Senate Republicans needed a partisan gerrymander to help maintain and possibly build on their new majority status while the House Democrats, with their safe majority, attempted to protect their own incumbents. In terms of constraints, the Indiana legislators faced almost none with the constitution having essentially no redistricting restrictions. In Kentucky, the laws provided a specific rule against splitting county boundaries. In both states, informal agreements between the chambers lessened the theoretically compromising role of divided government. Overall, the similarities in the two states redistricting environment provides for an interesting comparison for the power of constitutional constraints in limiting partisan gerrymandering.

Redistricting Law and History

Indiana

The Indiana Constitution gives the power of redistricting to the General Assembly, but provides few other guidelines for the decennial undertaking. The constitution only refers to the process in one brief section (Article 4, Section 5), and in that section, the constitution calls for contiguous districts with equal population. Indiana law does not provide any further guidance for redistricting and vests full control of the process to the legislature to set its own procedures and processes. Interestingly, the state vests power in a back up commission to handle congressional redistricting if the legislature fails to enact plans, but does not put any backup system in place for legislative districts.

In the pre-reapportionment revolution era, Indiana was similar to many other states by implementing legislative plans based on the congressional model, senate districts representing political units and house districts based on population. Prior to 1960, legislators used counties as the primary unit for drawing Senate lines, but once the courts ruled population equality as the standard for both chambers the legislature discarded this practice.[3] Until 1984, the Indiana Constitution specified that counties were not to be split during the redistricting process. However, an amendment struck this provision from the constitution in the

1984 election and this traditional principle is longer an important part of the redistricting process.

Prior to the 1990s, legislators commonly used multi-member districts in the legislative plans. However, after the case of *Bandemer v. Davis*, the legislature did not consider the use of multi-member districts in either the 1990 or the 2000 plans.[4] In *Bandemer*, the original suit focused on the dilution of Democratic voting power by multi-member districts; however, the Supreme Court's final ruling emphasized the constitutionality of partisan gerrymandering and not the use of multi-member districts. There remains no legal stipulation barring this practice, but the use of multi-member districts no longer appears part of the process.

The court's history in Indiana redistricting is once again similar to many other states during the reapportionment revolution. The federal courts became involved in 1963 to force the end of the malapportioned districts from the then current 1921 plan. The Republican state Supreme Court became involved in 1964, in ruling the veto of the Democratic governor of the legislative redistricting plan unconstitutional, on a technical point, and implementing the "little federal plan" (House representation based on population and Senate representation a mix of population and county units) of the Republican legislature.[5] In 1965, the federal courts implemented the final plans for the 1960s after selecting from a set of alternatives provided by the legislature. In the 1970s, the courts ruled on the fairness of multi-member districts to minority voting interests, but were not involved in anyway with the plans enacted by the Republican legislature. The 1980s saw the famous *Bandemer* case on partisan gerrymandering. A federal court initially ruled that the Republican plan was an unconstitutional gerrymander against Democratic interests; however, the Supreme Court reversed this ruling and kept the legislature's plans in place. After this ruling, court involvement in redistricting came to a stop as not a single case was filed against the 1990 legislative plans.

Overall, the legislature dominates the process in Indiana with little interference from either legal or constitutional rules or the courts. While the courts have played an important role in the past in Indiana, the current climate is one where the courts are not involved in the process. The major constraint on the legislature appears to be the legislators themselves with divided government and fierce partisanship in the state. However, even this appears mitigated as the state has a long-standing tradition of each chamber independently doing their own plans with an agreement in place between the chambers, regardless of partisan control, to approve each other's plans with minimal interference.[6]

Kentucky

Kentucky law puts the legislature in charge of redistricting with oversight via the gubernatorial veto. Redistricting plans proceed as regular legislation through the lawmaking process. Section 33 of the Kentucky Constitution specifies that the General Assembly has the power to draw the legislative seats into single member, contiguous districts that do not split county boundaries when a county's population is smaller than the ideal district size. The constitution also specifies for the House that, when possible, no district shall contain more than two full counties; although this is secondary to reaching population equality standards.

Historically, legislative remappers focused on the traditional principle of not dividing political subdivisions given the importance of the county unit in Kentucky's government, politics, and culture.[7] Traditionally, this principle has played an important role in legislative redistricting. According to Richard L. Engstrom, legislators reported they had a strong preference for protecting county boundaries while redistricting.[8] Up through the 1960 plans, the primary concern was not splitting counties rather than district population equality. However, unlike Indiana, Kentucky did not discard the use of the principle after "one-man/one-vote" became the guiding redistricting principle. The state continued to enforce the rule in the 1970s and 1980s with the courts becoming involved to overturn the 1970 plans based on malapportionment while upholding the constitutionality of the split county provision. Then in the 1990s the courts invalidated the first maps submitted by the legislature specifically because the plans split too many counties and not for population equality reasons. In *State Board of Elections v. Fischer*, the state Supreme Court ruled unconstitutional plans that divided 19 of 120 counties in the Senate plan and 48 counties in the House plan.[9]

In all previous redistricting cycles, the majority Democrats had control over the process in the legislature with little the Republicans in the either chamber could do to influence the outcomes. As such, the Senate and House Democrats put into place a friendly agreement, similar to Indiana, to allow each chamber to handle redrawing their own lines with no interference from the other chamber. While informal, this arrangement became accepted practice and the norm for how the legislature handled redistricting. However, unlike their Hoosier counterparts, Kentucky legislators faced constitutional requirements and past court involvement that showed not only the courts would interfere with the legislature's maps but also uphold the constitutional requirement against splitting counties.

The 2000 Redistricting: Context and Perception of the Plans

Indiana

Despite divided government, the majority parties anticipated little interference with their redistricting plans. In both chambers, the majority party anticipated the continuation of the norm of allowing the Senate Republicans and House Democrats to draw their maps independently and then include the maps in one bill to limit the chance of a gubernatorial veto.[10] With this apparent free rein, the chamber majorities set out on separate and quite different approaches to the new districts. For the Senate Republicans, the need for a partisan gerrymander was not pressing with the comfortable majority they held in the chamber, with the caveat, that if they picked up two seats, they would have a quorum and be able to conduct business without the Democrats present. For the House Democrats, a partisan gerrymander was the clear motive to protect their slim majority.

The Senate Republicans touted their plan as being fair toward incumbents, respecting minority populations, and communities of interest with the new maps based on legal and not political goals.[11] The plan did not put any incumbents, including Democrats, into the same district and the Republicans claimed the plan left each incumbent's core district in place. While the Republicans did not push a partisan gerrymander, population shifts were in their favor for attempting to subtly pick up the two seats needed to reach a quorum. In the traditionally strong Democratic areas of Gary and Indianapolis population growth was not keeping pace with the largest growing areas of the suburban counties surrounding Indianapolis, Republican strongholds. The Senate Republicans focused on equalizing population in these areas with the benefit of these areas helping their chances of picking up a couple of seats. Patricia Miller, the Republican's leader on redistricting discussed their priorities, "The first thing we looked at was population and to get districts that are equal representation. That has to be our top priority."[12] Republican Senator Brandt Hershman summed up their plans as such, "We made fair and reasonable decisions for everyone. The decisions made sense and reflected changes in population, not political gamesmanship."[13]

However, the Senate Democrats saw the maps a little differently. Lindel Hume, the Senate Democrats' spokesperson on redistricting, decried the maps would limit any influence of the Democrats in the Senate because the plan put forth by the Republicans would cause the Democrats to lose at least two, and possibly more, seats in the 2002 elections. In the end, the Democrats did not put up much of an argument with the plans after the Republicans allowed them to shift their district boundaries within the areas they controlled.[14]

The House Democrats had the clear motive of a partisan gerrymander to protect their majority. Ed Mahern, the Democrat in charge of the plans, was very open with the Democrats primary intentions of protecting current incumbents and not focusing on issues such as communities of interest or moving districts due to population shifts. In a hint of the gerrymander to come, Mahern stressed that keeping the districts core intact was "impossible due to a large extent because of population shifts."[15] Mahern put forth plans that protected incumbents and the traditional areas of Democratic strength. The Democrats did not push the Republicans too far by not putting any incumbents into the same districts with the exception of one retiring Democrat who's district was carved up for other incumbents.

The other main component to the Democrats' plan was to protect their traditionally strong areas of minority support in Gary (Lake County) and Indianapolis-Marion County. Unlike the Senate Republicans who presumably gained from the states suburban population growth, the House Democrats faced the prospect of losing seats in these areas. To address this question, an interesting dichotomy emerged between the parties. The House Republicans called for concentrating the minority populations into a few districts, a strategy that may help Republicans. The Democrats took a different strategy of keeping the same number of districts in the heavily minority areas despite population losses arguing that representation was best served by more districts rather than fewer, concentrated districts. Mahern acknowledged these population losses, especially in Lake County, but he said, "I'm going to do everything possible to make sure that Lake County has the same number of representatives as they have now," in addition, the new maps added one district in Indianapolis.[16]

Unlike the Senate Democrats, the House Republicans entered their own plans into the record as a preemptive attempt to get some of their wishes integrated into the new map, and publicly challenged the majority's plans. The main argument the Republicans had against the Democrats' plan was they split too many counties and communities of interest and produced districts of "bizarre configurations."[17] As pointed out by one journalist, the Democrats were in a good position to do this since, "Then as now, the party in power can ignore county and municipal boundaries and draw the districts to produce as many safe seats for its members as possible."[18] In pushing their plans, House Minority Leader Brian Bosma said, "It's our hope that the Democrats will hear our calls for fair, compact, commonsense districts."[19] However, Mahern and the Democrats quickly dismissed the Republican pleas,

"'Communities of interest,' championed by the Republicans, can be defined all different ways. Usually in drawing maps, 'community of interest' comes up when it furthers what (legislators) want."[20] Mahern said he did not intentionally divide counties or communities and that he did not attempt to keep the districts pretty, but was focused on equalizing population.[21]

The Democrats did not give the Republicans much say into the maps until the House Republicans refused to take the floor threatening to stall not only redistricting but the state budget. However, the Republicans agreed to some minor changes and took the floor for the straight party vote, but not without some final parting shots. Rep. Matt Whetstone summed up the Republican position, "One of the things that distresses us most is the fact that these maps are based on incumbents. They are based on the fact that voters are not the most important thing, but the incumbents are the most important thing."[22] Bosma added, "If you're a Democratic incumbent, this is the best map that could possibly be drawn."[23] Mahern concluded the new plans probably gave the Democrats forty-five safe seats up from forty-two in the old plans.[24]

In the last days of the session, both plans passed each chamber on straight party line votes and the majorities were able to implement their strategies with relatively few constraints. Divided government appeared to produce an institutional arrangement to favor the majorities rather than limiting partisan influence in the process. Most observers saw the process play out with relatively little acrimony or partisan bitterness, or at least much less than was expected heading into the session, according to House Majority Leader Mark Kruzan, "The general consensus was this was going to be a blood bath, and in fact, all it resulted in was some slight bruising in the end."[25]

Kentucky

The traditional norm of allowing each chamber to draw their own plans was in doubt heading into the 2000 round of redistricting as the Republicans had a slim majority in the Senate for the first time in Kentucky's history. The Democrats came out early in the process and said each chamber should have input in the other's maps while the Republicans contended the traditional practice should continue. Given the acrimonious atmosphere in Frankfort since the Republicans gained power of the Senate in 1999, this squabble set the stage for a partisan fight over one of the most political parts of politics. During 2001, Republican leaders requested embattled Democratic governor Paul Patton to call a special redistricting session in hopes of forcing the issue.[26] The Republicans worried the Democrats would stall on redistricting during the 2002 regular session in hopes of creating an impasse and forcing the use of the Democratic plans from the 1990s. Patton rejected this request, and the Republicans countered by asking the courts to set a deadline for redistricting to be completed. This opened the door for the potential of court drawn plans if the parties could not reach a compromise.

Complicating matters for the House Democrats was the issue of regional representation. While they still had a comfortable seat margin in the House, Democratic members were not in complete agreement on how to redraw their own boundaries as both Louisville-Jefferson County and the mountains of Eastern Kentucky were due to lose a seat because of population losses. How to deal with these population losses divided some Democrats based on how and where the seats should go. Jefferson County Democrats did not want to lose a seat and attempted to put together a plan that pushed the maximum population deviation threshold to keep from losing a seat.

Despite the House Democrats' regional issues, they put together plans without compromising with the Senate Republicans and introduced their own legislation with plans for both the House and Senate districts, officially breaking with tradition. This led to an even more partisan split in the legislature as redistricting loomed over the entire session and threatened gridlock over the state's lawmaking body. The Republicans countered with their own plans. The first month of the 2002 regular session displayed a heated and public debate that highlighted the nastiness of the relationship between the parties in the legislature. However, in the end, as the session neared a close both sides reached a compromise with some closed door negotiations and the Democrats' basically backing off the Senate plans they proposed. The new plans avoided the courts getting involved in drawing the lines and were put into place shortly before the filing deadline for the primary elections. In the end, the Republicans got most of what they wanted for the Senate and the Democrats for the House, and it appeared likely the bill strengthened the hand of the narrow Republican majority in the Senate and the longstanding Democratic advantage in the House.[27]

The Role of Traditional Districting Principles

Indiana and Kentucky have completely different histories with the use of traditional districting principles. These principles have no significant place in Indiana as the state only regulates that districts be contiguous. In Kentucky, both the constitution and the state courts place an important role for keeping county boundaries intact. Given Indiana's lack of requirement against splitting counties and Kentucky's specific and court enforced law, I expect to find the Indiana plans split many more counties into multiple districts than the Kentucky plans. Moreover, given the rhetoric of the Indiana Senate Republicans about respecting county boundaries and the House Democrats indication this was not important to them, I expect to find the House plan splits more counties than the Senate's. As shown in appendix 2, the Indiana House split a total of 69 out of 92 counties and the Senate split only 44. In Kentucky, the House split 27 out of 120 counties while the Senate only split 3. More importantly is the number of counties split that fell below the ideal population size for a district. The Indiana House Democrats split 45 out of the 68 counties below the ideal district size up from 41 in the 1990 plan. The Indiana Senate Republicans split 34 out of 82 counties down from 43 in the 1990 plan. In Kentucky, the House Democrats only split 6 out of the possible 99 counties in 2000 compared to 3 out of 100 in the 1990 map. The Senate Republicans did not split any of the 117 counties smaller than the ideal size in 2000; whereas, the 1990 Democratic plan split 2 of these counties.

These differences strongly suggest the importance of this constraint on limiting legislators' ability to draw districts. These findings also support the rhetoric coming from the Indiana legislators. The House Democrats, who did not even pretend to respect political boundaries, clearly drew their maps without any constraint on splitting the counties into multiple districts. The Senate Republicans stressed they drew plans that respected county boundaries and in comparison to the 1990 plans and the 2000 House plans this is true. The Senate Republicans split 41 percent of the counties below the ideal district size much below the 66 percent split by the House Democrats. They also split 11 percent fewer counties than their 1990 plan. However, when compared to the Kentucky plans this talk of respecting communities of interest falls a little flat. The House Democrats only split 6 percent of those counties below the ideal size while the Senate Republicans did not split a single county. Even with only 6 percent of counties below the ideal size split, the House Democrats faced the potential for the courts to rule the map unconstitutional.

House Floor Leader Greg Stumbo noted this by saying they [the Democrats] found some latitude in the courts ruling and were not introducing an unconstitutional plan with more county splits than the court said was allowable. In the past, the courts granted some latitude for House plans based on geographic concerns in mountain areas. The most notable of these splits was in Letcher County, along the Virginia border, where the House Democrats attempted to split the county into three districts in an attempt to place Republican incumbents in unfavorable positions. This would have violated not only the population clause of the constitution but also the clause against placing a county into more than two districts, broadly construed. However, the final plan only split the county into two districts after the Republicans balked at this during the final days of the session.[28]

The findings on split counties show the power of traditional districting principles under clearly defined conditions. In Kentucky, the constitution not only clearly specified the definition of when it was applicable to split counties, but the legislators also had to respect the constraint for fear of the courts ruling their plans unconstitutional. This is an important finding that shows the limits the Kentucky legislators had to work under when putting their plans together. This is especially important for the Senate Republicans who faced the larger constraint given the fewer counties the constitution permitted them to split and their pressing need for a partisan gerrymander.

Districts Changes and the Search for Gerrymandering

To determine how successful the parties were in achieving their redistricting goals, I examine the district changes between the old and new maps. For both the House Democrats in Indiana and the Senate Republicans in Kentucky, a partisan gerrymander was a primary goal. Both parties had small majorities and in the case of the Kentucky Republicans, the party was hoping to build on their newfound majority while the Indiana Democrats were hoping to hang on to their majority as the state turned more Republican. The controlling Indiana Senate Republicans and Kentucky House Democrats went into redistricting with safe majorities and did not face the need for partisan gerrymandering, but rather appeared to focus more on protecting their own incumbents. The remappers faced unique challenges in each state. The Kentucky Senate Republicans hoped to find a way to draw favorable districts around the constraining rule against splitting counties and gaining approval from the House Democrats and a Democratic governor. The Indiana House Democrats did not have any such formal statutory constraints, but had to implement a plan that the kept the minority House Republicans from walking out of the chamber and one the Senate Republicans would approve. As discussed earlier, both parties in Indiana took a hands-off approach to the other chambers plan, making it easier for the House Democrats to implement their plan. More importantly for the House Democrats was the shifting population and partisan swings toward the Republicans.

To look for the types of plans implemented, I look at first the physical change for the districts by examining how much of the new districts were kept intact with their parent districts and then by examining the partisan change by seeing how much change the new districts underwent from their parent.

Physical Change

For the Indiana Senate Republicans, who claimed they tried to protect communities of interest and the previous district core, the geographic change for the districts should be the least. On the other hand, in attempt to protect their own incumbents and partisan interests, the House Democrats did not pretend to protect communities of interest or the previous district boundaries and the geographic change should be the most extreme of the four chambers. In Kentucky, the amount the parties could rearrange geography appears more limited due to the constraint against splitting counties; however, there are 120 counties in the state that can be reconfigured in many ways as long as the districts remain contiguous and with whole counties (except of course for those above the ideal district size). The Senate Republicans' position was much like the House Democrats in Indiana. They wanted to pursue a partisan gerrymander to help protect and attempt to gain on their slim majority. As so, we should see more geographic changes especially since the Republicans were redrawing the districts based on old Democratic plans. In the House, the Democrats were in much the same position as the Indiana Senate Republicans. They had a safe majority and mostly wanted to keep incumbents happy and equalize population. As such, we should see less geographic change.

As shown in appendix 1, these expectations are generally met. The chambers with the least to gain in a partisan gerrymander, Indiana Senate and Kentucky House, kept the districts the most intact at 12 percent more than the partisan gerrymander chambers. On average, both the Indiana Senate and Kentucky House districts stayed nearly 85 percent intact while both the Indiana House and Kentucky Senate plans kept 73 percent of the districts intact. While the overall change is interesting, a better picture emerges for partisan motives by breaking down the new districts by partisanship of the parent districts. These results follow the expectation of the parties protecting their incumbents and giving the out party more new constituents in their districts. The Indiana House follows this pattern with the Democratic incumbents having their districts 7 percent more intact than the Republican incumbents, a statistically significant difference. The Kentucky House Democrats also protected their own by giving their incumbents 11 percent more of their old districts than the Republican incumbents. The Senate Republicans in Frankfort kept their incumbents districts 7 percent more intact although this is not a statistically significant difference. In the Indiana Senate, the Republican plans held fairly true to their rhetoric as they left all incumbents' districts 84 percent intact with the smallest standard deviation of all the plans.

Since an important aspect to keeping districts intact is population change, table 4.1 examines the district changes in the key urban areas in both states (the Louisville-Jefferson County metro in Kentucky and Lake County and the Indianapolis-Marion County metro in Indiana). These urban centers all lost population to or did not grow as fast as the surrounding suburbs and received plenty of media attention during the process. Furthermore, at least in Kentucky, the urban areas gave the parties the ability to gerrymander without the constraint against splitting counties coming into play. Despite the population decline, relative to the rest of the state, in both Lake and Marion Counties neither one lost any districts, in fact, both counties picked up a seat under the Democrats' House plan. On the other hand, Jefferson County lost a seat in the House plan and two in the Senate plan. Urban districts in all four plans underwent more change than the non-urban districts with both the partisan gerrymander chambers producing the most change in these areas. The Indiana House Democrats were able to slip two more districts into these counties and had to rearrange the average district by nearly 40 percent to do so. In the Kentucky Senate, Jefferson County districts underwent 16 percent more changes than the non-urban districts as the metro area lost two districts and the Republicans had to reshuffle the remaining districts to account for this. More importantly, they also used the area as their primary attempt at partisan gerrymandering. I will return to this shortly.

Table 4.1. Geographic Change in Urban Districts

	Urban Districts				Non-urban Districts		
Chamber	*2002*	*2000*	*Intact*	*SD*	*N*	*Intact*	*SD*
Indiana House	26	24	63.09	18.71	74	77.78	16.20
Indiana Senate	13	13	79.69	7.71	37	85.65	10.01
Kentucky House	18	19	76.87	17.90	82	87.65	15.31
Kentucky Senate	8	10	60.05	16.97	30	76.69	17.81

Notes: 2002 = Number of urban districts in 2002 plans
2000 = Number of urban districts in old plans
Intact = Percentage of parent district left intact
SD = Standard deviation of intactness
Urban areas defined as Lake County and Indianapolis-Marion County metro in Indiana and the Louisville-Jefferson County metro in Kentucky

These geographic results show that all four chambers conformed to the basic expectations. The Indiana Senate Republican plan did not differentiate between parties when redrawing lines and kept not only the most territory intact but also did not change around any of the parent districts for the incumbents. One slight surprise was the ability of the Kentucky Senate Republicans to give the average district over a quarter of new territory given the fact they only split three counties.

Partisan Reconstruction

I examine the partisan change in the plans to look for evidence of partisan gerrymandering by packing and cracking districts. To examine the district level changes table 4.2 presents the partisan reconstruction in each plan. In the Indiana House, the new plan basically fits the expectations for a partisan gerrymander. The House Democrats made their safe districts nearly 10 percent less friendly while making the Republican competitive districts nearly 4 percent more Democratic and slightly packing the safe Republican districts with more Republican supporters. However, the competitive Democratic districts did not become more Democratic. The Democrats attempted to crack their safest districts and distribute these supporters to a few select competitive Republican districts. As the voters

Table 4.2. Partisan Reconstruction by District Typology

District Type	*BV Kept*	*BV Added*	*2002 BV*	*Parent BV*	*Intact*	*N*
Indiana House						
Control/Safe	80.77	55.08	70.58	79.61	64.82	8
Control/Competitive	48.62	44.82	47.26	48.40	79.17	46
Out/Safe	32.01	31.43	31.54	33.02	72.30	40
Out/Competitive	42.83	45.89	45.01	41.90	57.30	6
Indiana Senate						
Control/Safe	34.54	35.96	34.57	35.19	84.76	28
Control/Competitive	42.27	37.70	41.02	42.38	78.89	4
Out/Safe	79.25	62.24	75.51	78.41	78.92	5
Out/Competitive	47.13	43.88	46.75	47.31	85.70	13
Kentucky House						
Control/Safe	73.90	55.03	68.81	73.78	70.91	9
Control/Competitive	43.92	42.84	43.71	43.81	92.34	56
Out/Safe	32.04	33.44	32.51	32.77	80.10	29
Out/Competitive	49.87	47.63	47.03	44.98	72.77	6
Kentucky Senate						
Control/Safe	34.54	36.46	34.42*	35.00	77.97	16
Control/Competitive	42.28	38.49	43.00*	42.39	69.99	3
Out/Safe	74.80	65.01	71.77	70.37	64.01	3
Out/Competitive	47.23	41.54	45.74	46.75	70.74	16

Notes: BV Kept: Percent Democratic vote of those precincts from the parent district
BV Added: Percent Democratic vote of those precincts from outside the parent district
2002 BV: Percent Democratic vote in the 2002 district
Parent BV: Percent Democratic vote of the parent district
Intact: Percent of the precincts the 2002 district shares with its parent
*The 2002 base vote falls outside of the range between the Democratic base vote kept and Democratic base vote added because in each case some of the districts within the typology did not gain any new precincts. Therefore, the Democratic base vote added is calculated only with those districts that gained precincts. Due to this, the average base vote for all districts within these typologies falls outside of the range.

added to these districts were nearly 3 percent more Democratic than the constituents that remained in the districts. While the Democrats were not able to increase support in their competitive districts, they appeared to rely more on incumbency to keep these districts Democratic. The 46 competitive Democratic districts remained nearly 80 percent intact over 20 percent more than the competitive Republican districts. The incumbents in these districts may not have gained Democratic supporters but they did keep their old constituents.

The Indiana Senate plan does not show much of a pattern and this falls into line with the House Republicans claim that they did not gerrymander. The one partisan goal the Republicans could hope to accomplish was picking up two seats to reach quorum without the Democrats present. To that end, the one Democratic incumbent clearly from a Republican district actually gained supporters, but they did take away nearly 4 percent of support from a competitive Democratic district. Overall, the Senate map did not produce any significant evidence of packing and cracking.

The Kentucky House plan follows a similar pattern to the Indiana House; although the House Democrats did not have a pressing need to partisan gerrymander. The safe Democratic districts lost partisan support, but not to the degree of the Indiana districts. The competitive Republican districts also underwent the most constituent change as well as becoming slightly more Democratic. Whereas, the competitive Democratic districts did not undergo any partisan shifts, but remained 92 percent intact. Another interesting aspect to the Kentucky House plan is that on average the competitive Republican districts are more Democratic than the competitive Democratic districts. However, there are only six competitive Republican districts as compared to fifty-six Democratic districts.

The Kentucky Senate Republicans had a pressing need to partisan gerrymander, but as shown earlier, constraints limited their ability to split counties. There are virtually no partisan shifts within the district typologies, as each typology remained within 1.5 percent of the average base vote in the old plan. From this, it appears the constraints in place limited the Republicans' ability to produce a statewide partisan gerrymander.

To test for evidence of systematic gerrymandering, I examine the changes to district partisanship and model the factors that contributed to these changes. Figures 4.1 and 4.2 plot the 2002 district partisanship and parent base partisanship. In these figures, a key indication of a gerrymander is a pattern to the district shifts. If a widespread partisan gerrymander is in place, then the safest districts should lose some partisan support while the competitive districts should gain partisan support.

Looking first at the Indiana House, figure 4.1 shows the Democrats clearly cracked their safest districts as shown by the cluster of the strongest Democratic districts that fall well below the "no change" line. However, it is not exactly clear what they did with this partisan support. Several of the Republican competitive districts did become more Democratic with one clearly above the line. They also shifted several of their most competitive districts more Democratic. Overall, the House Democrats appeared to spread their support as far as possible in an attempt to keep their tenuous majority.

The Indiana Senate does not show any such pattern. This finding conforms to the rest of the analysis up to this point. The Senate Republicans had no need to gerrymander and they did not. Besides, as figure 4.1 shows, most Indiana Senate districts favor the Republicans with only a handful of safe Democratic districts.

In the Kentucky House, the Democrats were in a similar position as the Indiana Senate Republicans. Figure 4.2 shows some shifting of the safest districts more Republican with a few Republican districts in the 40 percent range shifting slightly more Democratic. Overall, along with the earlier findings, the Democrats did not appear to implement a systematic partisan gerrymander throughout the state.

In the Kentucky Senate, the Republicans had a clear need for a partisan gerrymander, but also appeared to be the most constrained. Figure 4.2 shows they slightly packed a couple of safe Democratic districts with more Democratic partisans while shifting three Democratic districts from slightly less than 60 percent Democratic parent districts to 44 to 50 percent Democratic in 2002. The majority of the districts clustered around the 40 percent mark with no clear pattern of change in these districts.

Another test for gerrymandering is to examine the factors that influence the partisanship of a district. The regression results from appendix 1 show the base model with parent district partisanship explaining most of the variance in the 2002 districts and, as expected, the more Democratic the parent district the more Democratic the 2002 district. The second and third models provide more details for the influence of redistricting. In the In-

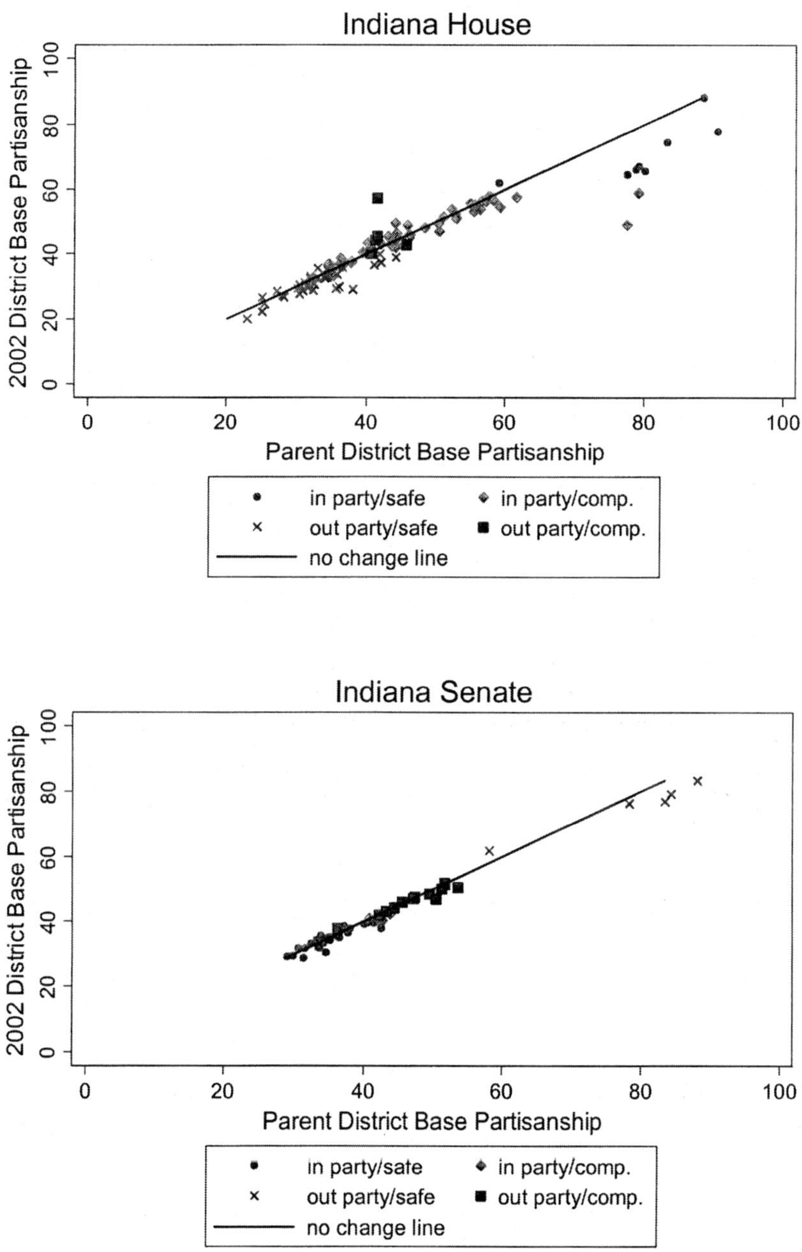

Figure 4.1. Indiana: Comparison of 2002 and Parent District Partisanship by District Typology

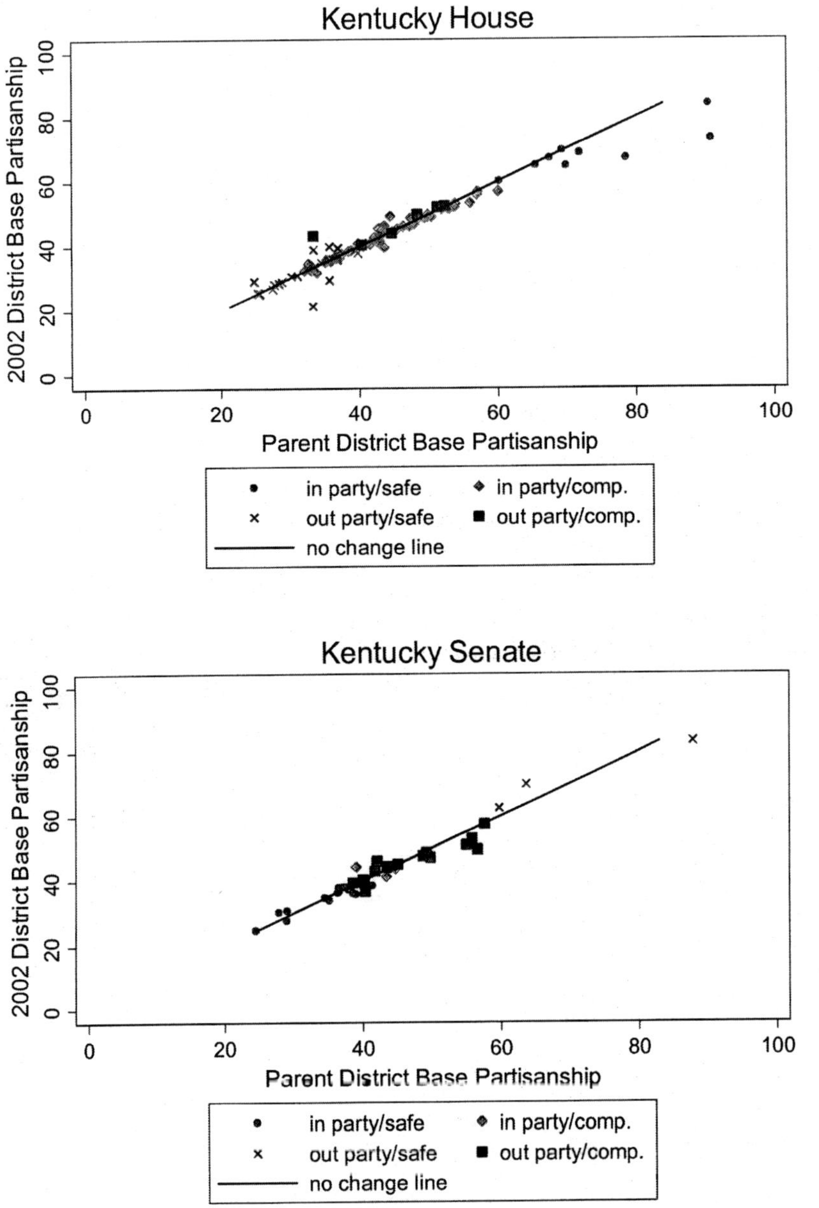

Figure 4.2. *Kentucky: Comparison of 2002 and Parent District Partisanship by District Typology*

diana House, the base model accounts for .88 of the variance. While this accounts for the vast majority of the district partisanship, compared to the other three chambers it was clearly the lowest. This left some room for partisan factors to shape the partisanship of the new districts. Models 2 and 3 offer some support for a Democratic gerrymander. In both models, competitive districts became more Democratic than safe districts while district control was not important. Model 3 also finds a significant influence for district intactness as more Democratic districts remained more intact. In the Indiana Senate, the base model explains .98 of the variance and shows that the new districts did not undergo much partisan change from the previous plan. Models 2 and 3 show statistical support for Republican and competitive districts shifting more toward the controlling Republicans, but substantively this does not provide much information since model 1 accounted for nearly all the variance in the data.

In the Kentucky House, competitive districts became more Democratic than safe districts showing the Democrats were able to shift partisan support in the competitive areas, but overall the parent district partisanship accounts for most of the 2002 partisanship. In the Kentucky Senate, competitive and in-party districts once again moved in the hypothesize direction, but model 1 provides most of the explanation for the 2002 district partisanship.

Up to this point, these findings support the earlier discussion that the Indiana Senate and Kentucky House plans were not partisan gerrymanders. The findings suggest the Republicans in the Kentucky Senate attempted where possible to implement a Republican friendly plan, but the constraint against splitting counties limited any widespread gerrymander. The strongest finding for a partisan gerrymander comes from the Indiana House where the Democrats' plan met important theoretical conditions. They cracked their safest districts and made the competitive Republican districts more Democratic. However, they were not able to do this to a dramatic extent, as they appeared to spread their supporters into as many districts as possible.

The above analysis indicates some level of partisan gerrymandering in the Indiana House while the Republicans in the

Kentucky Senate did not appear to have much success in their attempts. However, a closer look at two key examples gives a better view of the strategies in these chambers. The House Democrats' strategy was to target a few select competitive Republican districts in an attempt to sustain their slim majority. The case of the 86th district perhaps best illustrates the Democrats strategy in the Indiana House. Heading into the 2000 redistricting the 86th was a competitive Republican-leaning district in northwestern Marion County that had elected Republican Jim Atterholt in the previous two elections. Despite Atterholt's previous strong electoral showings, the Democrats focused on the 86th as an opportunity to pick up a seat.

The new 86th district is a prime example of targeting a district for partisan gain. As shown in maps 4.1 and 4.2, the new 86th took the old 86th and flipped it on its side so that the new district reached more centrally into Marion County. Specifically, this allowed the new 86th to pick up strong pockets of Democratic support in the Broad Ripple area of Indianapolis. The old 86th actually did not become the new 86th's parent district, or the parent to any district for that fact. The parent district for the once competitive Republican district was the strongly Democratic (80 percent base vote) 99th district. The new 86th picked up 32 percent of the old 99th, but of the 32 percent, 95 percent were Democrats. The new 86th kept 30 percent of the old 86th and barely drew Atterholt's residence into the district. The new 86th displaced nearly 70 percent of Atterholt's old electoral friendly constituents and made his new district nearly 30 percent more Democratic while cracking the 99th of 28 percent of its Democratic supporters. David Orentlicher emerged as the Democratic candidate and defeated Atterholt by less than fifty votes after several recounts and challenges to the outcomes. This well-publicized example provides a clear example of partisan gerrymandering at work.

A closer look at the Kentucky map reveals the Senate Republican's strategy. Dan Seum, an incumbent Republican from Louisville, holds the key district. Seum was one of two Democrats who switched parties just prior to the 2000 legislative session and gave the Republicans majority control for the first time

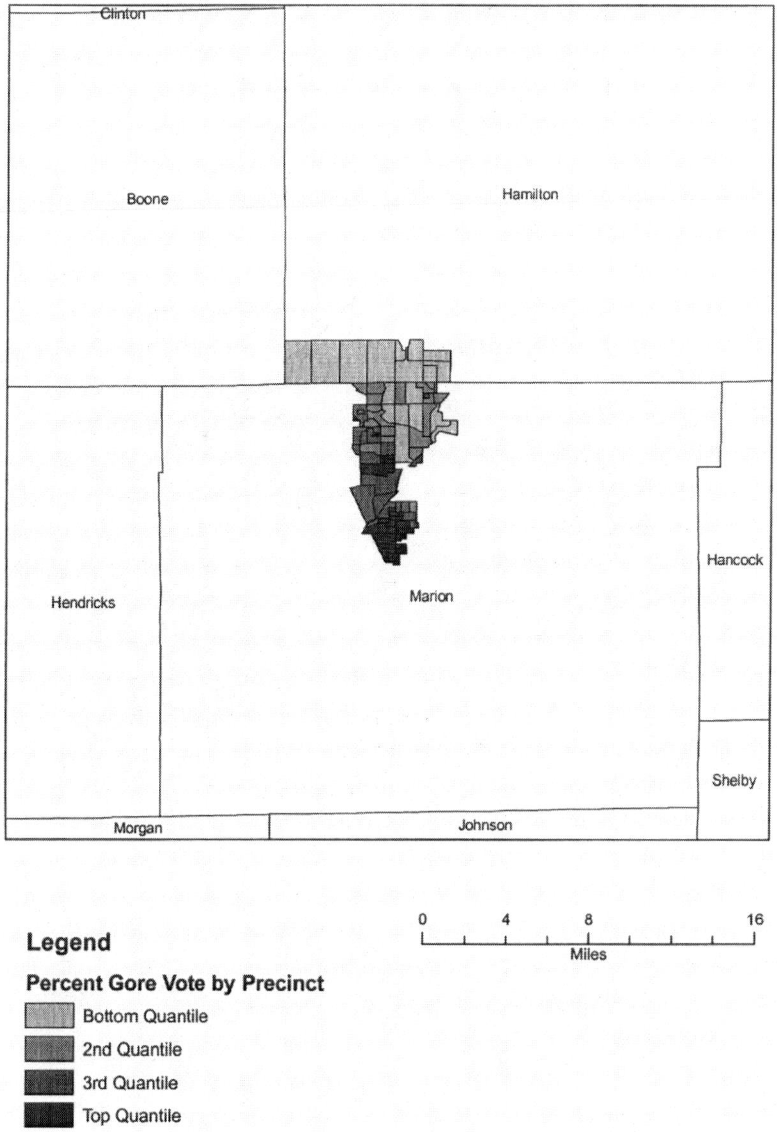

Map 4.1. 2002 Indiana House: 86th District

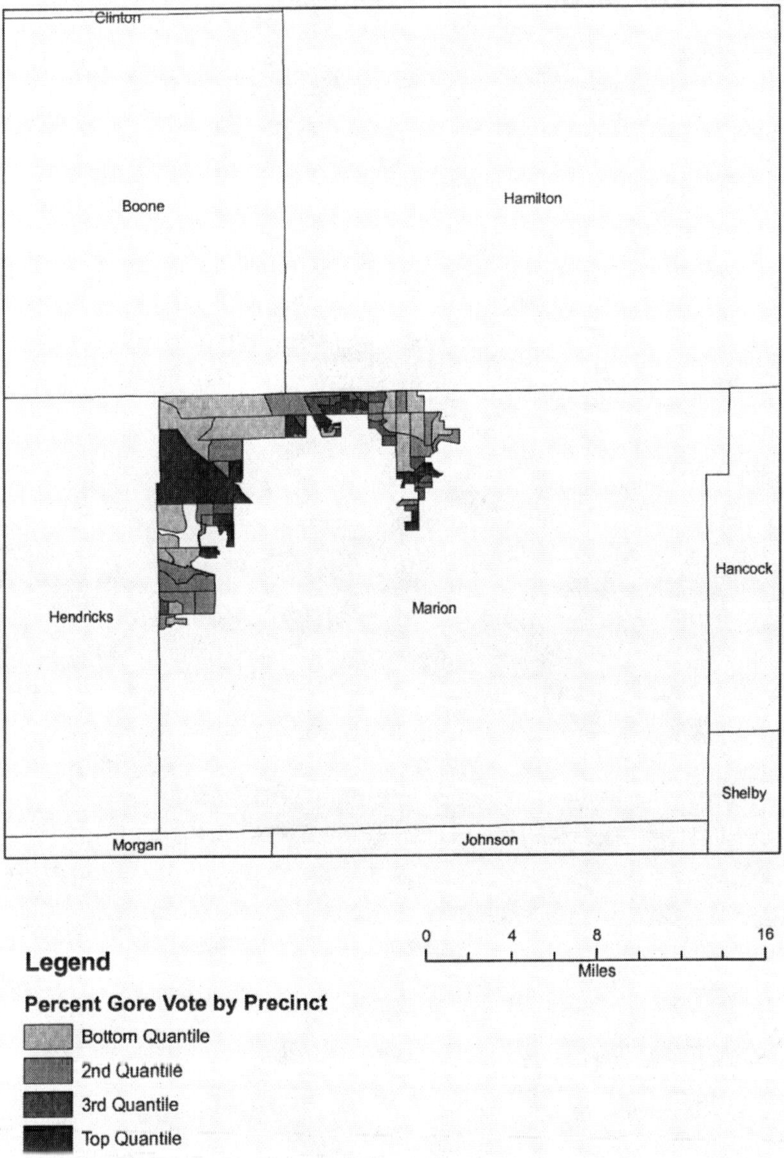

Map 4.2. 2000 Indiana House: 86th District

in the state's history. As a result, the Democrats made a concerted effort to retake those seats because the voters in these districts would obviously elect Democrats. Dan Seum's new Jefferson County district picked up nearly 60 percent new territory, but was not packed with more Republicans. In fact, the district became nearly 4 percent more Democratic. These changes were for two reasons. First, Seum changed residences within Jefferson County and the party had to accommodate his move without disrupting their other incumbents. Second, and more importantly, Seum's district was redrawn to avoid a specific challenger. Because of the late completion of redistricting, potential candidates either had filed for the primaries or were raising money and the parties, of course, had this information. A strong, well-funded, Democratic challenger was planning a run against Seum, but the Republicans drew her out of his district. The Republicans gave up partisan support for protection against a potential candidate. This is in stark contrast to other party switcher Bob Leeper of Paducah, whose 2nd district did not undergo any changes during the redistricting process. Leeper represents a moderately Democratic district in far western Kentucky that comprises all of three counties. He barely won reelection in 2002 by less than 400 votes. Clearly, Leeper could have used some of the help Seum received during redistricting, but the Republicans could not do anything because none of the counties in far western Kentucky approached the 106,000 population necessary to split counties constitutionally. Further, the counties contiguous to the 2nd district were all equally or more Democratic than those in the district.

From examining the district reconstruction in each of these chambers, the findings support a relatively constraint-free partisan gerrymander in the Indiana House. The Democrats split the most counties and the findings pointed to attempts at packing and cracking districts, although the strength of Republican support statewide and the population growth in the strongest Republican areas limited their ability. In the Indiana Senate, the Republicans said they did not partisan gerrymander and the evidence supports it. They did not appear specifically to target any vulnerable Democrats and showed no partisan bias in how they split counties, kept the districts intact, or changed the underlying district partisanship, with the one exception of making their incumbent's from competitive districts slightly safer (around 2 percent). However, it is important to note, most Senate Republicans already came from safe districts. In the Kentucky House, the Democrats with their comfortable sixteen-seat majority also did not overtly partisan gerrymander. Instead, the district changes suggest they targeted a few select Republican districts when accounting for population changes. Finally, the Kentucky Senate Republicans were clearly constrained by not being able to cut across county boundaries. They could not and did not produce a plan with widespread partisan gerrymandering. However, as the example shows, their will to partisan gerrymander was there and they did what they could to help themselves within the constraints they faced.

Electoral Outcomes

After establishing the intentions of the plans, I now examine the impact of the new maps in terms of the parties' bottom line: seat changes. The final analysis looks at the Election Day outcomes and compares the predicted outcomes based on redistricting and the actual seat changes as well as examining the seats/votes relationship.

To begin, table 4.3 lays out the position of the parties before the 2002 elections along with the actual seat changes broken down by what types of seats changed hands. These four chambers showed little turnover in the 2002 elections with the Democrats losing two seats in the Indiana House and one seat each in both chambers of the Kentucky legislature. The Indiana Senate showed no turnover. A closer look shows the most turnover in the Indiana House, where three incumbents lost, two Democrats and one Republican. No incumbents lost in the other three chambers. The Indiana House also demonstrated the most open seat turnover where the Democrats lost three seats and the Republicans only two. In Kentucky, the Democrats lost one open seat in the Senate, and in the House, the Democrats lost three

Table 4.3. 2002 Seat Changes

	Pre-Election		*2002 Election*		
Chamber	*D*	*R*	*D*	*R*	*Net Change*
Indiana House	53	47	51	49	+2 R
Indiana Senate*	10	15	10	15	No change
Kentucky House	66	34	65	35	+1 R
Kentucky Senate*	7	12	6	13	+1 R

Note: *= Only half the seats were up for election in 2002

open seats and the Republicans only two. From this perspective, redistricting appeared to do little. In the partisan gerrymandered chamber of the Indiana House, the controlling party actually lost seats, and there was virtually no change in the other chambers. However, the influence of redistricting is better understood in the context of the predictive analysis.

Table 4.4 shows the seat predictions based on the results in appendix 3. Table 4.4 clearly shows the importance of incumbency in both states and the tenuous majorities of the parties in three of the four chambers. In this table, the top portion shows the number of previous seats the Democrats held in each chamber, the actual number of seats won, and then the predicted number of seats won under varying conditions. The percent of the winners correctly predicted is in parentheses. The 2002 and 2000 conditions predict over 90 percent of the races correctly in each of the four chambers while in the no-incumbents condition this falls to between 60 and 80 percent.

Substantively, in the Indiana House the Democrats held onto their slim majority but actually lost two seats. This was better than each of the three conditions predicted. The 2002 model predicted the Democrats to lose four seats and the majority while the 2000 condition predicted a loss of three seats and a return to split control in the chamber. The no-incumbents situation predicted the Democrats would have only won twenty-seven seats. This suggests the Democrats' majority was mostly due to the strength of their incumbents and that they were able to hang on to the majority in a state where Republicans are much stronger.

Table 4.4. Seat Predictions

Chamber	Previous Seats	Seats Won	Predictions: 2002 Districts	2000 Districts	No Incumbents
Indiana House	53	51	49 (94)	50 (95)	27 (76)
Indiana Senate	10	10	9 (96)	9 (96)	0 (60)
Kentucky House	66	65	62 (97)	61 (96)	52 (79)
Kentucky Senate	7	6	6 (100)	7 (94.74)	13 (63.16)

Notes: "Seats won" equals the actual number of seats won by the Democrats in the 2002 elections. Predictions based on varying district conditions and computed from the regression results in Appendix 1. "2002 districts" are the districts used in the elections, "2000 districts" assumes 2002 elections held under the old maps, and "No incumbents" assumes all open seats in the 2002 districts. Percent of total races predicted correctly are in parentheses.

In the Indiana Senate, no seats changed hands during the 2002 elections. The 2002 and 2000 conditions each predicted the Democrats to lose one seat showing the Democrats did slightly better than expected. The 2002 and 2000 plans show no variation by predicting the same winners and highlight the lack of change between the two plans. Interestingly, with incumbents forced out, the Republicans would have swept all twenty-five races. It is important to note that the seats from traditional Democratic strongholds of Gary and inner city Indianapolis were not up for election in 2002. Overall, this again stresses the importance of incumbency in Indiana's legislative elections and the continuity of the districts between the old and new plans.

The Kentucky House followed the pattern of the Democrats winning slightly more seats than predicted. The House Democrats lost one seat in the election, but the model predicted a four-seat loss under the 2002 plans and a five-seat loss in the 2000 districts. Once again, the power of incumbency is evident. If the elections were held with all open seats, the Democrats were predicted to lose fourteen seats and go from being safely in the majority to holding a bare majority.

The predictions for the Kentucky Senate are quite interesting. The Republicans were able to pick up one seat and add to their slim majority. The model predicted this with the 2002 districts while under the 2000 districts the Democrats would have held onto this seat. Interestingly, taking away the influence of incumbency would have helped the Democrats. Under this condition, they would have won thirteen out of nineteen seats. The power of incumbency helped the Republicans hang on to their majority. These findings also show Senate Republicans were not able to gerrymander effectively to redistribute the voters in their favor.

The last area to examine is the responsiveness of the plans. To do this, I use the hypothetical swing ratio to see how stable the seat totals are given uniform vote swings across the districts. As shown in appendix 3, the Indiana House plan is the most volatile with the Democrats barely hanging on to their majority. If the state moved even 1 percent more Republican than the Democrats would expect to lose two seats and their majority. If the state moved 5 percent more Republican then they would lose up to six seats, but they would only gain one seat if the move went in their favor. This suggests the Democrats maximized their support. The other plans show more stability with the Senate Democrats unable to improve upon their ten seats won, and would only expect to lose one seat with Republican shifts. In Kentucky, the House Democrats would not see any losses with a Republican shift, but could pick up a couple of seats if the state moved more Democratic, and the Kentucky Senate shows a similar pattern. These findings show a lack of responsiveness in these three chambers that suggest the districts were quite safe for the parties in control.

Conclusion

For someone simply looking at the outcomes from the 2002 elections, they would not see much of a change in the partisan make up in Indiana or Kentucky. However, a closer look reveals important aspects of gerrymandering and legislative constraint. In the Indiana House, a two-seat loss would not appear to provide a successful partisan gerrymander. However, given all the factors involved, I argue the Democrats were successful at producing a map that allowed them to hang on to control of the chamber given the pro-Republican factors within Indiana. The state's population shifts clearly favored the Republican suburban areas and the voters are strongly Republican in presidential elections. In the end, the Democrats were able to draw the maps to win a razor thin majority of the seats with a bare minimum of the statewide votes.[29] In both the Indiana Senate and Kentucky House, the legislators were content with protecting their own while dealing with population changes and not pushing for partisan gerrymanders. The Indiana Senate Republicans were content with their safe majority of mostly safe districts and did not provide much of a push to change the status quo. The Kentucky House Democrats had to deal with population losses in areas of partisan support and put together a plan that mostly protected their own incumbents while making futile attempts to hurt a select few Republican incumbents in the areas of population decline. In the end, the Kentucky House Democrats appear safe for the time being, but the writing is on the wall for growing Republican gains as the current Democrats leave office. Finally, the Kentucky Senate provided the clearest example of how constraints can limit partisan gerrymanders and legislative manipulation of the maps. The Republicans were clearly in a position to partisan gerrymander and unlike the Indiana House Democrats were presumably in a position to reap the benefits of growing suburban areas and statewide voting shifts toward the GOP. However, the constitution severely limited their ability to split counties and thus attempt to rearrange favorable districts for themselves. In the end, they were able to manipulate the Louisville-Jefferson County districts to protect a vulnerable party switcher and crack the districts of two of the most liberal Democrats. This only suggests what they would have done if they could have had free rein over the maps.

Turning back to the important theoretical issues, these two states represent the legislative control/divided government case. In the end, the chambers with partisan gerrymandering expectations did attempt to do so while the less competitive chambers pursued a strategy of not upsetting the status quo and protecting their own. Divided government appears to have placed limits on the parties, but they were also able institutionally to work out compromises that limited the constraining influence of the division. This was specifically true in Indiana where the legislators did not face any other key constraints. The use of traditional districting principles clearly stands out as important in these cases as the legislators in Kentucky were primarily limited by the political subdivision principle, and the court's willingness to uphold this principle. The Indiana legislators did not face this constraint and took advantage of it, especially the House Democrats. Finally, the case of the Indiana House Democrats represents how a partisan gerrymander can work when measured in terms of limiting the party's losses and not gaining seats. More importantly, even given the freedom to partisan gerrymander, legislators could not capitalize on unfriendly conditions such as population shifts. Finally, and most importantly, traditional districting principles can limit legislators' abilities to control their destinies if provided in a clear standard the courts can easily uphold.

Notes

1. As quoted in Shannon Lohrmann, "Legislators Take on Mapping Boundaries," *Lafayette (Indiana) Journal and Courier*, 9 April 2001, http://www.lafayettejc.com/Census/0409|01.shtml (accessed 26 January 2005).

2. As quoted in Mark R. Chellgren, "NAACP Shares Redistricting Idea," *Cincinnati Enquirer*, 15 January 2002, http://www.fairvote.org/redistricting/reports/remanual/ohnews2.htm#naacp (accessed 8 September 2003).

3. James L. McDowell, "Indiana," in *Reapportionment Politics: The History of Redistricting in the 50 States*, ed. Leroy Hardy, Alan Heslop, and Stuart Anderson (Beverly Hills, Calif.: Sage Publications, 1981), 110–15.

4. 478 U.S. 109 (1986).

5. McDowell, "Indiana."

6. McDowell, "Indiana" and Mike Smith, "House Democrats Put Maps into Play," *Associated Press State and Local Wire*, 10 April 2001.

7. J. Allen Singleton, "Kentucky," in *Reapportionment Politics: The History of Redistricting in the 50 States*, ed. Leroy Hardy, Alan Heslop, and Stuart Anderson (Beverly Hills, Calif.: Sage Publications, 1981), 130–33.

8. Richard Lee Engstrom, "Political Cartography in Kentucky: Legislative Redistricting, 1971" (Ph.D. diss., University of Kentucky, 1971).

9. 910 Ky. S.W.2d 245 (1995).

10. Smith, "House Democrats Put Maps into Play."

11. Mary Beth Schneider, "GOP Offers New Maps for Legislative Districts," *Indianapolis Star*, 6 April 2001, http://www.fairvote.org/redistricting/reports/remanual/innews.htm (accessed 8 September 2003) and Mike Smith, "GOP Senators Propose Redistricting Plans; Motivated by Desire to Keep Current Districts Intact," *South Bend (Indiana) Tribune*, 6 April 2001.

12. Smith, "GOP Senators Propose Redistricting Plans."

13. Lohrmann, "Legislators Take on Mapping Boundaries."

14. Martin DeAgostino, "Legislators Scrutinize Proposed Maps for Pros, Cons; Redistricting Plans Shift Boundaries for Lawmakers," *South Bend (Indiana) Tribune*, 8 April 2001 and Martin DeAgostino, "Democrats Cry Foul Over Remap in Senate," *South Bend (Indiana) Tribune*, 21 April 2001.

15. Smith, "GOP Senators Propose Redistricting Plans."

16. Mike Smith, "Population Shifts Present Puzzle for Redistricting; Growth around Indianapolis Means Central Indiana Districts Must Shrink," *South Bend (Indiana) Tribune*, 18 March 2001.

17. Smith, "GOP Senators Propose Redistricting Plans" and Mike Smith, "General Assembly Moves toward Adjournment," *Associated Press State and Local Wire*, 30 April 2001.

18. John Strauss, "Future Losses May Offset Democrats' Showing in Elections," *Indianapolis Star*, 13 November 2002, http://www.fairvote.org/redistricting/reports/remanual/innews.htm (accessed 8 September 2003).

19. Smith, "GOP Senators Propose Redistricting Plans."

20. Lohrmann, "Legislators Take on Mapping Boundaries."

21. Smith, "House Democrats Put Maps into Play."

22. Smith, "House Democrats Put Maps into Play."

23. Mike Smith, "House Approves Map for Congressional, Legislative Districts," *Associated Press State and Local Wire*, 12 April 2001.

24. Smith, "GOP Senators Propose Redistricting Plans."

25. Smith, "General Assembly Moves toward Adjournment" and Martin DeAgostino, "Session Went to the Wire, but Got the Job Done; Budget, Redistricting Handled with 'Low Level' of Acrimony," *South Bend (Indiana) Tribune*, 20 May 2001.

26. Patton was in the middle of a sex scandal that saw his approval ratings plummet.

27. This recount is a synthesis from several newspaper articles. Please see Al Cross and Joseph Gerth, "Legislators, Governor Approve New Districts: Plan Aids Senate GOP and House Democrats," *Louisville Courier-Journal*, 1 February 2002, http://www.fairvote.org/redistricting/reports/remanual/kynews.htm (accessed 8 September 2003); Al Cross, "With Ample Room for Conflict, Expect a Heated Session," *Louisville Courier-Journal*, 6 January 2002, http://www.fairvote.org/redistricting/reports/remanual/kynews.htm (accessed 8 September 2003); Al Cross, "Democrats Reach Deal on Redistricting Plan," *Louisville Courier-Journal*, 9 January 2002, http://www.fairvote.org/redistricting/reports/remanual/ kynews.htm (accessed 8 September 2003); Al Cross, "GOP

Lawmakers Assail Redistricting Bill; Democrats' Plan Appears to Defy Court's Guidelines," *Louisville Courier-Journal*, 10 January 2002, http://www.fairvote.org/redistricting/reports/remanual/kynews.htm (accessed 8 September 2003); Al Cross and Mark Pitsch, "Senate Aims for Quick Vote on GOP Redistricting Bill," *Louisville Courier-Journal*, 25 January 2002, http://www.fairvote.org/redistricting/reports/remanual/kynews.htm (accessed 8 September 2003); Joseph Gerth, "Democrats Continue to Work on Redistricting Bill," *Louisville Courier-Journal*, 16 January 2002, http://www.fairvote.org/redistricting/reports/remanual/kynews.htm (accessed 8 September 2003); Joseph Gerth, "Remarks Spark Senate Squabble; Democrat's Comments Bring Threat of Censure from GOP's Williams," *Louisville Courier-Journal*, 18 January 2002, http://www.fairvote.org/redistricting/reports/remanual/kynews.htm (accessed 8 September 2003); Joseph Gerth and Al Cross, "Lawmakers Far Apart on Redistricting: Decisions Could be Left Up to Courts," *Louisville Courier-Journal*, 13 January 2002, http://www.fairvote.org/redistricting/reports/remanual/kynews.htm (accessed 8 September 2003); and Courtney Kinney, "New Districts Give N. Kentucky More Clout," *Kentucky Post*, 1 February 2002, http://www.fairvote.org/redistricting/reports/remanual/kynews.htm (accessed 8 September 2003).

28. Cross, "Democrats Reach Deal" and Cross and Gerth, "Legislators, Governor Approve New Districts."

29. The Indiana Democrats lost control of the House after 2004 elections, but regained the majority following the 2006 elections.

5

Partisan Commission Control

Texas and Ohio

> The dominant political party treated all members of the opposing party as if they were "enemies of the state" instead of respected state leaders, many with a great wealth of governmental knowledge and ability that has and could inure to the benefit of Texas.
>
> —Federal Judge John Hannah in his opinion upholding the Republican Legislative Redistricting Board's plans[1]

> What most people don't realize is the constitution has great detail in what you're allowed to do . . . It really has specifics.
>
> —Paul Tipps, Ohio redistricting expert and former chairperson of the Ohio Democratic Party[2]

Partisan commissions represent the wild card of the theoretical typologies of redistricting control. By design, partisan commissions take away the direct power of redistricting away from the legislature, but keep the partisanship. These commissions represent an interesting case where partisanship may dominate the process, but without a direct say by the legislators. In Texas, the commission became involved only after the legislature could not complete the process, but the commission has original jurisdiction in

Ohio. In both cases, the Republicans controlled the commissions with the Texas commissioners looking at a partisan gerrymander while the Ohio commission was remapping with safe Republican majorities in both chambers. This chapter shows the political dynamic between the commissions and the legislature and, in the case of Texas, highlights the ability of a commission to partisan gerrymander when facing relatively few constraints. The Texas case also shows the importance of state legislative redistricting in relationship to the congressional process. Led by Tom DeLay's strategy, the Republicans countered years of Democratic congressional gerrymandering with their own partisan map.[3] The Ohio case shows a model of redistricting that fundamentally limits partisan gerrymandering with its specific and partisan neutral rules for redrawing legislative boundaries.

Redistricting Law and History

Texas

Article 3, Section 28 of the Texas Constitution vests initial redistricting authority in the hands of the legislature. The legislature has the first regular session after the publication of the census to introduce new plans into law. If the legislature is unsuccessful in completing this task during the first session, the power moves to the Legislative Redistricting Board (LRB).[4] The LRB is comprised of five members: the lieutenant governor, the Speaker of the House of Representatives, the attorney general, the comptroller of Public Accounts, and the commissioner of the General Land Office. The latter three are statewide elected officials, while the Speaker of the House represents the lower legislative chamber. The lieutenant governor plays a dual role in Texas as both the traditional second in charge of the executive and the constitutional president of the Senate.[5]

Between 1921 and 1951, the legislature practiced a "silent gerrymander" by refusing to redraw the legislative lines.[6] In 1948, in response to gubernatorial pressure, the legislature submitted a constitutional amendment to the voters calling for the creation of the Texas Legislative Redistricting Board to deal with the issue of malapportionment. After the voters passed the amendment, the LRB went into effect to serve as a backup commission to redistrict in the event that the legislature was unable to complete the job. In reality, the LRB was put into place to force the legislature to redistrict in an era before the courts forced timely redistricting.

The legislature responded to the creation of the LRB by finally redistricting in 1951. During the preceding thirty years, the population in Texas shifted from a mostly rural population to having a majority of Texans living in urban centers.[7] As a result, the legislative plans in place for the past thirty years severely overrepresented rural interests primarily in east and central Texas. These rural legislators dominated the leadership in the one-party Democratic state. While the legislature redistricted in 1951, the new plan did not accurately correct for the malapportionment that favored the rural areas present in the old plans. The urban areas did gain some seats, but not as many as a plan with equal population would provide. However, this unequal distribution of seats was as much because of Texas law as it was the political desire to protect rural seats. The Texas Constitution dictated the distribution of seats primarily on county and not population standards. The constitutional formula for house seats gave the lesser-populated counties a disproportionate number of seats compared to the counties with the largest populations. In the Senate, the constitutional rule even further diminished urban representation by limiting any county to one senator regardless of population.[8]

The legislature once again redistricted under the county-unit rules in 1961. However, in 1965, a federal court invalidated the provisions of the Texas constitution that limited representation based on counties. The court ordered the legislature to redraw the 1961 maps using equal population guidelines, and in 1967, the legislature adopted new plans for both chambers.

The 1970s marked the first time the LRB played a part in the process. Following the 1970 census, the Democratic legislature adopted a new House map, but was unable to reach an agreement on new Senate plans. The House plan was quickly ruled unconstitutional for unnecessarily splitting counties in violation of the Constitution.[9] In 1972, the LRB drew new districts for both chambers, but both plans were challenged in federal court. A federal district court ruled the Senate plan legal and was in place throughout the decade with no further challenges. The court then ruled the House plan unconstitutional for population deviations and use of multi-member districts to dilute minority voting strength. The court ordered the legislature to redraw the map for use after the 1972 elections.

In the 1980s, the Democratic legislature originally adopted plans for both chambers. Soon after, the state Supreme Court ruled the House plan unconstitutional and the Republican governor, the first in over 100 years, vetoed the Senate plan. The LRB then adopted plans in the fall of 1981, but the Justice Department rejected the plans for diluting minority voting strength. The courts then put temporary plans in place for the 1982 elections and ordered the legislature to adopt new plans following the election. In 1983, the legislature implemented the court's plan without changes in the House and with a few minor changes in the Senate.[10]

The 1990 round of redistricting was wrought with court action, but the LRB did not get involved. The lawsuits began before the legislature even considered new plans, with various interest groups challenging the use of census figures without statistical adjustments for minority undercounts. The redistricting process turned into a decade-long wrangling between the legislature, Justice Department, state courts, and federal courts. The courts ordered revisions to the 1992, 1994, and 1996 plans primarily for reasons involving minority voting rights.[11]

Throughout the previous century, incumbency protection was the most important factor in Texas legislative redistricting.[12] Partisanship was not a key factor as the state reflected the one-party Democratic south through the early 1990s. Urban-rural divisions quickly faded after the 1960s court decision to force redistricting based on equal population. Rather, a core group of conservative white Democrats fought to protect their place in legislature by focusing on individual incumbents during the redistricting process.

Current redistricting law gives the legislature initial responsibility, and the LRB is the backup commission in the event that the legislature cannot complete this task in the first legislative session following the release of the census. In either case, slightly different rules apply to the drawing of Senate and House districts. Most notably, the constitution does not provide much guidance for the drawing of Senate districts. Section 25, Article III calls for single member districts composed of contiguous territory. The remainder of the article discusses the distribution of seats by county and the use of "qualified electors" in place of total population.[13] However, both provisions were ruled unconstitutional by court decisions in the 1960s. For House districts, Article 26, Section III provides more detailed guidelines. The districts are to be apportioned among the counties based on population with the following rules:

a. a county with sufficient population for exactly one district must be formed into a single district;
b. a county with a population smaller than the population needed for a whole district must be kept whole and combined with other contiguous counties to form a district;
c. a county that can hold a multiple of whole districts must be apportioned those districts, with no district extending into a another county; and
d. each county with a population sufficient for one or more whole districts plus a fraction of another district must be divided into that many whole districts, with the excess population added to other adjacent counties to form a district.[14]

Overall, the guidelines for Senate districts do not contain as many constraints as the rules for the House districts. The key difference is that the House plan must follow the traditional districting principle of upholding county boundaries while no such constraint is in place for Senate districts. While the LRB was initially put into place to force the legislature to deal with malapportionment, it now exists as the backup in the event that the legislature fails to act in a timely manner. The LRB may take away legislative influence but the membership does not remove partisanship from the process.

Ohio

In contrast to the Texas Constitution, Article 11 of the Ohio Constitution provides detailed instructions for redistricting and apportionment of the legislature. The Constitution of 1851 vested sole responsibility in the hands of the Ohio Apportionment Board making the board the longest running redistricting commission in the United States.[15] The board operated with three members until 1967 when the legislature amended Article 11 to add two additional legislative members. The current membership includes the governor, state auditor, secretary of state, one member selected from the majority party in the legislature, and one member from the minority party.

From 1851 to 1961, the board reapportioned the legislature every ten years under the rules of the 1851 constitution, and in doing so avoided the malapportionment issues plaguing most states throughout the country. Prior to 1851, the legislature handled redistricting and the Democrats and Whigs encountered fierce conflict over the issue. This conflict was the primary issue that led to the constitutional convention of 1850. The majority Democrats were successful in implementing their primary goals of protecting their rural interests. To do this, they took the power away from the legislature and put into place a representation ratio that used counties, not population, as the primary unit of representation. By doing this, the Democrats built in an advantage for themselves over the Whigs, who had mostly urban support in the then most populated city of Cincinnati. This ratio guaranteed smaller counties overrepresentation in the legislature, which in turn protected the Democratic majority.[16]

With this county-unit ratio in place, the Apportionment Board handled the process for the next hundred years with few problems. The rules prevented them from splitting across county boundaries to partisan gerrymander and the legislature accepted the rural bias built into the system. Ironically, as partisan loyalties realigned, this rural bias, initially designed to help the

Democrats defeat the Whigs, became a Republican bias as the Democratic stronghold shifted to urban areas in the mid-twentieth century.[17]

The one-man/one-vote revolution of the 1960s forced changes upon the Apportionment Board. Between 1964, when the courts found the county-unit provisions unconstitutional, and 1967, the legislature wrangled with new provisions that placed equal population as the primary guideline for the board to consider. In 1967, the legislature amended the constitution to comply with the equal population standard. This move altered the balance between rural and urban districts and significantly benefited minority representation in the legislature.[18] However, the most important component in Ohio redistricting remained political control of the board.

In 1970, the voters elected a Democratic governor and state auditor, thereby shifting control of the Apportionment Board away from the Republicans. The Apportionment Board put into place a Democratic friendly plan that placed several important Republicans into the same districts, including the Speaker of the House. The Republicans quickly challenged the plans, but the courts upheld the constitutionality of the new maps. In 1972, the Democrats gained control of the legislature and the new Democratic majority shifted power away from the rural areas to the urban parts of the state. In 1974, the Republicans took back control of the board, with the election of a Republican governor, and attempted to redraw the lines. However, the courts upheld the constitutional provision stating the board could only implement one plan a decade.[19]

The Republicans controlled the board in both the 1980s and 1990s and as a result the board implemented pro-Republican plans. The 1990s saw the Apportionment Board in court defending their plans for the most of the decade. The line of decisions in the *Voinovich* cases focused on both racial gerrymandering and the relationship between equal population and traditional districting principles. The legal battle began in 1992 with *Voinovich v. Ferguson* in which the Ohio Supreme Court found the board's plan constitutional. The issue involved one senate district that deviated below the 95 percent of the ratio of representation prescribed in the constitution. However, the court found the sections involving upholding county boundaries had equal legal status to the population clause and ruled the plan legal. Later that year in *Quilter v. Voinovich*, a federal district court ordered the board to reconsider the plan after the board did not adequately consider issues of majority-minority districts covered under the Voting Rights Act. After the board submitted a revised plan with additional documentation on their reasoning behind the plan's use of majority-minority districts, the district court was not satisfied the board met the legal standard and ordered a special master to create a new map for use in the 1992 elections. The U.S. Supreme Court then got involved and stayed the district court order. The district court then ordered that the 1992 elections be held under the board's original plan, and the board to reconvene after the elections to correct the problems in the plan.[20]

The court battles continued for the rest of the decade. The district court, on remand from the U.S. Supreme Court, eventually ruled on the population deviation issue by finding the board's plan did not violate the one-man/one-vote provision, despite its population deviation above 10 percent, because the state advanced a rational state policy in upholding county boundaries.[21] On the racial gerrymandering issues, in 1995, the district court ruled the plan unnecessarily packed minority voters and reduced minority influence throughout the state, but the Supreme Court vacated the judgment in light of the recent decisions in *Bush v. Vera* and *Shaw v. Hunt*.[22] Finally, in 1997, once again on remand from the Supreme Court, the district court found the plan did not dilute minority influence. This decision was grounded in the Supreme Court's recent decisions finding that race was one factor to be considered within the constraints of the traditional districting principles within a state.[23] By the end of the decade, the Apportionment Board's plan withstood judicial scrutiny with an important emergence for the legal place of traditional districting principles.[24]

Fresh from the judicial entanglement of the 1990s, the Republicans once again controlled the Apportionment Board for the 2000 round of redistricting with four of the five seats. The constitution, as amended in 1967, required the board to uphold the following detailed standards:

a. population not less than 95 percent nor more than 105 percent of the "ratio of representation," except in those cases where reasonable effort is made to avoid dividing a county[25]
b. single member districts
c. the board is only permitted to issue one plan for the decade
d. the Ohio Supreme Court retains sole jurisdiction for state court adjudication

Specifically for House districts:

e. compact and contiguous
f. districts are not to split county boundaries, but when necessary the board should attempt to uphold townships, municipalities, and city wards (in that order)
g. counties within 95–105 percent of the ratio of representation must form one entire House district and counties between 90–95 percent and 105–110 percent may form one entire House district

Specifically for Senate districts:

h. Senate districts are composed of three contiguous House districts.[26]

To summarize, the design of the Apportionment Board does not remove partisanship from the process. Indeed, from it's inception it was designed to remove legislative influence. The Ohio Constitution lays out some of the most specific guidelines anywhere in the country, with a particular focus on upholding political boundaries. In recent years, the courts have played a significant role in the process by reinforcing these constitutional requirements. Overall, the Republicans had no legal restraint against partisan gerrymandering as long as they could fit it into the guidelines already in place.

The 2000 Redistricting: Context and Perception of the Plans

Texas

The 2000 round of redistricting marked a new era in Texas as the Republicans stood in a position of power for the first time in over a century. The Republicans gained a one-seat majority in the Senate in 1996, marking the first time since Reconstruction that the GOP held the majority in either chamber. Heading into the 2001 legislative session, the divided legislature prepared for redistricting. The House Democrats pushed for a speedy resolution to redistricting while the Senate Republicans were content to stall on the issue. This was because the Republicans won the attorney general, the comptroller of Public Accounts, and the commissioner of the General Land Office in the 1998 elections. With the addition of the Republican Lieutenant governor, the Republicans held a 4–1 majority on the LRB. In the 2001 legislative session, the House Democrats passed new legislative plans, but the Senate Republicans did not let the House plans get out of committee. The Republicans never considered compromising. In fact, many observers considered the entire session one of the most partisan ever, and the redistricting debates some of the most mean spirited of all time. Some of the antics included a legislator coming to the House floor in a life vest to demonstrate his displeasure over his proposed new district that put thirty miles of water between his home and the rest of his district along the Corpus Chirsti Bay, and a priest praying for the end of the partisanship in the redistricting process during the daily invocation on the House floor.[27]

As the 2001 session closed, the LRB prepared to complete the process. On July 24, 2001, the LRB adopted new House and Senate plans by a 3–2 vote. The three statewide officers voted for the plans while the two legislative members voted against the new maps on grounds the plan paired too many incumbents together. The plans then went to the Justice Department for preclearance before they could be used for the 2002 elections. In October, the Justice Department granted the Senate plan preclearance, and in

November denied the House plan preclearance due to issues of Latino representation. In the final action before the 2002 elections, in late November 2001, a federal district court upheld the Senate plan and ordered changes to the House plan so that it would comply with the Justice Department recommendations.[28] The court's ruling kept 98 percent of the LRB's House plan intact with adjustments to areas of Latino concentration in South Texas that added an additional Latino majority-minority district.[29]

The entire process was very acrimonious between the parties, incumbents, and the LRB. Republican Party leaders saw the new maps as correcting the course of Texas history by assuring a Republican majority in the House. The Republicans held back nothing in attempting to gain the majority, and specifically used a strategy of pairing incumbents in order to guarantee open seats. The Republicans confident of a majority after the 2002 elections specifically targeted the Speaker's position and other Democratic leadership positions.[30] The state GOP leaders feared that longtime and popular Democratic Speaker Pete Laney could possibly hang on to the Speakership despite a new Republican majority due to his good relationship with rural Republican legislators. Specifically, those rural Republican legislators felt their concerns were not heard by the LRB. As a result, the LRB targeted Laney's (who was a member of the board) district for elimination by taking his old district and removing twelve of the fourteen counties he represented. The new House plan did not please many incumbents, including Republicans. The new plan paired nearly forty incumbents together, and upset many legislators who believed the LRB did not consider previous bipartisan cooperation in the legislature.[31]

Overall, the opinions of most involved thought the House Republicans would win the majority after the 2002 election with many predictions having them winning as many as eighty-eight seats or picking up sixteen seats. The Senate plan received much less media attention in part due to the lack of a legal challenge, but also because the Republicans were only attempting to build on their majority. Most accounts predicted a one-to-three seat Republican gain under the new map. At the end of the process, the two parties had distinct views on the outcomes. The Democrats called it purely political and categorized the plans as Republican attempts to maximize the number of seats they could win, while the Republicans argued the maps simply corrected the previous gerrymandering of the Democrats and accurately reflected the voter's preferences.[32]

Ohio

The Republicans secured their control of the Apportionment Board in 1998 with victories in the gubernatorial, secretary of state, and state auditor races. These statewide victories put the Republicans back in charge of the process following a successful redistricting in 1990 that saw the GOP become the majority in the House for the first time in over twenty years.[33] This time around, the Republicans spoke mostly in terms of protecting their incumbents and protecting their majority. Brett Buerck, chief of staff for House Speaker Larry Householder, said the board's goal "is not to expand the (Republican) majority. The goal is to maintain."[34] The Republicans appeared content with their majorities and acknowledged any additional seats may be hard to pick up as Republican caucus coordinator Scott Borgemenke said, "You do get to a point where 21 seats (the House majority) is a maximum."[35] Publicly, the Republicans predicted anywhere from a net loss of four to five seats to a gain of one or two seats. The Democrats hoped to challenge more seats than they had in the past decade, but conceded the Republican majority was safe and they would probably make few, if any, gains. The board consistently argued throughout the process, that regardless of their motives, the specific guidelines in the state constitution limited their ability to show political favoritism.[36]

The Apportionment Board on a partisan vote of 4–1 completed its constitutional duty by officially implementing new legislative maps on October 5, 2001. The new plans did not appear to draw a widespread partisan gerrymander, but rather targeted specific districts at the behest of the legislative leadership. In the House, Speaker Larry Householder openly discussed the desire to take back two seats the Democrats won in 2000. The first was a western Ohio district where eighteen-year-old Derrick Seaver won in a highly Republican district and the other was a Cincinnati district held by Wayne Coates. Coates won an open seat race in a district that the Republicans held for the previous twelve terms. In the Senate, the Republicans focused on Democratic incumbent Michael Shoemaker. The Republicans drew the district specifically in mind for Rep. John Carey, who was forced out of the House due to term limits.[37]

The issue of minority voting strength was the Democrats' main contention with the new maps. Democrats and the Ohio Black Caucus quickly challenged the new maps on the grounds "the Apportionment Board failed to follow the Voting Rights Act requiring states to draw the maximum number of districts that give a minority candidate an equal opportunity to win [influence districts]."[38] While Ohio does not need Justice Department preclearance before implementing new districts under the Voting Rights Act, the federal law bound the board. The Democrats contended the new maps did not produce enough influence districts, typically those with a 40 percent minority population or above, but instead packed minority voters into majority-minority districts to limit minority influence throughout the state. The Republicans countered the new maps kept the same number of influence districts as the previous maps and any attempts to add new districts would have violated earlier Supreme Court rulings in *Shaw v. Reno* forbidding race as a predominant factor. Additionally, the Republicans argued that the Democrats were more concerned with electing Democrats than black legislators.[39]

Anticipating arguments regarding the majority-minority districts, the Republicans gained the endorsement of the NAACP before releasing the new maps. However, this move generated controversy when it was discovered that Floyd Johnson, the NAACP representative who signed off on the board's plan, had signed a contract with the Republicans and accepted state money to consult with the Apportionment Board. The Democrats contended the money prevented a conflict of interest for Johnson that limited and compromised his ability to represent the NAACP and minority voting rights throughout the state. However, the controversy quieted down when the president of the Ohio chapter of the NAACP supported Johnson and the board's plan by saying, "It's well representative of African-American communities and the minority communities that we serve."[40]

In early 2003, a three-judge federal panel, with two Democratic appointees, found the board's plan constitutional and ruled that the Democratic plaintiffs did not prove that the plan diluted minority voting strength or used race as a predominant factor. After an appeal, the U.S. Supreme Court upheld the district courts ruling, thus ending the litigation for the Ohio legislative districts and securing the maps use for the remainder of the decade.[41]

Overall, the Apportionment Board implemented new maps that clearly favored the majority Republicans. However, the new districts did not represent a drastic shift from the pro-Republican districts in place throughout the 1990s. The board appeared to follow the constitutional guidelines, especially with regard to not splitting counties and communities of interest and adhering to the constitutional formula for apportioning seats by population throughout the state.[42] In the end, the plans did not face any litigation concerning the constitutionality of the districts based on the specific state guidelines the board followed and passed constitutional muster on the issue of federal minority voting rights. The Apportionment Board appeared to maintain Republican strength within the legal framework.

The Role of Traditional Districting Principles

Both states have several districting principles in place. In Texas, Justice Department preclearance under the federal Voting Rights Act served as the primary factor. This external constraint played an important role as the Justice Department upheld the Senate plan but ordered changes in the House plan. In the end, the courts upheld the LRB plans with minor reshaping to accommodate the Justice Department's suggestions. Ohio does not fall under the VRA although the Democrats challenged the new plans on grounds of minority vote dilution. The courts upheld the plans and ruled the plaintiffs did not prove the plans hindered minority representation.

The other important component in both states was the principle calling the remappers to uphold political subdivisions. In Ohio, the constitution provides specific details for when a county can be split and then calls for the remappers to uphold township, city, and ward boundaries to the extent possible in the split counties. In Texas, the constitution puts this principle in place for the House but not the Senate. In Ohio, this rule played an important role in previous redistricting cycles and the board appeared eager to follow it again. In Texas, this principle did not receive as much attention although the concept of county representation has played an important role in the past.

Looking at the results in appendix 2, the patterns of split counties show two important results.[43] The first is for the examination of partisan gerrymandering by comparing the old and new plans in each chamber. The second is to look for the constraining nature of the principle by comparing across states. In terms of partisan gerrymandering, in Ohio both sets of plans show nearly the same amount of county splits. The 2000 House plan split four more counties than the 1990 plan and the Senate plan split two more than the 1990 map. This is not surprising as the Republican board redistricted based on their old maps. In Texas, the Republican LRB actually split fewer counties than the legislative Democrats in 1990. The House plan only split four fewer counties while the Senate plan, where the rule is not applicable, split 16 fewer counties than the old Democratic map. While this does not show the Republicans did not gerrymander, it does fall into line with the Republican claims they had to correct for the 1990 Democratic gerrymander.

Comparing the two states, in Ohio, the board actually split more counties below the ideal district size than the LRB in Texas. This goes against expectations. The Ohio Apportionment Board split 15 of 66 counties below the ideal district size in the House, up from 12 in 1990 while in the Texas House the LRB only split one of 230 counties below the ideal district size. In the Senate maps, the Apportionment Board split 8 of 81 counties below the ideal size, up from 6 in 1990, while the LRB only split 10 of 247 counties down from 26 in the 1990s. This shows the LRB followed this principle quite faithfully despite their strategy of a full partisan gerrymander. There are several possible explanations. One explanation may be that the board respected the constitution, and the rule was an effective constraint. Interestingly, the LRB followed this rule in the Senate even though it did not apply. Another reason may be that the LRB was able to accomplish their goals without slicing through individual counties. This is possible given the large number of counties in Texas, the relative small geographic area of most counties, and the sprawled geography of the state.

In Ohio, the Apportionment Board actually split slightly more counties in 2000 than 1990 and split over 20 percent of counties below the ideal size in the House. This does not match the level of importance the board gave to this principle. However, upon further investigation, the board split across county boundaries, but did not split across township boundaries. The board split a township into multiple districts in only one of the fifteen counties split below the ideal district size. The board followed the constitution and did not haphazardly split through these counties. Instead, the board upheld township boundaries, a political subdivision that holds a prominent place in Ohio.

Both states show the potential constraining nature of traditional districting principles. In Ohio, the board followed the constitutional prescription for upholding political subdivisions, especially at the township level, but at the same time was not in a position where a partisan gerrymander needed to violate the constitution. In Texas, the LRB followed these guidelines even in the Senate where the rule was not in place. This suggests the Republicans were able to implement their partisan gerrymander without cutting through county boundaries.

District Changes and the Search for Gerrymandering

To test how successful the partisan commissions were in reaching their goals, I examine district change between the old and new plans. In Texas, the Republicans clearly wanted a partisan gerrymander while in Ohio the Republicans appeared more content with maintaining the status quo while targeting a few select races. The Republican LRB in Texas was attempting to gain the majority in the House and needed at least a four-seat swing to unseat the Democrats, while in the Senate the Republicans were hoping to build on their one-seat majority. In this analysis, I expect to find evidence of a successful partisan gerrymander as the Republicans proclaimed victory after the courts upheld the LRB's plans with only minor changes, and most accounts predicted not only a Republican takeover in the House but a sweeping victory of between ten and fifteen seats in the 2002 elections. The interesting question becomes how they accomplished this gerrymander while respecting traditional districting principles and putting a plan into place both the Justice Department and courts found acceptable. Specifically, I expect to find widespread changes both in terms of physical and partisan district change as the LRB drew pro-GOP maps from the 1990 Democratic plans.

In Ohio, I do not expect to find widespread evidence of a partisan gerrymander nor do I expect to find evidence of a bipartisan incumbent protection plan. The Republicans did not appear to push for a partisan gerrymander as they had comfortable majorities in both chambers. At the same time, the Apportionment Board had no need to work with Democrats in implementing the new plans. The Republicans, especially in the House, targeted a few select districts the Democrats won in 2000 to try and pick back up. Given the specific rules the board had to follow in drawing the lines and the lack of a need for a partisan gerrymander, I expect to find less district change in Ohio than Texas. However, I expect to find the Republican board strategically changed those select targeted districts to their advantage.

Parent Districts

The 2002 Texas Senate plan matched each new district with the same numbered old district so that thirty of the thirty-one old districts became the parent district for the same numbered district in 2002. That left one district that did not become a parent district and one district a parent for two new districts. The

House plan produced more maneuvering of parent districts as 99 of the 150 districts shared the same number as its parent district. The remaining fifty-one districts did not share the same number as its parent district. Additionally, seventeen old districts became a parent district for two new districts while one old district became a parent district for three new districts. This left nineteen old districts that did not form a parent district and were essentially eliminated. Of those districts that did not form a parent district, thirteen (68 percent) were Democratic districts.

In Ohio, the Senate map showed little change as each of the thirty-three old districts formed the same numeric parent with the new districts. The House plan showed an interesting pattern. Of the ninety-nine districts, only five shared the same number as its parent district. However, only one old district became a multiple parent and only one old district did not form a parent. The Apportionment Board kept a nearly one-to-one match between the old and new districts using a different numbering scheme. The Apportionment Board did not randomly pick district numbers, rather it followed the specific number scheme set out by the constitution. The constitution dictates that the board assigns the first district numbers to those districts that include only one county and then number districts that fall entirely within a county, and then assign numbers to districts from the largest to smallest populated counties. Population changes shifted this numbering formula and caused the renumbering of most districts. The Senate districts were able to keep the same numbers since the constitution does not provide a numbering formula for the Senate. While most House districts received new numbers, this does not necessarily translate into widespread physical or partisan change.

Physical Change

Examining the district intactness is the next step of testing for gerrymandering. I expect to find the Texas districts underwent more change than the Ohio districts as the Texas LRB was attempting a partisan gerrymander from an old Democratic map. Specifically, if the plans are partisan gerrymanders, I expect

Democratic districts to undergo more change than Republican districts as one method of partisan gerrymandering is to give the out-party incumbents many more new constituents.

According to the results in appendix 1, as expected, the Ohio chambers showed more district intactness than the Texas chambers as the districts in Ohio were left 20 percent more intact than in Texas. Looking at partisan control, interesting results emerge. In Ohio, the Republicans left their districts over 10 percent more intact than the Democratic districts, a statistically significant difference in both chambers. This shows the Apportionment Board was not neutral in assigning new constituents as they left their incumbents with more of the same territory to represent. In Texas, the Republicans did indeed leave their districts more intact; however, this was only at 61 percent intact as compared to the 83 percent intact in the Ohio House. Additionally, the Republican districts were only 7 percent more intact than the Democratic districts. Surprisingly in the Texas Senate, the LRB actually gave their incumbents more new territory than the Democratic districts as they left the Democratic districts 67 percent intact and the Republican districts only 62 percent intact. However, this difference is not statistically significant. While the Texas Republicans changed the maps more, they did not greatly favor their own incumbents by leaving their districts drastically more intact. Another explanation could be these changes were not partisan in nature but rather reflected the need to account for population shifts. However, there is no correlation in Texas between the population deviations of the parent districts from the ideal district size in 2002.[44] The LRB did not gerrymander in such a way that their incumbents kept more of their old constituents nor did they keep districts intact based on population.

Partisan Reconstruction

From table 5.1, the Ohio plans show little partisan change as no district type underwent more than a 2 percent shift in partisan base vote suggesting no widespread partisan gerrymandering in the plans. The Texas plans show signs of a partisan gerrymander. In

Table 5.1. Partisan Reconstruction by District Typology

District Type	*BV Kept*	*BV Added*	*2002 BV*	*Parent BV*	*N*
Ohio House					
Control/Safe	34.60	36.90	34.83*	35.10	29
Control/Competitive	45.09	45.22	45.19*	45.10	31
Out/Safe	75.69	68.95	73.31	74.03	22
Out/Competitive	50.90	44.79	49.50	50.56	17
Ohio Senate					
Control/Safe	34.86	41.03	35.79*	36.68	10
Control/Competitive	45.80	46.45	46.04*	47.20	11
Out/Safe	75.63	60.44	70.64	72.17	6
Out/Competitive	55.59	52.59	54.34	54.36	6
Texas House					
Control/Safe	28.28	33.03	29.46*	28.71	70
Control/Competitive	43.74	47.04	44.95	39.57	6
Out/Safe	72.96	64.05	69.66	68.38	26
Out/Competitive	47.15	42.00	44.76*	48.87	48
Texas Senate					
Control/Safe	30.42	32.50	31.04	30.77	15
Control/Competitive					0
Out/Safe	74.90	58.69	68.97	68.89	3
Out/Competitive	49.52	38.77	46.23	50.08	13

Notes: BV Kept: Percent Democratic vote of those precincts from the parent district
BV Added: Percent Democratic vote of those precincts from outside the parent district
2002 BV: Percent Democratic vote in the 2002 district
Parent BV: Percent Democratic vote of the parent district
*The 2002 base vote falls outside of the range between the Democratic base vote kept and Democratic base vote added because in each case some of the districts within the typology did not gain any new precincts. Therefore, the Democratic base vote added is calculated only with those districts that gained precincts. Due to this, the average base vote for all districts within these typologies falls outside of the range.

the House, the LRB made the Democratic competitive districts over 4 percent more Republican fitting the theory for a partisan gerrymander. However, they did not accomplish this by making the Democratic safe districts more Democratic. Instead, they made the competitive Republican districts 4 percent less Republican, although this was only six districts. In the Senate, the LRB also made the competitive Democratic districts 4 percent more Republican while making the Republican safe districts slightly more Democratic. This also fits with the expectations of a partisan gerrymander. It appears the LRB was successful in making competitive Democratic districts more winnable for the Republicans.

To test for evidence of systematic gerrymandering, I examine the changes to district partisanship and model the factors that contributed to these changes. Figures 5.1 and 5.2 plot the 2002 district partisanship and parent base partisanship. In these figures, a key indication of a gerrymander is a pattern of change by district typology. For example, theoretically, with a partisan gerrymander, I expect out-party/competitive districts to become less friendly for the out party. In both states this translates to competitive Democratic (out-party) districts becoming more Republican (or falling below the "no change" line). If the plans are not a partisan gerrymander, then there should not be a pattern to the districts or they should all fall close to the "no change" line.

The Ohio chambers, figure 5.1, do not demonstrate any pattern of partisan gerrymandering as the Republican districts fit the line quite well and the Democratic districts show more variability but not in any clear pattern. However, figure 5.2 shows a clearer pattern of partisan gerrymandering in Texas. The House and Senate districts both show that most competitive Democratic districts became more Republican and many of the safest Republican districts lost some safety. Fitting with the theory, these districts remained safe for the controlling party. The Texas chambers show the result of the Republican-led gerrymander. It also highlights the results of the previous Democratic gerrymander. In the 1990s, to maintain control, the Democrats packed many safe Republican districts while making many of their districts more competitive. In 2000, with Republican control of the LRB, the Republicans were able to maintain their safe seats and crack many of the competitive Democratic districts to their favor.

Another test for partisan gerrymandering is to examine the factors that influence the partisanship of a district. The results in appendix 1 show little support for a partisan gerrymander in Ohio. Republican controlled districts in chambers became slightly more Democratic in House, but the parent district partisanship is the dominant factor in structuring the 2002 partisanship. In both the Ohio and Texas Senate, the models do not

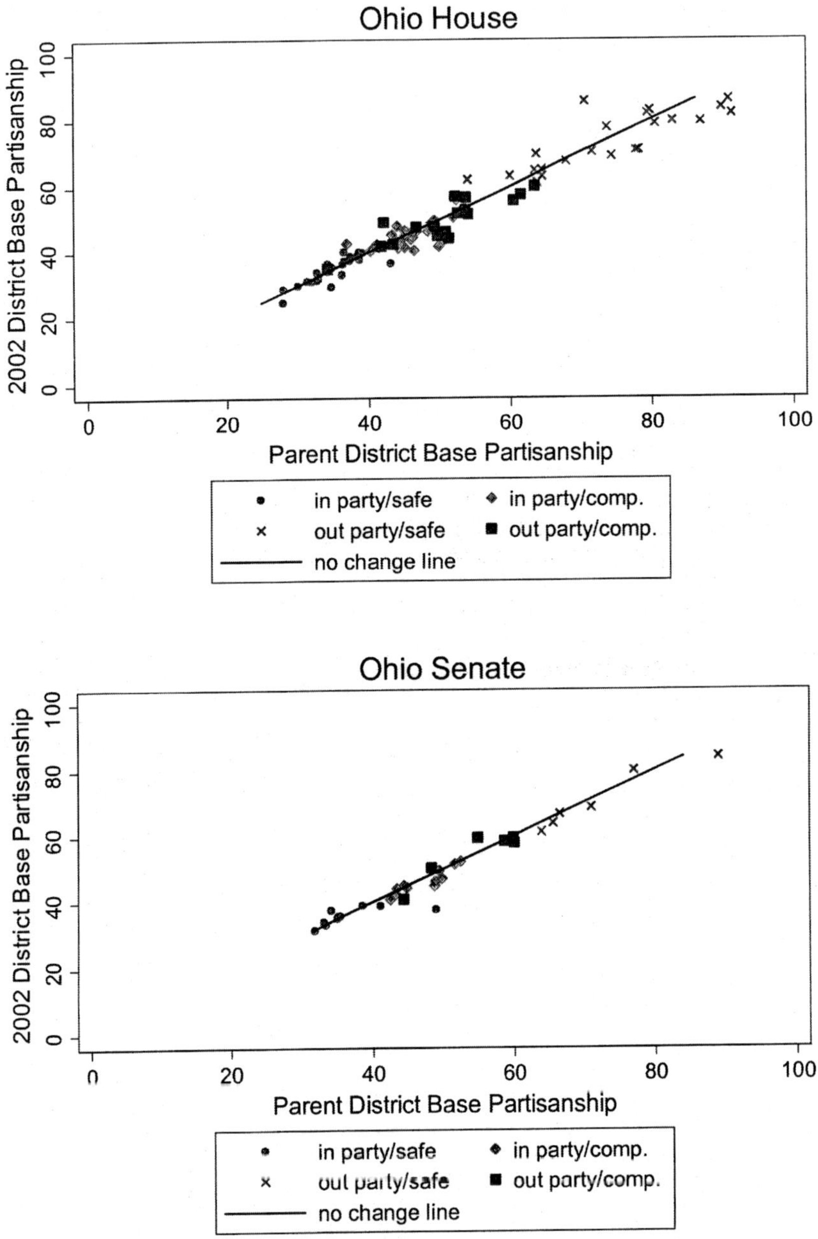

Figure 5.1. Ohio: Comparison of 2002 and Parent District Partisanship by District Typology

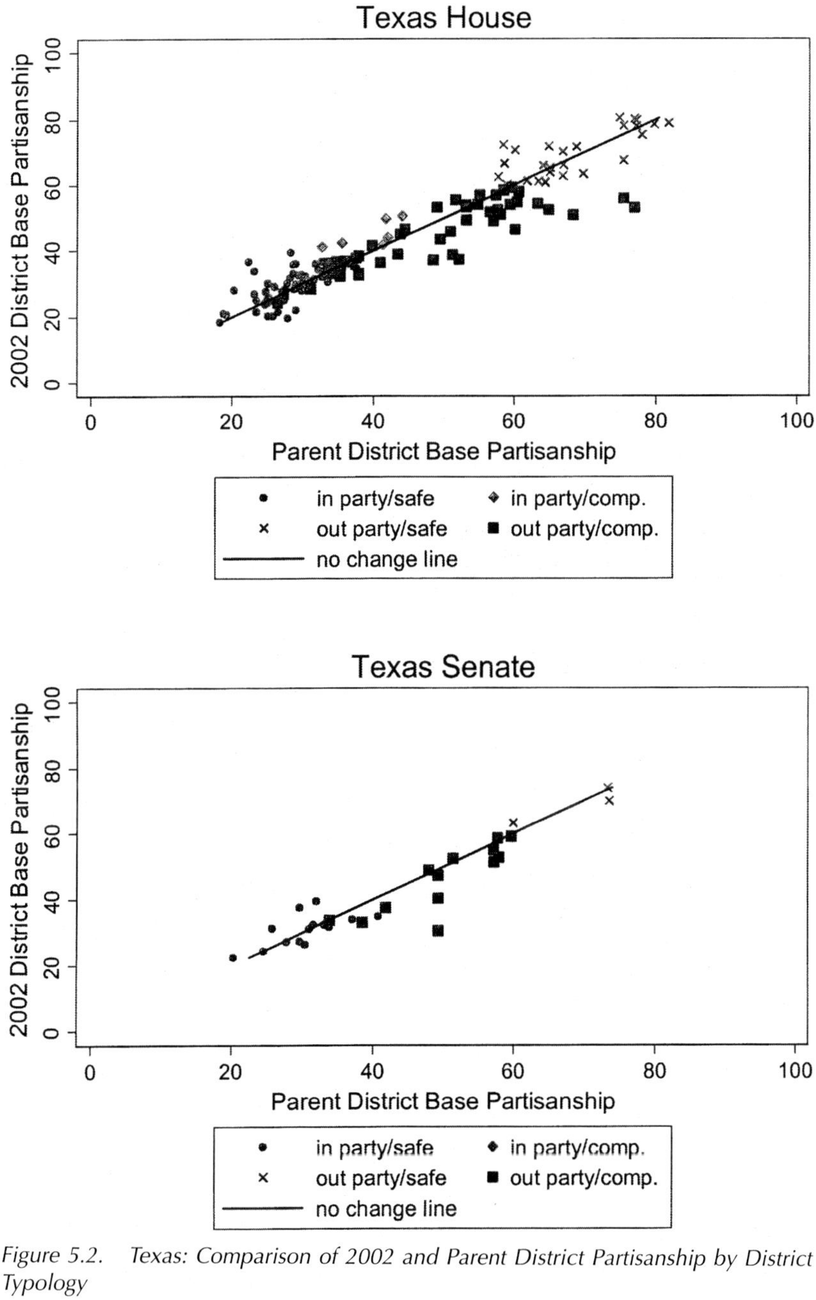

Figure 5.2. Texas: Comparison of 2002 and Parent District Partisanship by District Typology

support a partisan gerrymander, as only the base partisanship variables reach statistical significance. However, I am not confident in the robustness of the Senate models due to the lack of variation among the district typologies and small sample size. In the House, the models do support a partisan gerrymander as competitive and in-party districts move in the hypothesized direction and the model fit shows the most improvement out of the four chambers.

Paired Incumbents and Targeted Districts

Another strategy for partisan gerrymandering is to target incumbents by pairing them into the same districts. Table 5.2 shows the breakdown of paired incumbents by chamber and reveals the primary strategy of the Texas LRB. The Republicans needed to pick up four seats to gain the majority and the LRB appeared to facilitate this by creating twenty-two open seats by pairing incumbents into eighteen districts. The LRB paired two Democrats into six districts, three Democrats into two districts, two Republicans into two districts, and put both a Democrat and Republican in seven districts, and one district with two Democrats and one Republican. The Senate only had one "paired" district with a Democrat and Republican moved together. In Ohio, the Apportionment Board did not pair any incumbents in the Senate and put two Democrats into two districts while putting one Democrat and one Republican into three districts.

Coming back to the Texas House plan, a closer look exposes the extent of the partisan gerrymander. The LRB used an incum-

Table 5.2. Number of Districts with Paired Incumbents by Chamber

Chamber	*Democrats*	*Republicans*	*Mixed*	*Total*
Ohio House	2	0	3	5
Ohio Senate	0	0	0	0
Texas House	8*	2	8**	18
Texas Senate	0	0	1	1

Notes: *= Two districts paired three incumbents
**= One district paired two Democrats and one Republican

bent pairing strategy to achieve the Republicans' partisan needs. Table 5.3 provides the partisanship of the open seats created by incumbent pairings versus the districts with incumbents and the partisanship of the paired districts. The twenty-two open seats created by the LRB are 4 percent safer for the Republicans than all other districts. Looking at the paired districts, the LRB once again helped the Republicans by making those "mixed" districts with both a Republican and a Democratic incumbent safely Republican. Those eight districts were 10 percent more Republican than the average district. Overall, the LRB strategically paired incumbents to favor the Republicans and then took the created open districts and drew them to favor the Republicans as well. Assuming the Republicans only won half of these open and mixed paired districts, the GOP would easily win the majority in the House.

However, the strategy achieves more than just winning the majority. The Republicans were quite confident in their ability to win the majority so they turned their attention to leadership. The LRB placed eleven Democratic committee chairmen into paired districts in an attempt to open up those slots come the 2003 session. Additionally, they targeted Speaker Pete Laney as some Republicans worried he could retain the Speaker position given a group of Republican Laney loyalists if they were not able to capture an overwhelming majority. However, given Laney's far-flung, West Texas district, the LRB was not able to hurt him that much. His district was already safely Republican and geography prevented them from easily pairing his district with another Democratic incumbent. In the end, they gave him 40 percent

Table 5.3. Partisanship in Texas Paired Districts

District Pairing	*Partisan Base Vote*	*N*
Open Seats Created	38.82	22
All Other Districts	42.48	128
Mixed Pairings (Dem and Rep)	32.74	8
Democrat Pairings	47.98	8
Republican Pairings	23.20	2
All Other Districts	42.42	132

new constituents and made his new district slightly more Republican (from 31 percent Democratic to 28 percent Democratic).

In Ohio, the Republican Apportionment Board was more content with targeting a few districts the party wanted to pick up or protect in the 2002 elections. Table 5.4 shows the board had mixed success. In the House, Speaker Larry Householder specifically wanted to pick up two districts. One belonged to Derrick Seaver, a fresh out of high school eighteen-year-old, who shocked the state in 2000 by defeating a Republican incumbent and becoming the youngest legislator in the history of Ohio.[45] However, the board was not able to do much with Seaver's district. His district actually became slightly more Democratic while remaining 94 percent intact. This was due to the constraints in the Ohio Constitution. First, the board had to follow the prescribed scheme for assigning districts based on population and upholding political subdivision boundaries. Seaver's district had to include two full counties and a few townships from a third county based on the population of the rural district, as such, the board was unable to split through areas to alter his district. The other targeted district belonged to one-term incumbent Wayne Coates. In 2000, Coates won an open seat in Cincinnati that traditionally belonged to the GOP. Here the board was able to do more since Coates lived in urban Hamilton County. The board had more freedom to draw through Cincinnati to alter his district. Coates' new district became 5 percent more Republican while gaining 30 percent new constituents.

Table 5.4. Changes in Targeted Ohio Districts

Targets	*2002 District*	*2000 District*	*2002 BV*	*Parent BV*	*Intactness*
House					
Wayne Coates (D)	28	32	44.92	49.60	70.71
Derrick Seaver (D)	78	85	35.01	34.09	94.44
Senate					
Jeffry Armbruster (R)	13	13	52.19	52.50	91.29
Kevin Coughlin (R)	27	27	51.40	51.58	87.32
Michael Shoemaker (D)	17	17	40.77	44.38	57.25

In the Senate, the Republicans tried to protect two vulnerable incumbents, Jeffry Armbruster and Kevin Coughlin, from suburban Cleveland. Once again, the constitution constrained the board as they could not implement many changes to the districts. Armbruster's 13th district had to include two full counties and townships from a third. Most importantly, Armbruster lived in Lorain County, which includes the traditionally liberal Oberlin College. The board was unable to draw Oberlin Township, which voted 83 percent for Gore, out of the district. Due to population, Kevin Coughlin's 27th district had to remain completely within Summit County (Akron). So, the board attempted to give him the strongest Republican precincts in the county, but could not provide much help in the traditionally strong Democratic area. Finally, the board was able to target successfully Democratic incumbent Michael Shoemaker. The board drew Shoemaker's 17th district to include eight complete counties and townships from two other districts in southeastern Ohio. Due to the smaller county populations in the area, the board was able to maneuver the district so that Shoemaker only kept 47 percent of his old constituents while losing nearly 4 percent of his Democratic supporters. Most importantly, term limits forced out a popular Republican House incumbent, John Carey, who lived in the area. The Apportionment Board strategically drew Carey into Shoemaker's district.

The Texas case highlights an apparent successful partisan gerrymander. The LRB was able to adhere to the constraints in place—traditional districting principles and Justice Department preclearance—and still implement a clear pro-Republican plan. Perhaps most interestingly, this case also shows that commissions may facilitate a gerrymander rather than constrain it. The partisan LRB was able to target incumbents to help the Republican cause while not having to deal directly with the legislature. The LRB did not have to compromise with anyone. Under legislative control, it is much more difficult to implement such a far-reaching incumbent targeting strategy as the legislators themselves, in almost all situations, have some institutional recourse to force a compromise. This lack of compromise helped the LRB and the Republicans tremendously.

The Ohio case highlights how constraints can play a limiting role in redistricting. While the Apportionment did not have a glaring need like the Texas LRB to partisan gerrymander, the Republican board did not attempt a neutral plan, as they wanted to help the Republicans where necessary. However, the specific guidelines in the Ohio constitution limited the board's ability to have free rein over the maps. Specifically, the combination of upholding political subdivisions, below the county level, and the specific rules for how to distribute House seats limited the board.

Electoral Outcomes

Table 5.5 shows the Republicans were the winners in both states. In Ohio, the Republicans picked up three seats in the House to increase their majority to twenty-five seats and picked up one seat in the Senate. Turning back to the targeted races discussed earlier, in the Senate, both Kevin Coughlin and Jeffry Armbruster barely held on to their seats as Coughlin won with 53 percent of the vote while Armbruster won with 50.3 percent of the vote, or by just 526 votes. The seat pick up came in the race between Democrat incumbent Mike Shoemaker and Republican challenger John Carey. Carey won with 54 percent of the vote in the district the board drew specifically for him. In the House, the Republicans were able to defeat the targeted Wayne Coates and won two of the three Democrat v. Republican incumbent races. However, the other target of Speaker Larry Householder, Derrick Seaver, cruised to an easy victory. In Texas, the Republicans made the largest seat gain in the nation by picking up sixteen seats in the House and easily taking over the majority. They also managed to pick up three seats in the Senate to add to their one-seat majority. In the House, the Republicans picked up fourteen of the eighteen seats forced open by incumbent pairing and won seven of the eight races with incumbent Democrats and Republicans paired together.[46] The incumbent pairing strategy worked almost perfectly for the Republicans as not a single incumbent was defeated.

Table 5.5. 2002 Seat Changes

	Pre-Election		*2002 Election*		
Chamber	*D*	*R*	*D*	*R*	*Net Change*
Ohio House	40	59	37	62	+3 R
Ohio Senate*	9	8	8	8	+1 R
Texas House	78	72	62	88	+16 R
Texas Senate	15	16	12	19	+3 R

Note: *= Only half the seats were up for election

Turning to the predictive analysis, table 5.6 provides the seat predictions based on the results in appendix 3. Table 5.6 shows the Republicans fared slightly better than expected in the 2002 elections as the Democrats lost one seat more than the 2002 districts predicted in the Ohio House and Texas Senate and three more seats than predicted in the Texas House. Interestingly, if the 2002 elections were held under the 2000 districts not much would have changed. This is most important in the Texas House where the LRB pushed an aggressive partisan gerrymander. However, using the old Democratic districts only predicts two more Democratic victories. This suggests the Republicans were going to gain the majority with or without redistricting. Taking away the power of incumbency shows the Democrats would have lost an additional two seats in the Ohio House and eleven more seats in the Texas House than they actually did. This suggests the 2002 maps did heavily favor the Republicans in both states, as the Democrats needed the power of incumbency to hang on to many of their seats. Overall, the Republicans were in good shape with or without partisan gerrymandering, but the new districts only helped particularly in open seats. In Texas, the experts were very successful in their predictions for the Republicans, and the LRB's focus on drawing Democratic committee chairs out of office appears to be an extra reward of having control over the process.

The last area I examine is the hypothetical seats-votes relationships in each plan. As shown in appendix 3, each of the four

Table 5.6. Seat Predictions

Chamber	*Previous Seats*	*Seats Won*	*2002 Districts*	*2000 Districts*	*No Incumbents*
Ohio House	40	37	38 (92.93)	40 (92.93)	35 (89.90)
Ohio Senate	9	8	8 (100)	8 (100)	10 (88.24)
Texas House	78	62	65 (94)	67 (92.67)	51 (86)
Texas Senate	15	12	13 (96.77)	14 (93.55)	13 (90.32)

Notes: "Seats won" equals the actual number of seats won by the Democrats in the 2002 elections. Predictions based on varying district conditions and computed from the regression results in Appendix 1. "2002 districts" are the districts used in the elections, "2000 districts" assumes 2002 elections held under the old maps, and "No incumbents" assumes all open seats in the 2002 districts. Percent of total races predicted correctly are in parentheses.

plans demonstrates a lack of responsiveness. In both the Ohio House and Texas Senate, a 10 percent vote swing would not have shifted any seats while in the Ohio Senate only a two-seat swing would have occurred at the extremes and a four-seat swing in the Texas House. This shows the 2002 elections had few competitive races in mostly safe districts. In Texas, part of this is due to the extremely high number of uncontested seats, but this was not the case in Ohio. Overall, this finding shows the remappers packed districts so that unpredicted statewide swings would not greatly influence the party's fortune.

Conclusion

In Texas, like most other southern states, the key for completing the transition from the traditional one-party Democratic rule to Republican control is forcing the Democratic incumbents out of office. The Republican support is already there as many incumbent Democrats continue to win in Republican districts. This is exactly what the LRB did in the Texas House by taking the old Democratic plan and strategically displacing Democratic incumbents. The model predictions did not show much of a difference in seats won or lost based on the old or new district configurations, but taking away incumbency clearly advantaged the Republicans. The Texas case illustrates a successful partisan gerrymander that built on favorable conditions already found in the state. In Ohio, the Republicans built on their old maps at the margins while not making widespread districting changes.

These commissions showed high levels of partisanship under different conditions in putting together their plans. This shows that taking the power directly away from the legislature does not necessarily insulate the process from partisan gerrymandering. Both commissions clearly implemented successful pro-Republican plans. While the Texas LRB achieved a blatant partisan gerrymander, the Ohio Apportionment Board was able to tweak the old districts in support of the GOP needs, and thus produced a subtler outcome in favor of the Republicans.

Turning back to the constraints in place, the Texas LRB accomplished their goal while adhering to the Texas Constitution of not splitting county boundaries and meeting the Justice Department's goals of not diluting minority voting strength. Fortunately for the LRB, the large number of counties, and vast size of the large ideal district sizes of both the House and Senate districts, allowed them to maneuver the districts with whole counties in ways that paired incumbents together. Most important for the efforts of the LRB was the overall Republican support throughout Texas. They could easily draw many pro-Republican districts and pack a small number of safe Democratic districts while focusing on targeting incumbents for elimination. The Texas case shows how constraints may not hinder a partisan gerrymander especially when the remappers in control do not have to compromise with anyone during the process. The LRB had to implement plans that would pass constitutional muster in the courts, but did not have to directly compromise with anyone during the process.

The Ohio system highlights a case where constraints make a difference. Like the LRB, the Apportionment Board did not have to compromise with anyone during the process, but had to follow much stricter constitutional guidelines. The Ohio Constitution is one of the most detailed in terms of redistricting rules and demonstrates how constraints can work if properly prescribed. However, these constraints did not completely limit the Apportionment Board. In the examples described in this chapter, the board was able to help the Republicans in two of the five districts. These two districts fell within the legal guidelines and the board was able to pursue these without compromising with anyone during the process.

Notes

1. As quoted in Jim Yardley, "Once-Heralded Bipartisanship Fades in Texas House," *New York Times*, 30 December 2001.

2. As quoted in John McCarthy, "Republican Legislative Districts Get Bigger," *Associated Press State and Local Wire*, 14 May 2001.

3. For good overviews of the Texas congressional redistricting, please see Seth C. McKee and Daron R. Shaw, "Redistricting in Texas: Institutionalizing Republican Ascendancy," in *Redistricting in the New Millennium*, ed. Peter F. Galderisi (Lanham, Md.: Lexington Books, 2005), 275–312 and Seth C. McKee, Jeremy M. Teigen, and Mathieu Turgeon, "The Partisan Impact of Congressional Redistricting: The Case of Texas, 2001–2003," *Social Science Quarterly* 87 (2006): 308–17.

4. According to Texas Legislative Council, *Guide to 2001 Redistricting* (Austin: Texas Legislative Council, 2000), the LRB has a ninety-day constitutional window to act. The Texas Supreme Court interpreted this to mean the LRB has power if the legislature fails to act or if the governor vetoes or the courts overturn a plan during this ninety-day period. After this period, the power returns to the legislature (Texas Legislative Council 2000).

5. Texas elects the governor and lieutenant governor separately.

6. Ronald Claunch, Wesley S. Chumlea, and James G. Dickson, Jr., "Texas," in *Reapportionment Politics: The History of Redistricting in the 50 States*, ed. Leroy Hardy, Alan Heslop, and Stuart Anderson (Beverly Hills, Calif.: Sage Publications, 1981), 311–17.

7. Claunch et al., "Texas."

8. Claunch et al., "Texas."

9. Claunch et al., "Texas."

10. Charles Eckstein, personal correspondence with author, 9 May 2005.

11. Texas Legislative Council, *Guide to 2001 Redistricting.*

12. Claunch et al., "Texas."

13. The qualified elector provision was a reference to those voters who met certain poll tax and literacy requirements. The 1960s Civil Rights legislation invalidated the provision.

14. Texas Legislative Council, *Guide to 2001 Redistricting.*

15. Kathleen L. Barber, "Ohio," in *Reapportionment Politics: The History of Redistricting in the 50 States*, ed. Leroy Hardy, Alan Heslop, and Stuart Anderson (Beverly Hills, Calif.: Sage Publications, 1981), 256–65 and Michael P. McDon-

ald, "A Comparative Analysis of Redistricting Institutions in the United States, 2001–2002," *State Politics and Policy Quarterly* 4 (2004): 371–95.

16. Barber, "Ohio."

17. Barber, "Ohio."

18. Barber, "Ohio."

19. Barber, "Ohio."

20. *Voinovich v. Ferguson*, 63 Ohio St. 3d 198 (1992) and *Quilter v. Voinovich*, 794 F. Supp. 695 (N.D. Ohio) (1992).

21. *Quilter v. Voinovich*, 857 F. Supp. 579 (N.D. Ohio) (1994).

22. *Quilter v. Voinovich*, 812 F. Supp. 1006 (N.D. Ohio) (1995); *Bush v. Vera*, 116 U.S. 1941 (1996); and *Shaw v. Hunt*, 116 S. Ct. 1894 (1996).

23. *Quilter v. Voinovich*, 981 F. Supp. 1032 (N.D. Ohio) (1997).

24. For more details on the individual cases, please see National Conference of State Legislatures, *Redistricting Case Summaries from the '90s* (Denver: National Conference of State Legislatures, 1998).

25. The ratio of representation is simply the ideal district size based on dividing the state population by ninety-nine for the House and thirty-three for the Senate.

26. The Ohio system is interesting in that it uses a form of coterminous districts, but not the typical one Senate member and two House members sharing one district. Instead, the board draws the House districts based on the above criteria and then takes the House map and outlines Senate districts that include three whole House districts. The board draws two sets of maps, but the Senate map must derive from the House map.

27. Hugh Aynesworth, "GOP Plan Aims to Oust Texas Speaker," *Washington Times*, 30 July 2001, http://www.fairvote.org/redistricting/reports/remanual/txnews3.htm (accessed 8 September 2003) and Bob Richter, "High Stakes, Close Split Heat up Remap Battle," *San Antonio Express-News*, 14 May 2001.

28. Texas Legislative Council, "Texas Redistricting: 2000–2004 News Items," http://www.tlc.state.tx.us/redist/doc/00-03redistnews.htm (accessed 9 May 2005). Interestingly, the court confirmed the Democratic plaintiffs' claim of partisan gerrymandering, but did not find that made the plans unconstitutional.

29. Kelley Shannon, "New Boundaries for Texas House Ordered," *Baltimore Sun*, 28 November 2001, http://www.fairvote.org/redistricting/reports/remanual/txnews5.htm (accessed 8 September 2003).

30. Aynesworth, "GOP Plan Aims to Oust Texas Speaker."

31. Sam Attlesey, "Taking Stock of the Fallout from Redistricting," *Dallas Morning News*, 2 December 2001; Deon Daugherty, "Redistricting Remains Contentious Issue," *Amarillo Globe-News*, 12 August 2001, http://www.amarillo.com/stories/081201/tex_redistricting.shtml (accessed 10 July 2005); and Yardley, "Once-Heralded Bipartisanship."

32. Terrance Stutz, "GOP Expects to Control House, Redistricting Has Titled Several Seats Away from Democrats," *Dallas Morning News*, 3 January 2002; Sam Attlesey, "Judges OK Maps that Favor GOP, Party Could Control State

Senate; Laney's Future as Speaker May Be at Risk," *Dallas Morning News*, 29 November 2001; and Yardley, "Once-Heralded Bipartisanship."

33. John McCarthy, "Republican Legislative Districts Get Bigger," *Associated Press State and Local Wire*, 14 May 2001.

34. John McCarthy, "New Lines May Not Help Republicans Much," *Associated Press State and Local Wire*, 24 September 2001.

35. Liz Sidoti, "Redistricting, Term Limits Shake Up Legislative Races," *Associated Press State and Local Wire*, 21 February 2002.

36. Julie Carr Smyth, "GOP Goes All Out While Democrats Pick Their Battles," *Cleveland Plain Dealer*, 22 February 2002; Lee Leonard, "Redrawn District Lines Put Seats Up for Grabs; Democrats Battling Across the State to Cut GOP Majority in General Assembly," *Columbus Dispatch*, 23 September 2002; and William Hershey, "2000 Census Results to Force Shuffling of House Seats; Montgomery May Lose, Warren Should Gain," *Dayton Daily News*, 30 July 2001.

37. Liz Sidoti, "For Tab or Spot Use; Redistricting, Term Limits Shake Up Districts for Voters," *Associated Press State and Local Wire*, 15 October 2002.

38. Lee Leonard, "2001 Reapportionment; Redrawn Districts Ruled Constitutional," *Columbus Dispatch*, 18 November 2003.

39. Leonard, "2001 Reapportionment."

40. John McCarthy, "NAACP Director Had Contract with Republicans," *Associated Press State and Local Wire*, 27 September 2001.

41. John McCarthy, "Federal Judges: New Legislative Map Didn't Discriminate," *Associated Press State and Local Wire*, 24 May 2003 and Leonard, "2001 Reapportionment."

42. Lynn Hulsey, "Speakers: Keep Same, Legislative Districts; Redistricting Board Conducts Public Hearings," *Dayton Daily News*, 23 August 2001 and Hershey, "2000 Census Results to Force Shuffling."

43. The Ohio Senate plans are tied to the House plans with three entire House districts making one Senate district. I include the Senate plan here for comparison purposes although the split counties are inherently linked together such that a county may be entirely in one Senate district and be split by a House district, but a county may not be entirely in a House district and be split by a Senate district.

44. The correlation coefficients were .002 between percent of deviation and district intactness and -.03 for total population deviation and district intactness.

45. Ben Sutherly, "Young Seaver Ready to Serve," *Dayton Daily News*, 9 November 2000, County Editions.

46. These numbers are adjusted to account for four incumbents who moved into open districts before the 2002 primary.

6

Bipartisan Commission Control

Washington and Idaho

> Redistricting is just not one for which the legislative process is suited. Legislative majorities could not resist gerrymandering; they could not satisfy the natural survival instincts of politicians while creating fair districts in which voters have a chance to make their wishes known. . . .
>
> —Former Washington Secretary of State Ralph Munro speaking about the formation of the independent redistricting commission in 1983[1]

> You can't take the politics out of this process, and anyone would be naïve to think you could.
>
> —Ethan Morena, executive director of the Washington State Redistricting Commission[2]

The design of bipartisan or neutral commissions intentionally removes both direct legislative and partisan control from redistricting. When reformers discuss how to fix redistricting, the use of bipartisan or independent commissions is often the primary suggestion. In this chapter, I examine if these commissions actually operate in a bipartisan or neutral manner and if the plans implemented match the theoretical goals. In both Idaho and Washington, the commissions use similar formats for appointing members and the rules in place. An equal number of partisan appointments comprise the membership. According to the rules in each state, the commissioners must following specific traditional districting principles and compromise to implement new plans. The interesting finding in this chapter is that partisanship remains in the process, but is not necessarily reflected in the final plans implemented. The details of the process highlight the thinly veiled partisan overtones of both commissions. However, in the end, the rules in place limited the implementation of partisan plans, but not without a political struggle along the way.

Redistricting Law and History

Washington

The history of redistricting in Washington is a storied one with important events from the past half-century having helped shape the current laws. The most fundamental of these events came in 1983. In that year, the voters approved the legislature's proposal to amend the constitution to create an independent redistricting commission to begin operation in 1990.[3] Prior to this amendment, the legislature controlled the process much like most other states, albeit with more citizen involvement than found in many places. Before getting into the details of the commission, I will take a brief look at the previous decades.

In the decades before the reapportionment revolution, the legislature treated redistricting just like most states across the country by simply not redrawing maps or only doing so when the legislators felt the need. The legislature redrew the maps following the 1900 census but refused to do so after both the 1910 and 1920 censuses. By 1930, many citizens wanted action and managed to get a redistricting bill on the ballot via the initiative. The initiative passed at which point the legislature stepped in and enacted its own plan designed to override the citizens' plan. However, the governor vetoed the legislative plan "on the grounds that initiated statues were immune from repeal or modification for two years."[4] The citizens' plan stood in place for the remainder of the decade.

After the 1940 census, the legislature refused to take action once again and left the citizens' plan in place. Fed up with the process, members of the minority party introduced a bill to create an independent redistricting commission, but the bill failed.[5] By the 1950s, the twenty-year-old districts had become badly malapportioned, but the legislators once again refused to act. By 1956, citizen and civic groups were devoting much time and effort to the problem and the League of Women Voters put a plan on the ballot, which passed.[6] The media jumped on this story with headlines such as "Courageous Women Doing a Job Men Have Neglected [sic] 25 Years" and many legislators responded with bitterness as one Senator complained the plan was made from "a lot of women sitting around cutting paper dolls out of maps of the state."[7] In response to the plan, the legislature "amended" the initiative by restoring the old districts.

The 1960s brought the court's orders for both redistricting every ten years and the implementation of one-man/one-vote. The pressure of the courts forced the legislature to implement a plan in 1965, but only after a fiercely partisan battle. By the time of the 1970 census, the state had a divided legislature and a growing geographic split between the urban Seattle and Spokane areas, rural Eastern Washington, and the growing suburbs. As such, the legislature was unable to implement a plan in either the 1971 or 1972 sessions. At which time, the federal courts stepped in and hired a private redistricting master, a geography professor from the University of Washington, and gave him full control of quickly putting new maps together for the 1972 elections. Heading into the 1980s, groups such as Common Cause and the League of Women Voters were leading the charge for a redistricting commission. The legislature was able to put together constitutional legislative plans in 1981, but had trouble with the congressional maps. The congressional maps eventually went to a temporary commission in 1983, the same year the voters passed the constitutional amendment to permanently create a commission.[8]

The new independent commission went to work for the first time following the 1990 census and successfully implemented plans in a timely manner. The plans stood throughout the decade without being subjected to any legal challenges, and many observers in state concluded that using an independent commission "has so far avoided the lawsuits and political infighting common in other states."[9]

Turning to the 1983 constitutional amendment that created the apparently successful independent commission, Washington law calls for the Republican and Democratic legislative leaders to each appoint two members. None of the commission members can be elected officials or party leaders, registered lobbyists, or actively involved in a political campaign while on the commission. These four members then elect a non-voting chair who oversees the process. If the legislature cannot agree to their appointees or the appointees cannot pick a chair, then the state Supreme Court appoints either the four members or the chair. The law does allow for some legislative input by giving the legislature the ability to amend the commissions plans with a two-third vote in each chamber. This amendment power is limited by only permitting the legislature to change no more than 2 percent of any district's population. The amendment ability is meant for technical corrections. In addition, the law provides guidelines for the commissioners to follow when putting together their plans. The most important guideline is equal district population, and calls for the following guidelines, insofar as is practical to meet the equal population standard:

a. District lines should coincide with local political subdivisions (city and county boundaries) and "communities of interest." The number of counties or municipalities divided among more than one district should be as small as possible.
b. Districts should be convenient, contiguous (share a common land border or transportation route), and compact. Land areas are deemed contiguous if they share a land border or common transportation connection (e.g., ferry, bridge, tunnel, highway).
c. The state is to have forty-nine districts with one senator elected from each district and two house members. The House members are to run at-large.

d. Districts must not favor or discriminate against one political party or group and cannot consider incumbency when drawing a district.
e. District divisions should encourage electoral competition.[10]

The commission must work within these guidelines to implement a map that focuses on equal population while not splitting counties or communities of interest. They must also create competitive districts without considering incumbency or partisan factors.

Idaho

The 2000 round of redistricting brought a new era to the state of Idaho as it marked the first time a commission and not the legislature redrew the state's legislative districts. In 1993, the legislature and the people of Idaho amended Section 2, Article 3 of the state constitution by creating a citizen commission "to assume the responsibility for redistricting from the legislature."[11] Senate Joint Resolution 105 from Session Law 1993 created a six-person commission with three each appointed by the two major political parties within the state. The move to a bipartisan commission was in response to the general dissatisfaction of the partisan plan produced by the joint committee on redistricting from the 1990s.

However, the road to a commission begins as far back as the reapportionment revolution of the 1960s. Historically, the Idaho Legislature drew both legislative and congressional districts based on county boundaries and not population.[12] The U.S. Supreme Court essentially ruled this practice unconstitutional during the 1960s move toward the "one person, one vote" standard. As a response, the Idaho Legislature in the 1970s adopted a modified county-population system by drawing plans based on county lines to the extent possible. This system worked for the 1970 maps, and the legislature tried to implement the 1980s plan using the same formula.[13] However, the Idaho State Supreme Court took up a legal challenge and ultimately found the system unconstitutional. The court's reasoning did not follow the federal "one person, one vote" standard but rather ruled the plans did not pass constitutional muster since the plans split county boundaries in direct violation of the Idaho constitution which stated all counties must be kept intact for legislative boundaries.[14] After the legislature failed to meet a court deadline for passing a new plan, the state Supreme Court implemented the plans used for the 1984–1990 elections.

Heading into the 1990 redistricting, the legislature amended the state constitution to allow the division of counties in anticipation of the same legal problems from the 1980s. Now that the legislature had control of the process back, the majority Republicans also decided to complete redistricting by a joint committee without the input of the entire membership. The result was a highly partisan plan that upset most legislators at their exclusion from the process. As a result, in the 1994 session the legislature amended the constitution to create a bipartisan citizens' commission in a move that took power away from not only the leadership but the entire the legislature as well.[15]

After the passing of the constitutional amendment, Idaho law laid out the specifics of the commission in a similar manner as Washington's laws. Each party appoints three members, who must pass a plan with a majority vote. A member may not be a registered lobbyist, an elected official or party officer or candidate for office, and may not run for the legislature for five years after serving on the commission; additionally, the six members should come from the various regions of the state. The law defines eight criteria to govern the commission's duties:

1. Census data is the only permissible data
2. To the maximum extent possible, districts shall preserve traditional neighborhoods and local communities of interest
3. Districts shall be substantially equal in population and seek to comply with all applicable federal standards and statutes
4. To the maximum extent possible, the plan should avoid drawing districts that are oddly shaped

5. Division of counties should be avoided whenever possible. Counties should be divided into districts not wholly contained within that county only to the extent reasonably necessary to meet requirements of the equal population principle. In the event that a county must be divided, the number of such divisions, per county, should be kept to a minimum
6. To the extent that counties must be divided to create districts, such districts shall be composed of contiguous counties
7. District boundaries should retain, as far as practicable, the local voting precinct boundary lines
8. Counties shall not be divided to protect a particular political party or a particular incumbent[16]

From these criteria, it is clear the importance of protecting county boundaries in Idaho as the code specifically says that counties, and not districts, cannot be either partisan or incumbent gerrymandered. Equal population appears less important than in many other states as the commission guidelines rely more on the Idaho tradition of districting by county rather than population. The commission format follows the typical bipartisan method by appointing an equal number of members from each party. These commissioners then select a chairperson from within its own membership to oversee the process of neutral redistricting.

The 2000 Redistricting: Context and Perception of the Plans

Washington

There was reason for optimism in Olympia that the Washington State Redistricting Commission presented a viable option to the partisan and self-interested legislative control of redistricting. The bipartisan process successfully reached its goals in 1991 by designing plans that fostered close elections in competitive districts that swung back and forth between the two parties. However, not all involved in Olympia liked these outcomes. According to state GOP chairman Chris Vance, "At some point, there must be a dominant party, with a clear majority and a clear minority, for the process to work."[17] Democratic chairman Paul Berendt echoed similar sentiments, "Super-competitive districts across the state are not good for public policy. This is a huge problem if you believe in legislators working together for solutions. Due to having overly competitive districts, legislators are constantly looking over their shoulders and being worried about taking tough votes because of what might be coming at them in the next election."[18]

In early 2001, the second set of commissioners took office for the Washington State Redistricting Commission. The four citizen appointees (two Democratic and two Republican) quickly selected the chairperson to oversee the commission. The new commission began business in the summer of 2001 by holding meetings across the state to hear citizens' concerns over redistricting. In these meetings, most citizens discussed the desire for the commission to keep political subdivisions and local communities together and for as little change as possible to the districts.[19] However, this non-partisan mood quickly changed early in September when the commissioners introduced their first plans for debate.

Entering the fall, the commission came under attack from several groups. First by the parties themselves as Berendt ripped the commission by arguing it was the commission's fault for the virtual gridlock in the nearly evenly divided legislature: "We have a state full of districts that are a reflection of the commission, not of the geopolitical makeup of the state of Washington. This was not by accident. This was by design and it was the 1990 redistricting that created this mess, and I tell you it's going to happen again." The executive director of the Commission argued, "You can't take the politics out of this process, and anyone would be naïve to think you could."[20] In practice, the commission tried to protect incumbents and create districts that left them no worse off than they were by following a strategy of drawing roughly equal numbers of safe districts for the parties and making the rest competitive swing districts. In the end, the process remains "highly political and tends to protect incumbents, but it's scrupulously bipartisan and keeps the Legislature at arms' length." According to Vance, "Neither side can get away with doing anything ridiculous, so they don't even try."[21]

After the commissioners introduced their initial plans the negotiating began in the early fall and stalemate fell over the proceedings. During the fall, the commission's separation from the legislature fell apart as representatives from the four party caucuses set up offices right next door to the commission using the same data and computers. Perhaps most importantly, the built-in transparency of the commission's dealings went by the wayside as the commissioners negotiated in meetings of only two at a time to avoid triggering open meeting laws. In the final days of the process, the commissioners divided themselves into partisan camps and each party submitted a plan and negotiated from the two plans. Some papers went as far as calling the process "map farce" because of the partisanship in the process.[22] According to Commissioner Dean Foster the commission was considering political data, "Let's not fool ourselves—this is a partisan group, and we're going to look at those numbers. It's probably time to acknowledge that."[23] This was in direct violation of the constitutional and statutory criteria set up for the commission. Also, despite rules against considering incumbency, the commission seemed to focus on protecting incumbents as according to Foster, "We're not here to undo the elections by removing incumbents."[24]

The system was set up to give the commissioners strong motivation to make a deal. "They're supposed to know that compromise is far better than the alternative—a plan approved by the state Supreme Court."[25] As the December 15th deadline approached the commission worked nearly around the clock to produce an agreeable plan. The final plan produced such a compromise with a map that was fairly close to the old boundaries. It appeared to have the same number of safe and competitive districts and only drew two Democratic incumbents out of their districts to accommodate population shifts. However, the commission had a major problem as the legislative plan was not voted upon until the early morning hours of December 16th. The commission missed the constitutional deadline by hours for the legislative plan but they had not even produced a congressional map for a vote. This created a constitutional crisis in the state, but due to some confusion over statutory versus constitutional deadlines the legislature stepped in rushed through a bill to retroactively change the deadline from December 15th to January 1st. This allowed the legislative plans to stand and the commission to address the congressional plans which they also failed to produce before December 15th.[26]

According to media reports, "The commission had been lambasted by the state's media for tardiness, rampant partisanship, wasting tax dollars, stubbornness, and other sins." Despite these views redistricting expert Richard Morrill, the 1983 special master, argued that despite all the attention given to the deadlines and preliminary failures the plans are remarkably good since most voters will be in their same districts and few incumbents disturbed. "If anyone thought taking redistricting out of the hands of the Legislature would make the process any less partisan, messy and frustrating, the 2001 Redistricting Commission has proven otherwise."[27]

Idaho

The Idaho Commission on Redistricting officially formed for the first time on June 5, 2001, with six citizen commissioners (three Democratic appointees and three Republican appointees) charged with creating new plans for the legislature and the two congressional seats. While the new format resulted in completed plans, the commission did not achieve this without controversy and court intervention. On August 22, 2001, the commission, by a vote of 4–2, passed plan L66 for the state's 35 legislative districts and C15 for the state's two congressional districts. The congressional plan passed with two Republican ayes and two Democratic ayes and was implemented with little fanfare or controversy. The Legislative plan passed with three Democratic ayes and one Republican aye, and created nearly six months' worth of political maneuvering, judicial intervention, and partisan and regional animosity.[28] Groups from the southeastern counties of Madison and Bingham immediately challenged Plan L66 on grounds of county divisions and population deviations between districts. On November 29, 2001, the Idaho Supreme Court ruled in an unanimous decision that plan L66 was indeed unconstitutional on the grounds it "violates the Equal Protection clause of the Fourteenth Amendment to the United States Constitution because the population of its districts varies more than 10 percent constituting a prima facie case of discrimination and the State has offered no evidence of legitimate reasons for the deviation."[29] Because of this population deviation of 10.69 percent, the commission had to reconvene and adopt new plans.

In the decision, the court noted the commission's attorney, the state attorney general, did not provide any legitimate reasons why the population deviation advanced a rational state policy. The decision and the attorney general's office handling of the case upset members of the commission. Several commissioners argued they gave the attorney general's office reports that outlined upholding county boundaries was the rational state policy for going above the 10 percent population deviation. Republican appointee Dean Haagenson said, "We didn't get very good lawyering from our attorney general's office."[30] From most accounts, the lack of "good lawyering" was not by accident. Apparently, the Republicans made a decision to have the Republican attorney general not push the rational state policy argument in court as a protest to what the party perceived as Republican appointee Dean Haagenson's vote to approve a Democratic plan.[31]

After the court ruled Plan L66 unconstitutional, the commission reconvened in January 2002 with some membership changes to consider new plans. After some maneuvering to Plan L66, the commission produced Plan L91 on January 8, 2002. Once again, some southeastern counties challenged the plan. This time the lawsuit challenged the plan on grounds of multiple county splits to three counties. The lawsuit did not challenge the plan on grounds of population deviation despite the fact Plan L91 had an 11.79 percent difference. This time around the commissioners hired a private attorney to represent the commission in front of the state Supreme Court, but the court again agreed with the counties and ruled the plan unconstitutional. Finally, on March 9th, the commission adopted Plan L97 with a vote of 5–1 and only one Republican holdout. The plan had a population deviation of 9.71 percent, and the Idaho Supreme Court denied the final two petitions clearing the way for its implementation for the 2002 elections.[32] Plan L97 once again upset the county commissioners in eastern Idaho as the commission shifted several seats to the northern part of the state. The plan upset the Republicans since the changes forced several Republican incumbents into the same districts.

Public reaction to the commission's initial foray into redistricting was almost completely negative. The Republicans were so upset they pushed for the abolition of the commission format at their state convention. A delegate and local radio talk show host argued, "The commission answers to no one. The legislators have to answer to the citizens of the state and that is where the power should be."[33] The Democrats did not seem very upset by the commission's work, as all three of the commission's plans appeared to favor the Democratic areas, although the Democrats were still resigned to a tiny minority. Despite the failing of the commission to end partisan bickering, the jury is still out to whether or not the commission was able to reach the other nonpartisan goals for which it was charged.

The Role of Traditional Districting Principles

Traditional districting principles played an important role for the commissions in both states. However, the place of these rules in the actual workings of the commissions varied depending on the circumstances. In Idaho, the rule against splitting counties was first and foremost in the state as county commissioners sued over the first two plans and had the second plan successfully ruled unconstitutional specifically based on this principle. In addition, most newspaper accounts of the process focused on the plight of specific counties in each plan over partisan gains or losses. The commission did appear to struggle with how to balance protecting county boundaries with communities of interest with the three Democratic members wanting to protect counties from being split at all costs and the Republicans open to splitting counties in cases where they could uphold smaller communities of interest. In the end, the commission focused on not splitting counties and appeared to not, overtly at least, protect any specific partisan or incumbent interests.[34]

The Washington commission worked under similar guidelines as the Idaho commission, especially in terms of protecting county boundaries and not considering partisanship or incumbency. They also had the added instruction of enhancing electoral competition whenever possible. From most accounts, the commission did a good job of protecting county and city boundaries although the topic was not nearly as important as it was in Idaho. However, the commissioners did openly admit to referring to partisan and incumbent data in clear violation of their constitutional guidelines. In the end, the commission focused on producing equally populated and competitive districts and succeeded, at least in the eyes of the media, in both regards.

Given that counties have played a fundamental role in redistricting over the years in both Washington and Idaho, and both commissions had specific rules against splitting county boundaries unnecessarily, I expect to find few, if any, counties below the ideal district size split into multiple districts. I also expect to find a decrease in the number of split counties in Idaho as the commission redrew the legislature's 1990 plan and a similar number of splits in Washington as the commission also drew the old plan. Appendix 2 confirms these expectations. In Washington, the 2000 plan did not produce much change in terms of county splits with the 2000 plan splitting two fewer counties below the ideal size than the old plan while splitting six of the twenty-nine, or 20 percent, of the counties below the ideal size. In Idaho, the commission split 18 percent fewer counties than the legislature did in 1990 and only split two of the thirty-six counties below the ideal district size down from eight under the old Republican plan.

The role of traditional districting principles took on an important role for the neutral commissions in Idaho and Washington. The commissions dutifully upheld the principle against splitting county boundaries and in Washington tried to justify those county splits with the upholding of communities of interest.[35] The principle against splitting counties gave the commissions, and the courts in Idaho, a concrete measuring stick for drawing district lines. Overall, the principles received more attention in these two states than in most and functioned more as guideposts than constraints for the commissioners in completing their tasks.

District Changes and the Search for Gerrymandering

Parent Districts

The first step to examining the district changes in each state is determining the parent districts for the new plans.[36] In Washington, the changes appear minimal as each old district became the parent district for the same numbered new district. In other words, old district 1 formed the majority of new district 1, old district 2 became the parent for new district 2, and so on for all forty-nine legislative districts. The commission did not fundamentally eliminate any districts throughout the state. Idaho presents a different story. Of the thirty-five legislative districts only four shared the same number as its parent district. Additionally, as table 6.1 shows six old districts did not become a parent district while two old districts each became the parent for three new districts and two old districts each became the parent for two new districts. Once explanation for this could simply be population shifts among the districts. If this is the case, then heavily underpopulated districts may not form a parent district as the population changes may force the elimination of those districts. The overpopulated districts may then form into multiple parents as the remappers split the single old district to accommodate the population growth. However, this does not appear to be the case in Idaho as, of the six districts that did not form a

Table 6.1. Parent District Information

State	No Parent	Deviation	Base Vote	Multiple Parents	Population Deviation	Base Vote
Idaho	13	5,268	41.01	4	−2,436	35.97
	16	752	41.05	14	36,099	27.23
	17	−1,558	39.38	15	3,902	31.28
	18	2,761	25.21	19	−5,110	53.10
	28	−5,574	19.15			
	35	−6,130	33.43			
Washington	none			none		

Note: Districts refer to 2000 districts.

parent, three were below the ideal district size, meaning the districts needed to add population to reach equal population standard and three were above this ideal, meaning the districts needed to lose population to reach the standard. For the four districts split into multiple parents, once again two were underpopulated and two were overpopulated.

A second explanation for the switch in parent districts is a partisan one. If the commissioners attempted a partisan gerrymander than they may have targeted one party's districts for elimination while splitting the other party's more favorable districts into multiple parent districts. Table 6.1 shows that of the six eliminated districts four were more Democratic than the average district while three of the four multiple parent districts leaned Democratic. From this perspective, the commission did not appear to favor one party in this process or specifically change the old districts based on population. To test for any hint of partisan favoritism, the next step is to examine the partisan reconstruction in each plan.

Partisan Reconstruction

The first step is to determine how the plans break down the districts into the typologies of district control and partisan support. Given the use of neutral commissions, coterminous districts, and the implementation of only one plan, I use a modified typology categorization for both Idaho and Washington. Instead of the four categories of in party control/safe district, in party/competitive district, out party/safe district, and out party/competitive district, I divide each district into Democratic, Republican, Leaning Democratic, and Leaning Republican categories based on the incumbents' party of the three seats in each district. A Democratic district is one in which all three members (one senator and two house members) are Democrats, a Republican district is one where all three members are Republican. A district with two Democrats becomes a Leaning Democratic district and one with two Republicans becomes a Leaning Republican district.

Table 6.2 shows the partisan reconstruction for both states. If partisan gerrymandering is present then I should find shifts to help one party over the other, particularly in the competitive districts. This is clearly not the case in either state. In terms of the breakdown of districts by typology, there are few changes for either state. In Washington, there was an almost equal distribution of Democratic, Republican, and Leaning districts. In Idaho, the sheer dominance of the Republicans jumps out as Republican districts make up 75 percent of the map. The Democrats gained one district due to the multiple parent districts of a Democratic district in Boise.

Table 6.2 shows the partisan shifts for the new plans broken down by typology. In Idaho, the only noticeable change between the partisanship of the old and new districts was in the four Democratic districts, where on average they became 7 percent less friendly. The partisanship in the other districts did not change by more than 1 percent. The commission did not crack the Democratic districts to pack other districts with Democratic supporters. In terms of district intactness, the Democratic districts underwent the most change by keeping only 34 percent of their parent districts. Three of the four districts were in Boise where the commission had to reshuffle districts to accommodate population growth. Overall, the average intactness of a new district was only 56.07 percent of its parent. While the commission redrew the districts so that each district only kept about half of its old precincts, the partisanship in the districts changed little

Table 6.2. Partisan Reconstruction by District Typology

District Type	*BV Kept*	*BV Added*	*2002 BV*	*Parent BV*	*Intact*	*N*
Idaho						
Democratic	52.73	38.81	42.38	49.95	34.04	4
Leaning Democratic	40.86	25.11	39.81	39.59	89.19	1
Republican	25.97	27.48	26.67	25.72	59.19	26
Leaning Republican	32.06	32.53	31.17	32.70	49.53	4
Statewide	30.15	29.29	29.35	29.68	56.07	35
Washington						
Democratic	65.30	62.39	64.31	65.18	77.06	17
Leaning Democratic	52.16	55.14	52.23*	52.36	93.07	7
Republican	42.80	41.09	42.40	42.84	86.00	16
Leaning Republican	48.00	48.95	48.21	48.21	69.82	9
Statewide	52.90	51.80	52.47	53.06	80.94	49

Notes: BV Kept: Percent Democratic vote of those precincts from the parent district
BV Added: Percent Democratic vote of those precincts from outside the parent district
2002 BV: Percent Democratic vote in the 2002 district
Parent BV: Percent Democratic vote of the parent district
Intact: Percent of the precincts the 2002 district shares with its parent
*The 2002 base vote falls outside of the range between the Democratic base vote kept and Democratic base vote added because in each case some of the districts within the typology did not gain any new precincts. Therefore, the Democratic base vote added is calculated only with those districts that gained precincts. Due to this, the average base vote for all districts within these typologies falls outside of the range.

and without any evidence of a partisan bias. The Washington commission implemented even less change as none of the four district types underwent more than 1 percent partisan change and the districts remained 80 percent intact. This is not surprising given the perfect match of the parent districts to new districts. The commission did not fundamentally alter the old map, but rather tweaked the districts at the margins.

To test for evidence of systematic gerrymandering, I examine the changes to district partisanship and model the factors that contributed to these changes. Figure 6.1 plots the 2002 district partisanship and parent base partisanship. In Washington, the new map places most districts in almost the same partisan alignment as the old maps and most districts fall near the 50 percent mark. This indicates very little change between the plans and shows the commissioners followed the rule emphasizing drawing competitive

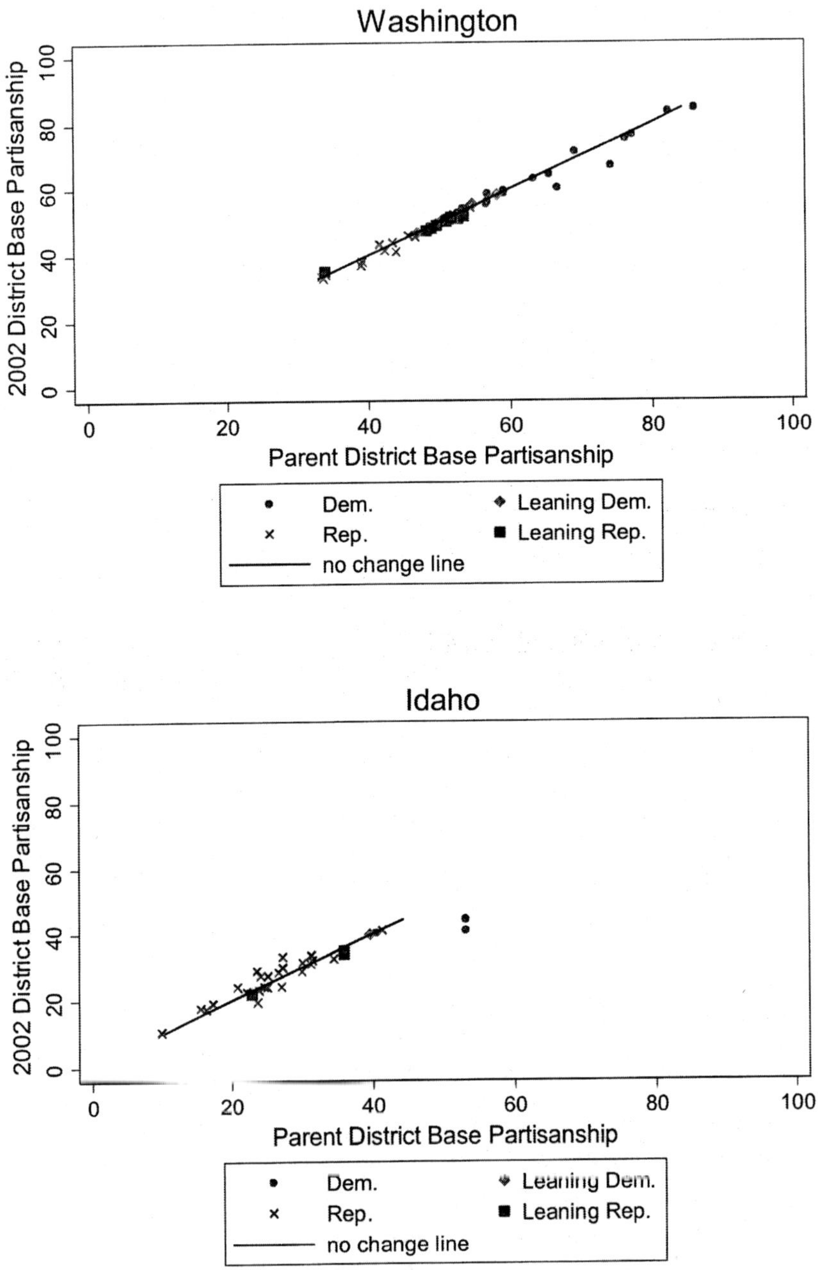

Figure 6.1. *Washington and Idaho: Comparison of 2002 and Parent District Partisanship by District Typology*

districts. In Idaho, the 2002 plan shows a little more change, but nothing to indicate a systematic partisan gerrymander. The sheer number of Republican districts stands out in figure 6.1; and while some of these districts did gain Democratic partisans, the overall partisanship of the districts favors the Republicans.

Looking at the model for district change found in appendix 1, I do not expect to find any evidence of partisan gerrymandering in the neutral commission states. Therefore, the partisanship of the parent district should be the main explanatory variable in these models. If the commissions followed the rules, then the other variables should not structure the partisanship of the 2002 districts or improve the fit of the model. The findings show that in Washington nothing outside of the parent district partisanship structured the district partisanship of the new plan. It appears, judging from the model fit of .98, that the new districts underwent little change from the old map. This suggests the commission did not play partisan favorites when producing the new map. In Idaho, the outcome is similar although the commission did produce more change. The base model once again is the guiding factor behind the new plans district partisanship. The typology model shows the Democratic districts became less Democratic in comparison to the partisanship of the other three district types. However, the significance of the typology falls out in the third model. In the third model, the parent districts deviation from the ideal district size shows a very small influence on district partisanship. This shows the parent districts with the most overpopulation became slightly more Democratic.[37] Overall, given the small improvement in model fit and the lack of significance for any of the key gerrymandering variables, the commissioners in Idaho implemented a plan that did not favor either party.

The final component of district change I examine for this case is the population deviation of the 2002 districts. In Washington, the commission put a primary focus on equalizing population for all forty-nine districts and they accomplished this goal almost to perfection. The ideal district size for a 2002 Washington legislative district was 120,288 people, and the smallest district had a population of 120,111 with the largest district having a population of 120,467.

The Idaho commission had its first plan ruled unconstitutional because the largest district deviation from the ideal was above the 10 percent standard, and its second plan also deviated above this standard. The final plan barely fit into the standard with 9.71 percent deviation. The Idaho commission put most of its focus on upholding county boundaries as regulated by its guidelines. The ideal district size for a 2002 Idaho legislative district was 36,970 people, and the smallest district had a population of 34,927 with the largest having 38,516 people. The commission pushed the 10 percent deviation standard, but not for partisan gain. There was no significant correlation between district population and partisanship. Rather, the commission used population deviations to keep as many counties intact as possible.

The pre-electoral analysis uncovered a lot of political and partisan bickering over the workings of the commissions, their motives, and the constitutionality of both the implemented plans and the statutory procedures under which the commissions operated. Despite the public acrimony, the findings show both commissions implemented plans that followed the most important guidelines in each state in a partisan neutral manner. The Idaho commission had to implement more changes to reach a neutral plan as they were undoing the Republican gerrymander of ten years before; whereas, the Washington commission implemented a map with very minor changes, in part as a compromise between the two sets of partisan appointed members and in part due to the neutrality of the plan implemented by the commission ten years before. These neutral plans came even as commissioners, in both states, spoke in terms of the partisanship of the process. However, each had well-defined and tangible guidelines from which to draw the maps and no one set of partisan commissioners could implement a map without compromise from the other commissioners.

Electoral Outcomes

Given the lack of partisan gerrymandering in both states, I do not expect to find much influence for redistricting on the electoral outcomes. This is particularly true in Washington where the commission produced new districts mostly unchanged from the previous plan. The electoral landscape changed little from 2000 to 2002. In Idaho, the shift from a Republican plan to the commission neutral plan was likely to produce some fallout. Specifically, the lack of district intactness and pairing of several Republican incumbents appeared to favor the Democrats in an attempt to gain some seats back from the Republicans' 1990 plan.

The Washington plan did not pair any incumbents into the same districts. Once again, this is not surprising given the small amounts of change between the plans. Of the state's 147 incumbents, the commission only moved two incumbents into new districts and forced one incumbent to move a few blocks to stay within her old district.[38] In other words, these two Representatives moved into a district with a different number and new parent district, but remained the only incumbent within the new district. In both instances, one House member in the district that picked up an incumbent decided to run for open Senate seats.

Idaho is a different story. Plan L97 displaced over half of the incumbents in the state into newly numbered districts and paired sixteen incumbents into eight seats (seven districts). Of these eight seats, seven paired Republicans together while the other district paired a Democrat and a Republican incumbent together. With fourteen incumbents paired together, it is easier to understand the issues the Republicans had with the commission. The Republican leadership implicated the commission as being pro-Democratic and cited these pairings as one of the primary reasons.[39] One reason for these pairings is simply the Republicans controlled nearly 90 percent of the seats in the state which left their incumbents the most vulnerable to be paired together. The commission's reasoning for these placements appeared to be population shifts and geography, and not partisanship, which the guidelines forbade. Five of the seven districts were from eastern Idaho, which suffered the slowest population growth, and the other two were large rural districts that encompassed large portions of northern and central Idaho. It does not appear the commission targeted Republicans specifically, but rather the underpopulated districts, which Republicans happened to represent.

Heading into the November 2002 elections, the electoral landscape could not have looked any different as the Washington legislature was in a virtual partisan deadlock and the Idaho legislature had essentially a one-party system. The Washington Democrats held the slimmest of majorities with a 25–24 seat advantage in the Senate and a 50–48 edge in the House. The House majority came as a result of picking up a seat in a 2001 special election breaking a three year 49–49 tie. In Idaho, the Republicans enjoyed the safest margins in the nation with a 32–3 advantage in the Senate and a 61–9 majority in the House. As table 6.3 shows, the 2002 elections produced gains for the Democrats in Idaho and split outcomes in Washington. The Idaho Democrats gained nine seats, five in the House and four in the Senate, to move from having 11 percent of the state's legislative seats to holding 22 percent. Of the Democrats' seven-seat swing, five came at the hands of challengers unseating Republican incumbents.

These gains bucked a decade-long trend of Republican gains under the old Republican redistricting plan and moved the House close to its 1990 delegation size. The Senate gains more than doubled the Democrats' delegation in the chamber. However, this remained well short of the party's 1990 total when the Democrats held a share of the majority.[40] Despite the seat pickups, the Democrats remained well short of having enough seats to have a procedural say in the business of the

Table 6.3. 2002 Seat Changes

	Pre-Election		*2002 Election*		
Chamber	*D*	*R*	*D*	*R*	*Net Change*
Idaho House	9	61	16	54	+5 D
Idaho Senate	3	32	7	28	+4 D
Washington House	50	48	52	46	+2 D
Washington Senate*	13	11	12	12	+1 R

Note: *= Only half the seats were up for election in 2002

legislature; although some state experts argued the gains may put the Democrats in a position to form some working coalitions with moderate Republicans.[41] In Olympia, the partisan changes were fewer but came with greater consequences. In the House, the Democrats successfully built on their 2001 special election win and added two seats to hold a six-seat majority, the largest majority since 1996. The Republicans made an important one-seat gain in the Senate giving them the majority in that chamber for the first time since 1996 and broke the Democrats' control of the government.

One specific guideline for the Washington commission was to foster electoral competition, although the rules did not specify what this meant. The Idaho commission had no such guideline. However, the Washington commission did no better at developing competitive elections than the Idaho commission. Considering races won with less than 60 percent of the vote as competitive, the Washington House had 20 out of 98 (20 percent) competitive, the Washington Senate had 6 out of 24 (25 percent), the Idaho House had 17 out of 70 (24 percent), and the Idaho Senate had 7 out of 35 (20 percent) fall into this category. The Washington plan did not lead to closer races than the Idaho plan.

The next question becomes what influence did redistricting have on these outcomes? Table 6.4 reveals some interesting predictions based on the regression results in appendix 3. First, the model predicts the winners quite successfully under all three conditions. In only the Idaho "no incumbency" condition did the percentage drop below 80 percent. For the remaining conditions, the seats correctly predicted were above 80 percent with the model predicting 11 of 12 races correctly in the Washington Senate. Substantively, the Idaho Democrats faired much better than expected. In the House, the model under the current map only predicted a one-seat gain from the seven they held going into the election. Under the 2000 districts, the Democrats would have faired much better, but still not matched their actual totals. The Democrats would have fared the worse if all the incumbents were prevented from running in 2002. In the Senate, the 2002 and 2000 districts both predicted only three wins, but the lack of incumbents would have improved the Democrats' chances. Under no condition, did the model predict the actual number of wins for the Democrats. In Washington, the House Democrats also fared better than expected as the 2002 and 2000 models predicted a slight Republican majority and absence the bonus of incumbency the Democrats would have only held thirty-four seats. This suggests incumbency plays a large part in the Washington Democrats' success. In the Senate, the Republicans picked up a seat to takeover the majority by knocking off an incumbent Democrat going against the 2002 and 2000 model predictions. Overall, these models do not show a huge redistricting advantage for either party. The Democrats in Idaho did better than the models predicted, but this does not appear to be due to the help of districting changes.

The final test for the influence of redistricting is to examine the seats-votes relationship for the 2002 elections. If the commissions avoided partisan plans then I should find the plans responsive to vote swings, so that partisan seat changes move with the vote swings. As shown in appendix 3, the two House chambers demonstrate high levels of responsiveness while the Senate chambers show the likelihood of less seat turnover. Only the Washington Senate appears to favor one party, as the Democrats could expect to pick up four seats with a pro-Democratic vote shift of more than 4 percent while the Republicans could not ex-

Table 6.4. Seat Predictions

Chamber	*Previous Seats*	*Seats Won*	*2002 Districts*	*2000 Districts*	*No Incumbents*
Idaho House	7	16	8 (82.86)	13 (78.57)	6 (74.29)
Idaho Senate	3	7	3 (88.57)	3 (88.57)	6 (74.29)
Washington House	50	52	48 (89.80)	48 (89.80)	34 (79.59)
Washington Senate	13	12	13 (95.83)	13 (95.83)	11 (95.83)

Notes: "Seats won" equals the actual number of seats won by the Democrats in the 2002 elections. Predictions based on varying district conditions and computed from the regression results in Appendix 1. "2002 districts" are the districts used in the elections, "2000 districts" assumes 2002 elections held under the old maps, and "No incumbents" assumes all open seats in the 2002 districts. Percent of total races predicted correctly are in parentheses.

pect this same advantage with a pro-Republican shift. The Washington House shows the largest expected seat changes of thirteen seats across the scale. Interestingly, the same district boundaries did not translate to the same responsiveness in the Senate elections. Overall, the hypothetical swing ratio shows the commissions implemented responsive plans that do not show partisan bias as the parties could expect to do equally as well depending on the vote swings.

Overall, this analysis does not suggest the new districts in either state greatly benefited one party over the other, at least not in any clear systematic manner. The Democrats' modest gains in Idaho appear not to be by design from the commission, and neither party gained an advantage for the majority in Washington. While the party leaders in Washington argued the commission put too much emphasis on creating competitive elections, the 2002 elections did not bear this out, as the races in Washington were no more competitive than those in Idaho, where the Republicans have a clear majority. The lack of clear evidence for partisan gerrymandering fits the expectations and shows the commission's plans did not have a biased partisan effect.

Conclusion

The bipartisan commissions implemented generally neutral plans, but the commissions dealt with partisan problems during the process. The outcomes generated by the commissions achieved the reformers goal of partisan neutral plans despite partisan bickering during the process. In both states, the commissioners eventually compromised and followed the rules to produce new districts. The success of these commissions represents one method for limiting partisan influence; however, the problems during the remapping also highlight potential problems with this method as well. In both states, partisanship was thinly veiled on the commissions and compromise was not easily reached. In Washington, the commissioners circumvented the transparency of the system by working around open meeting laws to meet in private and consider restricted political and incumbency data. In the end, the parties reached a successful compromise with little change in the districts. But, this was not before creating a constitutional crisis by missing the deadline for implementing the new plans.

In Idaho, the commission put a plan in place with more changes to correct for the Republican gerrymander in 1990. This upset the majority Republicans who accused the commission of favoring the Democrats. While these accusations did not pan out in terms of the plan implemented, the larger problem stems from the commission's inability to avoid litigation and adopting multiple plans. The commission was unable in its first two attempts to balance equal population and the state's historical importance against splitting counties against the regional issues in the state.

One important failing of this chapter is that these findings do not and cannot show whether the partisan neutral plans implemented came about because of the commission format or the rules the commissioners had to follow. Since both states have similarly strict guidelines in place, this chapter does not offer a comparison between a neutral commission with free rein over how they draw the maps and one in which the commission is constrained by the rules. As it turns out, all states with neutral commissions have also put into place heavily constraining rules for the commissioners to follow.

Overall, the redistricting plans from Washington and Idaho did not demonstrate any patterns of gerrymandering. The bipartisan commissions worked in that the commissioners had to compromise on their partisan interests and follow the traditional districting principles in place. However, this format did not remove partisanship from the process rather it simply removed it from the public's view.

Notes

1. As quoted in Washington State Historical Society, "Redrawing the Battlelines: A Virtual Exhibit," http://www.redistricting.wa.gov (accessed 25 October 2004).

2. As quoted in Beth Silver, "Who You'll Vote For is Up to Them, Redistricting: Impact on Elections Can Be Profound," *Tacoma (Washington) News Tribune*, 2 September 2001.

3. Washington State Historical Society, "Redrawing the Battlelines."

4. Hugh A. Bone and Richard Morrill, "Washington," in *Reapportionment Politics: The History of Redistricting in the 50 States*, ed. Leroy Hardy, Alan Heslop, and Stuart Anderson (Beverly Hills, Calif.: Sage Publications, 1981), 339.

5. Washington Redistricting Commission, "Redistricting: A Decade-by-Decade Glance," http://www.redistricting.wa.gov/pages/factsDecade.html (accessed 25 October 2004).

6. Bone and Morrill, "Washington" and Washington Redistricting Commission, "Redistricting: A Decade-by-Decade Glance."

7. Washington State Historical Society, "Redrawing the Battlelines."

8. Bone and Morrill, "Washington" and Washington Redistricting Commission, "Redistricting: A Decade-by-Decade Glance."

9. Washington State Historical Society, "Redrawing the Battlelines."

10. Washington State Historical Society, "Redrawing the Battlelines."

11. Idaho Redistricting Commission, "State of Idaho Redistricting 2001," http://www.idahoredistricting.org (accessed 9 September 2004).

12. Lily Wai, Elaine Watson, and Stephen Woods, "Idaho Librarians' Role in Census Redistricting," *Idaho Librarian* August, (2003), http://www.idaholibraries.org/newidaholibrarian/200308/contentsAhtm (accessed 13 September 2004).

13. Neil McFeeley and H. Sydney Duncombe, "Idaho," in *Reapportionment Politics: The History of Redistricting in the 50 States*, ed. Leroy Hardy, Alan Heslop, and Stuart Anderson (Beverly Hills, Calif.: Sage Publications, 1981), 96–100.

14. Wai, Watson, and Woods, "Idaho Librarians."

15. Wai, Watson, and Woods, "Idaho Librarians."

16. Idaho Redistricting Commission, "State of Idaho Redistricting 2001."

17. David Ammons, "High-Centered: Redistricting Adds Up to Tied-Up Feeling," *Olympian (Washington)*, 29 September 2001, http://www.fairvote.org/redistricting/reports/remanual/wanews2.htm (accessed 29 September 2003).

18. Ammons, "High-Centered: Redistricting."

19. Neil Modie, "Redistricting to Cut Seattle's Clout; Expanding, Bumping and Redrawing Lines Will Hurt Democrats in the City the Most," *Seattle Post-Intelligencer*, 2 August 2001, and Brad Shannon, "Redistricting Panel Gets an Earful: Commission Hears Opposition at Olympia Meeting," *Olympian (Washington)*, 8 June 2001, http://www.fairvote.org/redistricting/reports/remanual/wanews2.htm (accessed 29 September 2003).

20. Silver, "Who You'll Vote For is Up to Them."

21. David Ammons, "Redistricting: Sanitized, but Still Starkly Political," *Olympian (Washington)*, 26 August 2001, http://www.fairvote.org/redistricting/reports/remanual/wanews2.htm (accessed 29 September 2003) and Ammons, "High-Centered: Redistricting."

22. David Ammons, "Redistricting Woes: Citizen Panel Stumbles Badly; Process Turns out Messy, Frustrating," *Olympian (Washington)*, 30 December 2001, http://www.fairvote.org/redistricting/reports/remanual/wanews3.htm (accessed 29 September 2003).

23. Patrick Condon, "Baird's District Last to be Redrawn," *Olympian (Washington)*, 20 November 2001, http://www.fairvote.org/redistricting/reports/remanual/wanews2.htm (accessed 29 September 2003).

24. Neil Modie, "A Man and His District May Soon Part Ways: Redrawn 39th Could Put Pearson on the Outside Looking In," *Seattle Post-Intelligencer*, 5 October 2001.

25. Peter Callaghan, "Compromise Should Be at Heart of Redistricting," *Tacoma (Washington) News Tribune*, 18 December 2001.

26. Neil Modie, "Redistricting Reaches a Political Stalemate," *Seattle Post-Intelligencer*, 17 December 2001, and Beth Silver, "Lawmakers Not Eager to Get Into Redistricting," *Tacoma (Washington) News Tribune*, 18 December 2001.

27. David Ammons, "Redistricting Commission Finds 11th-Hour Solution: State High Court Must Now Decide Whether to Accept Last-Minute Plan," *Olympian (Washington)*, 6 January 2002, http://www.fairvote.org/redistricting/reports/remanual/wanews.htm (accessed 29 September 2003) and Ammons, "Redistricting Woes."

28. According to Leslie R. Alm, Ross E. Burkhart, W. David Patton, and James B. Weatherby, "Intrastate Regional Differences in Political Culture: A Case Study of Idaho," *State and Local Government Review* 33 (2001): 109–19 regionalism has played an important role in Idaho politics and the development of the state's political culture.

29. Idaho Redistricting Commission, "State of Idaho Redistricting 2001."

30. Brian Peters, "Do Over: Court Orders Redistricting Rebalanced; Idaho's Bipartisan Panel Charged with Apportioning North, Southeast More Fairly," *Lewiston (Idaho) Morning Tribune*, 30 November 2001.

31. For more details, please see Peters, "Do Over"; Corey Taule, "Redistricting Heading for Round Two," *Idaho Falls (Idaho) Post Register*, 4 December 2001; and Jim Fisher, "Make Redistricting Panel Whole, and Stand Back," *Lewiston (Idaho) Morning Tribune*, 5 December 2001.

32. Idaho Redistricting Commission, "State of Idaho Redistricting 2001."

33. Graham Garner, "State Republicans Blast Current Legislative Map," *Idaho State Journal*, 18 June 2002, http://www.fairvote.org/redistricting/reports/remanual/idnews.htm (accessed 29 September 2003).

34. Corey Taule, "Elusive Redistricting State Commission Still Can't Agree on Map," *Idaho Falls (Idaho) Post Register*, 5 January 2002.

35. Brad Shannon, "Latest Redistricting Plan Keeps Olympia Together; Plan to Meld West Olympia with Shelton, Bremerton Withdrawn," *Olympian (Washington)*, 6 November 2001, http://www.fairvote.org/redistricting/reports/remanual/wanews2.htm (accessed 29 September 2003).

36. Since both states use coterminous districts, the commissions only produced one plan with thirty-five districts in Idaho and forty-nine in Washington.

37. In practical terms, for every 10,000 people a parent district was overpopulated, the new district became 1 percent more Democratic. The growth in the Boise area drives this finding.

38. Warren Cornwall, "Redrawn Districts Shift Some Lawmakers; Campaign Trails Aren't What They Used to Be," *Seattle Times*, 4 August 2002.

39. Garner, "State Republicans Blast."

40. In 1990, the Senate consisted of forty-two seats of which the Democrats held twenty-one. The 1992 redistricting shrunk the Senate to its current size of thirty-five members.

41. Betsy Z. Russell and Erica Curless, "Democrats Make Gains in Capitol; Party Nearly Doubles its Numbers in Legislature," *Spokane (Washington) Spokesman-Review*, 7 November 2002, Idaho edition.

7

Conclusion

Making the Case for Redistricting Reform

In the wake of the Supreme Court's 2006 ruling in the Texas redistricting saga allowing mid-decade redistricting, the findings in this book become even more important. In the analysis, I have shown the importance political actors place on redistricting, but the ability of remappers to reap the electoral benefits is contingent upon the constraints within a state. Under some conditions, redistricting can be one of the most important determinants of elections. Yet, in other conditions, the constraints in a state virtually negate this influence. These findings suggest that research concluding that redistricting shapes electoral outcomes as well as the studies that find a negligible relationship are both partially correct.[1] This book reconciles these two conclusions by demonstrating the influence of redistricting is highly dependent on the conditions and constraints within a state. More importantly, the findings show that relying only on electoral outcomes to test the influence of redistricting, without considering the constraints within a state, does not capture the full effect or tell the complete story.

Political Winners and Losers

Politically, the remappers in those states with the least restrictive constitutional rules had the most success. Overall, the Texas

Republicans emerged as the overwhelming winners in the cases examined. With control of the Legislative Redistricting Board (LRB), the Republican leaders were able to bypass the legislature in implementing an incumbent-based partisan gerrymander. The Republicans targeted and paired incumbents and were ultimately able to turn a slim minority in the House into a clear majority. In so doing, the LRB upset many incumbents, from both parties, with their strategy. In terms of implemented plans, both the Georgia and Indiana House Democrats completed successful partisan gerrymanders. In Georgia, their strategy ultimately backfired as the Republicans had control of both chambers by 2004 in part due to Senate party switchers and the courts ruling their plan was unconstitutional. In the Indiana House, the Democrats were able to stretch their support far enough to retain their small majority in 2002. However, in 2004, with the same districts, the Democrats lost their majority, but then regained it in 2006. Their plan was at least a short-term success given the strong GOP support and population swings in the state.

In the remaining five states, the various constraints in place held partisan gerrymandering in check. In Ohio, where the Republicans controlled the Apportionment Board, the GOP did not have an overwhelming necessity to partisan gerrymander. Instead, the party leaders targeted a few select races to either protect or attempt to pick up from the Democrats. Their success was mixed as the detailed constitutional rules limited their ability to cut across county boundaries while specifying, based on population, how the districts had to be distributed throughout the state. In Michigan, the specific APOL criteria, which are quite similar to the Ohio rules, held the Republicans in check. The House Republicans were able to manipulate the system to implement a favorable plan. However, the plan did not constitute a statewide partisan gerrymander based on the changes between the old and new districts. In the Senate, the minority Democrats used the system to their advantage and forced a compromise plan that actually helped them. In Kentucky, the Senate Republicans were unable to implement a far-reaching partisan gerrymander due to their inability to split across county boundaries. They did manipulate the districts in their favor in the urban areas, but were limited to only dividing three of the 120 counties into multiple districts. This clearly limited their partisan goals.

The most constrained states were Washington and Idaho, where neutral commissions completed the remapping. Neither plan demonstrated any significant features of partisan or incumbent gerrymandering. The Washington districts changed little as the commission generally corrected for population changes from the commission's 1990 plan. In Idaho, the Republicans complained the new map was a Democratic gerrymander. However, it appears the commission implemented a neutral plan to replace the 1990 Republican gerrymander. As a result, the Democrats picked up a few seats in the 2002 elections, but this still left the Republicans with over 80 percent of the total seats. The neutral commission worked, but it is important to note that in both states the commissioners had to follow specific constitutional rules that incorporated many of the same criteria found in both Ohio and Michigan. Additionally, partisanship remained in the process. In Washington, the state faced a constitutional crisis as a result of the commissioners' inability to reach a compromise on time. In Idaho, partisan overtones were found everywhere in the process as the plans were often referred to as the Democratic and Republican proposals.

Effectiveness of the Constraints

Overall, the two most egregious gerrymanders occurred in those states where the controlling party had complete control of the process—the legislature in Georgia and the partisan commission in Texas. However, complete partisan control did not guarantee a successful partisan gerrymander. In both Michigan, with unified legislative control, and Ohio, with the partisan commission, the rules in the state effectively limited the implementation of widespread partisan gerrymanders. The effectiveness of these rules is evident across different types of redistricting control.

The constraint of divided government did not necessarily work as predicted. In both Indiana and Kentucky, the chamber's leadership stayed out of each other's plans. In Indiana, this was particularly true. The House Democrats allowed the Senate Republicans to redistrict their chamber as they pleased and the Senate Republicans did not interfere with the House plans. In Kentucky, the parties went against this tradition early in the process when the House Democrats introduced plans for both chambers; however, when negotiations began the Democrats backed off their Senate proposal and both chambers signed off on each other's plan. However, in both states, divided government did force compromise between the parties to the extent that they had to produce maps that were not so excessively gerrymandered the other chamber would not agree to them.

The use of traditional districting principles played an important constraining role. In this book, I specifically examined the use of the restriction against splitting political subdivisions. Indiana was the only state that did not have any restrictions against splitting county boundaries. As a result, the House Democrats were able to ignore county boundaries to create a plan that cut across 75 percent of the state's counties. In Georgia, the Democrats were able to ignore the provisions given the legal phrasing that said county boundaries should be upheld if possible. This apparent loophole allowed the Democrats to split more than 50 percent of the counties in both plans. Compared to the Democrats' 1990 plan, this was an increase of nearly 20 percent in the House and almost 40 percent in the Senate. Without enforcement of this traditional districting principle, the remappers had much more success at creating districts to their advantage.

In five of the other six states, this principle played an important role in limiting gerrymandering. In Kentucky, the Senate Republicans were unable to help a vulnerable incumbent due to their inability to cut across county boundaries and this was the primary factor in constraining the Republicans from a statewide gerrymander. In Idaho, the bipartisan commission reduced the number of counties split by almost 20 percent from the Republican's plan in 1990, when the legislature had amended the constitution allowing the splitting of county boundaries. In

Washington, the rules called for upholding political subdivisions and communities of interest, but placed a greater importance on creating competitive districts. As a result, the commission split a slightly higher number of county boundaries, but this did not appear to be a major problem as the commission justified this as necessary to keep districts competitive. It also appears that in some large counties, in terms of land area, the commission kept communities together while splitting through the counties.

The rules in Michigan and Ohio were the most specific in terms of how the remappers could split political subdivisions. In Michigan, the APOL criteria restricted the remappers from splitting counties, and in those counties, where it was necessary, the rules restricted the splitting of municipal boundaries. In Ohio, the rules specified a specific distribution of seats to counties and then disallowed the splitting of political boundaries down to the ward level. These specific rules, especially at the sub-county level, severely restricted the remappers' ability to gerrymander.

Texas represents the exception to these findings. The LRB split fewer counties in 2000 than the Democrats did in 1990, but were still able to implement a partisan gerrymander. With the large number of counties, a huge land area, and large ideal district populations, the LRB was able to manipulate the districts by shifting full counties between districts to achieve their goal of incumbent displacement. This case illustrates that remappers may follow the rules and, under the right conditions, still be able to implement a partisan plan.

Overall, the findings demonstrate the important role that traditional districting principles play in the redistricting process. More specifically, they show how important political subdivisions are in constraining partisan gerrymandering. However, not all scholars identify such an important role for traditional districting principles. Micah Altman argues that, politically, "violations of traditional districting principles are essentially harmless."[2] Richard L. Engstrom suggests that despite recent rulings suggesting the willingness of the courts to consider traditional districting principles, the courts remain unlikely to enforce these principles in cases of partisan gerrymandering.[3] In light of my findings, I maintain when traditional districting principles are written into a state's redistricting rules they are an important constraint on partisan gerrymandering.

The fourth constraint I include is the potential for judicial involvement. Theoretically, I argue remappers may be more likely to follow the rules in place and implement constitutional plans with the threat of potential judicial entanglement. My empirical results do not speak directly to this. Rather I have anecdotal evidence from my case studies that suggest those who control the process, either legislators or commissioners, did not want to lose power to the judiciary. Additionally, the courts played an important role in several states by enforcing the redistricting guidelines in previous years. In Kentucky, the legislators knew the courts had invalidated plans in the 1990s for splitting too many counties, and in Ohio, the courts validated the traditional districting principles in place during the 1990s. The courts also played an important role in states that required VRA preclearance. In both Texas and Georgia, this was an important hurdle the new plans had to clear before implementation. The best example of remapping without fear of judicial involvement came in Indiana, where the partisans in control of the process did not appear to consider the potential for court involvement. This was not surprising given the lack of litigation in the past and the lack of requirements they had to meet when putting together the plans. Overall, those in control were cognizant of potential court involvement and, more importantly, followed the rules prescribed in each state to meet the constitutional standards.

The findings support the theory that constraints limit partisan gerrymandering. However, this is contingent upon the specific conditions within a state. Remappers were able to implement partisan gerrymanders in states with unified legislative control, divided legislative control, and partisan commissions. But, at the same time, I find the ability to partisan gerrymander was also limited in states with unified legislative control, divided legislative control, and partisan commissions. Central in all of these situations were the rules in place, and not necessarily the control of the process. Many previous studies have simply assumed the type of control was a primary factor in whether or not the remappers could implement a gerrymander.[4]

The one condition that did not demonstrate any partisan gerrymandering was the use of bipartisan commissions. This format appeared to remove partisan gerrymandering from redistricting in Washington and Idaho. However, I am unable to determine if this was because of the use of the neutral commission or the rules in place Unfortunately, I cannot directly test for this as all of the states that use neutral commissions also provide very constraining rules for the commission to follow. There are no cases where the commissioners have free rein to draw the maps. I argue the outcomes were a result of both the use of a commission and the rules in place. Given the amount of partisanship surrounding both commissions, I argue the commission worked in spite of the reformers goals of removing partisan politics from redistricting. Compromise appeared to be the key as the formats in both states did not give one set of partisan appointed commissioners the votes to implement new plans on their own. As a result, the commissioners had to compromise from their original goals, and in Washington, this was important as the commissioners did not want to process shifting to the courts.

In particular, the use of traditional districting principles with clear and specific constitutional guidelines is the condition that placed the heaviest constraint against partisan gerrymandering. Under various redistricting strategies these rules limited gerrymandering. These rules worked in situations where the strategy was clearly a statewide partisan gerrymander as in the Kentucky Senate and in situations where the strategy was to target specific districts as in Ohio. However, the simple application of these principles may not always work as the Texas case shows. Overall, the constraints found within these states did an effective job of limiting, but not eliminating, partisan gerrymandering.

Looking Ahead to 2010: The Legal Landscape and Calls for Reform

In this section, I take a step back from my specific findings and discuss the American redistricting landscape heading into 2010.

Two cases from the 2000 round of redistricting stand out as having potentially long-term consequences. The first is the Georgia case discussed in chapter 3, *Larios v. Cox*.[5] A federal district court initially ruled the plans unconstitutional on grounds the population deviations in the Democrats' plan violated the one-person/one-vote standard. The Supreme Court later upheld the ruling in a summary affirmance and did not provide a rationale for their judgment.[6] In *Larios*, the district court did not directly rule on the issue of partisan gerrymandering for which the plaintiffs sued; instead the judges focused on the issue of population deviation. In the decision, the court went against nearly thirty years of precedent that assumed legislative plans with less than a 10 percent population deviation were constitutional. Throughout the years, the courts have even allowed plans with greater than a 10 percent deviation to stand as long as the state provided a legitimate state goal, such as protecting political subdivisions, for the deviations. This decision opens the door for challenges to plans with any amount of population deviation. It is not yet clear if this ruling will shift the precedent or if this case will stand out as a judicial outlier. If it does produce a shift, it would change one of the fundamental rules of legislative redistricting and force the states to provide specific reasons for any population deviations.

The second case is *Vieth v. Jubelirer*, which involved the Pennsylvania congressional districts.[7] In this case, Democratic voters challenged the Republican plan as an unconstitutional partisan gerrymander. The U.S. Supreme Court in a 5–4 decision ruled not to overturn the districts with a four judge plurality, lead by Justice Scalia, calling the issue of partisan gerrymandering "nonjusticiable" because "no judicially discernable and manageable standards for adjudicating such claims exist."[8] This case represented a crossroads in potential partisan gerrymandering cases. It had been eighteen years since the court dealt directly with the issue of partisan gerrymandering. In the *Bandemer* case, the court established that partisan gerrymandering was justiciable but set such a strict standard that no court had ever ruled a plan unconstitutional using this standard. Election law experts viewed the case as an opportunity for the court to either assert the standard established in *Bandemer* or abandon it altogether.[9] The Court appeared to abandon it and by doing so appeared to limit the chances of future plans being ruled unconstitutional on grounds of partisan gerrymandering.

The other important development in American redistricting is the growth in reform movements throughout the country. In early 2005, when California Governor Arnold Schwarzenegger proposed taking redistricting power away from the legislature and putting retired judges in charge, California joined at least ten states with recent or ongoing reform movements.[10] Although voters in both California and Ohio rejected reform initiatives in 2005, the issue remains an important one across the country.

For the past twenty-five years, Common Cause has been one of the leading proponents of redistricting reform, and during this time, the group has advocated for nearly the same set of reforms.[11] As of February 2005, the group proposed states use the following redistricting guidelines:

1. A nonpartisan and independent redistricting commission
2. Fair criteria that include:
   a. Equally populated districts
   b. Remappers comply with the Voting Rights Act
   c. Respect communities of interest, to the extent possible
   d. Compact and contiguous districts
   e. Using necessary election data to draw competitive districts, where possible
   f. Process shall be "incumbent blind"
3. Public participation and transparency
4. Completed only once every ten years, unless ordered by the courts
5. Judicial review
6. States should consider the use of proportional representation systems and multi-member districts.[12]

The reform movements in most states echo these guidelines with the public push being for independent redistricting in the form of a neutral commission. However, most supporters of neutral commissions do not claim they are a panacea of reform that will completely remove all the legislative evils from the process and automatically produce fair and equitable maps for all involved. Rather, the common view is that the move to commissions is a viable and practical, but not perfect, solution for removing the inherent conflict of allowing legislators to pick their own constituencies.[13] Kansas State Senator Derek Schmidt summed up this view when discussing a proposal in Kansas to move toward the use of a redistricting commission: "There is an inherent conflict of interest in allowing those of us in public office to draw our own districts, and we're trying to mitigate that conflict."[14]

With the growing push for independent commissions, I argue these reformers are stressing the wrong aspect of their proposals. Every proposal for independent commissions that I have seen includes a specific set of rules for the commissioners to follow. These rules usually include the use of traditional districting principles, and most call for either the prohibition of considering political and incumbency data or the push for competitive districts. According to my findings, the rules are the most important component to successful redistricting reform and not necessarily who controls the process.

I agree with these independent reformers that neutral plans should be the ultimate goal of redistricting, but I think it is impractical to suggest a switch to independent commissions will remove politics from the process. As I show in the cases of Washington and Idaho, the commissions clearly operated under the cloud of partisan politics. It is quite possible the use of bipartisan or neutral commissions simply subvert the partisanship away from public view.

Reformers also believe that neutral commissions will be more successful than the legislatures at implementing constitutional plans that withstand judicial scrutiny. However, results from the 2000 round of redistricting do not support this. In Idaho, the commission had its first two plans thrown out by the courts before finally implementing a third plan that withstood judicial scrutiny. In Arizona, the new independent commission, modeled after Washington's rules that stress competitive districts, had its first plan thrown out by the courts when the plaintiffs introduced plans with more competitive districts than the commissions. As a result, the 2002 elections were held under a court-ordered map. These cases suggest that a move to a neutral commission does not necessarily guarantee any greater success in the courts than legislative redistricting plans.

In terms of redistricting reforms to limit partisan gerrymandering, I suggest a general redistricting model that borrows heavily from Michigan and Ohio and is easily exportable to all states.[15] In addition to adherence to equal population, the Voting Rights requirements, and the use of contiguous districts this model specifically calls for

1. An apportionment formula that respects political subdivisions at the county level and below and allows a 10 percent population deviation to meet these principles
2. A method for allowing the introduction and evaluation of competing plans
3. Rules codified in the constitution

These three points are what I consider the most useful and practical rules for limiting partisan gerrymandering. I argue a specific apportionment formula similar to Ohio's, which determines the distribution of districts throughout the state, provides a central framework for the remappers to follow. In conjunction with respecting political subdivisions, these two rules should limit the type of gerrymander the Democrats used in both Georgia and Indiana that tried to squeeze as many districts as possible into their areas of strength. Additionally, a specific formula for when remappers may split counties and other political units and to what extent they can be split is critical to limiting gerrymandering. Both Ohio and Michigan specify respect for county and municipal boundaries. In Michigan, this includes a method for limiting the splits within the counties above the ideal district size. In light of the Georgia Democrats' strategy of under- and overpopulating districts, I argue states should be allowed to deviate from absolute population equality only to reach the specific goals of the state's apportionment formula and for respecting political subdivisions.

I take the second point directly from the APOL criteria currently in use in Michigan. This rule opens up the redistricting process and is designed to allow for some transparency in the process by forcing a comparison and evaluation of competing plans. As the Michigan case illustrates, this rule can lead to bipartisan compromise within one-party controlled redistricting environments and the implementation of relatively neutral plans. However, there is room for manipulation within this rule as the House Republicans successfully blocked the Democrats' plan for evaluation.

The final point is important for preventing exploitation of the redistricting system by those in charge, particularly the legislators. Amending a state's constitution to include the state's specific rules for redistricting is probably the best way to avoid manipulation of these rules. This would also allow the voters to have a say over the redistricting system in each state and provide more stability in the rules as the remappers and courts would know the exact criteria when producing and evaluating redistricting plans.

This model specifies rules for partisan neutral redistricting regardless of who controls the process. A move to independent commissions does not necessarily solve the problems of partisan gerrymandering. Instead, politics and partisanship will remain in redistricting no matter who drafts the plans. I think it is virtually impossible within the American system to find any potential line drawers, whether it is legislators, appointed commissioners, judges, interest groups, or even citizens, who could draw lines without some of form of self-interest entering into the process. Additionally, I do not think the removal of partisan and incumbency data is a practical constraint. These are important components of the American electoral system and removing these factors from consideration removes key components of the link between legislators and constituents.

I suggest this general model as a set of rules that may best allow for partisan neutral redistricting. This model would not completely remove the potential for partisan manipulation, but I do not think any system or set of rules could do this. I think the more practical approach is to focus on limiting partisan gerrymandering and putting into place a system that is partisan neutral and favors fair and equal districts for all voters.

The final question I discuss is can redistricting promote a healthier representative and electoral system by focusing on protecting the people and not the politicians. In terms of representation, a fair electoral system is paramount. To promote fair and equal representative districts, redistricting should promote the concepts of congizability and the continuity of representation.[16]

According to Bernard Grofman, a political scientist and notable redistricting expert, congizability is "the ability to characterize the district boundaries in a manner that can be readily communicated to ordinary citizens of the district in commonsense terms based on geographical referents."[17] Grofman's concept of congizability relies heavily on the central place of geography in the American political system. Central to Grofman's argument is the way that voters identify themselves with the geography within a state. Districting based on this concept would involve following natural geographic boundaries and political subdivisions within a state. An emphasis on congizability appears most closely related to the traditional districting principles discussed in this book and provides an option for partisan neutral redistricting. A focus on congizability appears to be a fair method to distribute districts so that all constituents are able to identify which district they vote in based on clear geographic units within a state. I argue that geographic units are inherently politically neutral and shift the focus from political considerations to those of the voters.

Throughout this book, I focused specifically on the use of county boundaries; however, this is not necessarily the best political subdivision for all states.[18] In many states, most citizens identify where they live in terms of the county. In the Midwest and New England, townships tend to be this unit. However, this leaves the door open for gerrymandering in urban areas where the population of a county or city is larger than the ideal district size. To deal with this, the Ohio model offers a solution by identifying, down to the city-ward level, the political units remappers must respect. The key is for each state to identify the units voters identify with and would easily recognize within a district description. An example within metropolitan areas may even be school districts as these represent clear political boundaries of which almost all citizens are aware.

Another potential method to increase the ease with which voters can determine who represents them is with the use of coterminous districts. The use of these nested districts should provide the voters with an easier time of identifying which house and senate districts they live in as they only have to consult one map to determine their legislators. This could also increase representation for the entire geographic area as the use of coterminous districts increases the number of legislators working for a defined area. With separate maps, there is often a haphazard overlap between House and Senate boundaries that does not facilitate cross-chamber cooperation to work for any clear geographic area. One limiting factor in the use of nested districts is the ratio of House to Senate seats in a state. For coterminous districts to work, the number of House seats must be a multiple of the number of Senate districts. Currently, nineteen states use some form of coterminous districts with another six having a divisible distribution of seats that could easily adapt to using nested districts. The other half of the states would have to alter the number of seats in one or both chambers to implement coterminous districts.

In combination with boundaries that respect political subdivisions, the use of coterminous districts could enhance the representation between legislators and constituents as it should alleviate some voter confusion and even provide the legislators with a clearer picture of exactly whom they represent. In districts that do not follow political subdivisions, the remappers often draw boundaries that leave both voters and legislators with an increased amount of work to determine either whom their legislator is or whom their constituents are. This is probably more of a problem today than ever before as the increases in computer and Geographic Information Systems (GIS) technology now allow remappers to easily divide districts in any number of imaginable configurations.

Moving to the issue of continuity of representation, political scientists Ronald Keith Gaddie and Charles S. Bullock III refer to it as the stability between incumbents and constituents from the old maps to the new maps. In my argument, I discuss this in terms of district intactness between the old and new maps and not necessarily in terms of incumbent stability. By focusing on geography, I remove the potentially biasing issue of incumbency from the discussion. I argue continuity of representation should reflect an attempt to keep as many voters as possible in the same district during redistricting. As such, redistricting should not be a game where those in control are able to completely undue the previous electoral boundaries and carve them up for their own political advantage. Rather, redistricting would better serve our democracy as a tool for updating the boundaries, where necessary, due to population shifts and keeping the old districts as intact as possible. This goes back to the primary argument that redistricting should focus on the voters and their ability to control the electoral system by knowing who represents them and keeping this as stable as possible. This would put citizens in a better position to elect their representative of choice and not essentially predetermine the outcomes based on how some partisan elite decided to draw their district.

Overall, redistricting can harm American popular sovereignty, but not to the extent many people fear. The current system of rules and constraints found in many states effectively limits the ability of remappers to gerrymander in a way that subverts citizen control over the electoral process. However, the examples that routinely make the news are in those cases where the remappers are able to implement a successful partisan gerrymander, like Texas and Georgia, and not the cases where the rules limited the partisan manipulation of the maps, as in Kentucky and Ohio. The key to protecting the voters from the dangers of redistricting is to establish clear and specific constitutional rules that focus on neutral guidelines that do not advantage those drawing the maps no matter their strategic and self-interested goals. Redistricting should emphasize the needs of all voters equally, primarily by providing easily recognizable districts with some level of continuity to as many citizens as possible.

Notes

1. For an example of studies that find little redistricting influence, please see Mark Rush, *Does Redistricting Make a Difference: Partisan Representation and Electoral Behavior* (Lanham, Md.: Lexington Books, 2000).

2. Micah Altman, "Districting Principles and Democratic Representation" (Ph.D. diss., California Institute of Technology, 1998), 59.

3. Richard L. Engstrom, "The Post-2000 Round of Redistricting: An Entangled Thicket within the Federal System," *Publius: The Journal of Federalism* 32 (2002): 51–70.

4. For examples, please see Harry Basehart and John Comer, "Partisan and Incumbent Effects in State Legislative Redistricting," *Legislative Studies Quarterly* 16 (1991): 65–79 and Richard Niemi and Simon Jackman, "Bias and Responsiveness in State Legislative Districting," *Legislative Studies Quarterly* 16 (1991): 183–202.

5. 124 S. Ct. 1503 (2004).

6. David E. Rosenbaum, "Justices Allow Redistricting in Georgia," *New York Times*, 1 July 2004.

7. 24 S. Ct. 1769 (2004).

8. Shannon P. Duffy, "U.S. Supreme Court Rejects PA Democrats Redistricting Suit; Splintered Decision Leaves Small Opening for Future 'Partisan Gerrymandering' Lawsuits," *Pennsylvania Law Weekly* 3 May 2004: 7.

9. Marcia Coyle, "High Court Will Weigh U.S. House Remapping; Gerrymandering Might Have Limits," *National Law Journal* 8 December 2003: 1.

10. Adam Nagourney, "States See Growing Campaign for Redistricting Reform," *New York Times*, 3 February 2005. According to this article, campaigns were ongoing in California, Colorado, Florida, Georgia, Maryland, Massachusetts, Pennsylvania, and Rhode Island. In other reports, I found recent reforms enacted in Arizona, an ongoing movement in Kansas, and a failed attempt in Ohio.

11. The major difference between the 2005 guidelines and the 1977 guidelines is the consideration of MMDs and electoral data to draw competitive districts. The 1977 guidelines called for the use of single-member districts only and the complete exclusion of any past electoral or registration data in the process. For more information on the 1977 guidelines, please see Bruce Adams, *Toward a System of 'Fair and Effective Representation': A Common Cause Report on State and Congressional Reapportionment* (Washington, D.C.: Common Cause, 1977).

12. For more information, please see Common Cause, "Common Cause Redistricting Guidelines," February 2005 http://commoncause.org (accessed 27 May 2005). Common Cause fits into the "independent" reformers group which considers partisan politics inappropriate to the process. This differs from the "good-government" reformers that usually acknowledge that partisan politics is a legitimate consideration in redistricting, but should not dominate the

process. For more information, please see Clark Bensen, "Substantial Political Consequences, A Practitioner's Perspective on Redistricting," *Extensions* Fall (2004): 5–8.

13. For further information on this view, please see Jeffrey C. Kubin, "The Case for Redistricting Commissions," *Texas Law Review* 75 (1997): 837–72 and Richard Morrill, *Political Redistricting and Geographic Theory* (Washington, D.C.: Association of American Geographers, 1981).

14. Chris Grenz, "Panel Would be Picked from Pool," *Topeka Capital-Journal*, 10 February 2003.

15. I also consider the use of coterminous districts as an important constraint to limiting partisan gerrymandering. However, given the unequal distribution of House and Senate seats in many states this is not exportable to all states. I discuss nested districts in greater detail in the concluding section of this chapter.

16. Bernard Grofman, "Would Vince Lombardi Have Been Right If He Had Said: 'When It Comes to Redistricting, Race, Isn't Everything, It's the Only Thing'?" *Cardozo Law Review* 14 (1993): 1237–76, introduces the term congizability and Ronald Keith Gaddie and Charles S. Bullock III, "The Political Consequences of an Uncontrolled Redistricting" (paper presented at the annual meeting of the Southern Political Science Association, New Orleans, January 2005), examine the continuity of representation.

17. Grofman, "Would Vince Lombardi," 1262.

18. Another potential argument is for respecting communities of interest. Generally, these communities are difficult to define. Most people tend to reference communities of interest in vague terms that are not as easy to identify on the map as political units. Districting based on media markets is one potential identifiable use of communities of interest. Please see Brian F. Schaffner, "House Members, Legislative Activities, and Local Coverage" (Ph.D. diss., Indiana University, 2002).

Appendix 1
Measuring Gerrymandering

District Intactness

To measure district intactness, I determine the proportion of constituents shared between a new district and its parent district. I develop this intactness score by calculating the number of precincts that the new district shares with its parent district and dividing by the total number of precincts in the new district. For example, if ten precincts fall into a district and nine of those came from the parent district then the new district would be 90 percent intact with its parent district. The use of precincts and not total population works for this measure since each precinct has approximately equal population within a state. Therefore, the percentage of a district left intact will be the same whether using the number of precincts of the population within those precincts. To check this, I computed the intactness using both precincts and total population for Kentucky and found a correlation of .93 between the two.

I use this district intactness score along with the district typologies to look for patterns of change. In a partisan gerrymander, the controlling party is more likely to keep their districts more intact while giving the out party incumbents more new constituents to represent. A bipartisan incumbent gerrymander should see all incumbents' districts remain more intact and a

Table A1.1. 2002 District Intactness

Chamber	*All Districts*	*D Districts*	*R Districts*	*Mixed*	*Difference*
Georgia House	57.86 (146)	62.50 (86)	51.57 (60)		10.93 (3.23)***
Georgia Senate	56.76 (56)	62.76 (32)	48.78 (24)		14.98 (3.60)***
Michigan House	70.89 (110)	68.66 (50)	72.74 (60)		4.08 (1.21)
Michigan Senate	64.31 (38)	63.80 (13)	64.58 (25)		.78 (.12)
Indiana House	73.96 (100)	77.02 (54)	70.38 (46)		6.64 (1.87)**
Indiana Senate	84.10 (50)	83.81 (18)	84.26 (32)		.45 (.16)
Kentucky House	85.71 (100)	89.40 (65)	78.85 (35)		10.56 (3.24)***
Kentucky Senate	73.19 (38)	69.97 (19)	76.71 (19)		7.04 (1.16)
Ohio House	77.79 (99)	69.84 (39)	82.95 (60)		13.11 (3.95)***
Ohio Senate	81.44 (33)	74.12 (12)	85.61 (21)		11.48 (2.34)**
Texas House	57.07 (150)	53.07 (74)	60.97 (76)		7.90 (2.53)**
Texas Senate	64.86 (31)	67.42 (16)	62.14 (15)		5.28 (.82)
Idaho	56.07 (35)	34.04 (4)	59.19 (26)	57.46 (5)	25.15 (2.29)**
Washington	80.94 (49)	77.06 (17)	86.00 (16)	80.00 (16)	8.94 (1.94)*

Notes: Idaho and Washington use coterminous districts. One senator and two house members are elected from one district. In these states, D Districts are those with three Democratic members, R Districts are those with three Republican members, and Mixed Districts are those with both parties holding at least one of the seats. Difference column is the difference between Democratic and Republican districts. T-test statistic is in parentheses.

*** $p < .001$
** $p < .05$
* $p < .10$

neutral plan should produce a systematic pattern of core retention across the district typologies.

Models of District Partisanship

Notes on Variable Specification

Dependent Variable in All Models: 2002 District Partisanship (Democratic)

Independent Variables: These vary slightly by state. Please see below for complete details.

Parent Base Vote: Democratic Vote for the Parent District (all models)

In-Party District: 1 if incumbent from the controlling party, 0 if not (all models except Idaho and Washington)

Competitive District: 1 if parent district partisanship was between 40 percent and 60 percent, 0 if not (all models except Idaho and Washington)

In-Party * Competitive: Interaction between In-Party District and Competitive District: 1 if district is an in-party and competitive district, 0 if not (all models except Idaho and Washington)

Typology Variables used for Idaho and Washington (Chapter 6) Models

Leaning Democratic: 1 if two of the three members in the parent district are Democrats, 0 if not

Leaning Republican: 1 if two of the three members in the parent district are Republicans, 0 if not

Republican: 1 if all three members in the parent district are Republicans, 0 if not

Democratic districts are the reference group

District Intactness: percent 2002 district intact with parent district (all models)

Dem. Inc. Personal Vote: percent vote the incumbent received in Democratically controlled districts (all models except Georgia House, Idaho, and Washington)

Table A1.2. Models of 2002 District Partisanship

Independent Variables	*Model 1*	*Model 2*	*Model 3*
Georgia House			
Parent Base Vote	.7602 (.0294)***	.4990 (.0471)***	.4905 (.0479)***
In-party District		17.81 (2.648)***	16.60 (2.748)***
Competitive District		17.38 (1.759)***	15.44 (1.981)***
In-party * Competitive		−28.40 (2.968)***	−26.10 (3.150)***
District Intactness			−.016 (.0270)
MMD			.3785 (1.453)
Pop. Deviation			−.304 (.1438)**
Constant	9.869 (1.472)***	14.61 (1.628)***	16.65 (2.594)***
N	146	146	146
Adj. R^2	.82	.90	.90
Georgia Senate			
Parent Base Vote	.7141 (.0413)***	.4650 (.0573)***	.5047 (.0658)***
In-party District		17.83 (3.174)***	23.74 (6.281)***
Competitive District		15.82 (1.965)***	16.61 (2.283)***
In-party * Competitive		−25.60 (3.304)***	−25.10 (3.825)***
District Intactness			.0420 (.0413)
Dem. Inc. Personal Vote			.0831 (.0497)
Rep. Inc. Personal Vote			.0262 (.0624)
Pop. Deviation			−.152 (.2191)
Constant	11.59 (2.142)***	15.09 (2.010)***	4.899 (5.704)
N	56	56	56
Adj. R^2	.84	.93	.93

Michigan House			
Parent Base Vote	.9872 (.0165)***	.8869 (.0303)***	.8636 (.0514)***
In-party District		−5.67 (1.555)***	−6.35 (6.260)
Competitive District		−4.93 (1.069)***	−4.88 (1.091)***
In-party * Competitive		6.520 (1.554)***	7.252 (1.649)***
District Intactness			−.012 (.0168)
Dem. Inc. Personal Vote			.0275 (.0596)
Rep. Inc. Personal Vote			.0262 (.0624)
Term Limited Parent District			1.248 (.6877)*
Constant	.3741 (.9455)	9.192 (2.406)***	9.289 (3.502)**
N	110	110	110
Adj. R^2	.97	.97	.97
Michigan Senate			
Parent Base Vote	.7558 (.0782)***	.3351 (.1229)**	.4170 (.3084)
In-party District		−28.2 (7.402)***	−33.4 (34.66)
Competitive District		−13.6 (5.110)**	−12.3 (6.125)*
In-party * Competitive		25.16 (7.902)**	22.06 (9.767)**
District Intactness			−.080 (.0703)
Dem. Inc. Personal Vote			−.214 (.3316)
Rep. Inc. Personal Vote			−.104 (.3308)
Term Limited Parent District			−.550 (2.597)
Constant	12.30 (4.462)**	48.01 (9.624)***	63.55 (15.12)***
N	38	38	38
Adj. R^2	.71	.79	.78
Indiana House			
Parent Base Vote	.8031 (.0292)***	.6321 (.0483)***	.6901 (.0540)***
In-party District		9.595 (2.667)***	6.450 (3.935)

(continued)

Table A1.2. (*continued*)

Independent Variables	*Model 1*	*Model 2*	*Model 3*
Competitive District		7.868 (1.670)***	8.115 (1.648)***
In-party * Competitive		−11.40 (2.891)***	−11.00 (2.817)***
District Intactness			.0676 (.0235)**
Dem. Inc. Personal Vote			−.013 (.0281)
Rep. Inc. Personal Vote			−.025 (.0303)
Constant	7.077 (1.369)***	10.65 (1.699)***	5.969 (3.954)
N	100	100	100
Adj. R^2	.88	.91	.92
Indiana Senate			
Parent Base Vote	.9264 (.0166)***	.7468 (.0385)***	.7416 (.0367)***
In-party District		−8.65 (1.784)***	−8.47 (2.503)**
Competitive District		−5.53 (1.384)***	−6.28 (1.333)***
In-party * Competitive		6.604 (1.774)***	7.820 (1.711)***
District Intactness			.0558 (.0219)**
Dem. Inc. Personal Vote			−.020 (.0157)
Rep. Inc. Personal Vote			−.030 (.0134)**
Constant	2.295 (.7571)**	16.95 (3.081)***	14.79 (3.961)***
N	50	50	50
Adj. R^2	.98	.99	.99
Kentucky House			
Parent Base Vote	.8746 (.0215)***	.8286 (.0391)***	.8195 (.0413)***
In-party District		2.321 (1.877)	5.144 (3.232)
Competitive District		4.410 (1.237)***	4.944 (1.313)***
In-party * Competitive		−4.67 (2.206)**	−5.08 (2.246)**

District Intactness			−.018 (.0197)
Dem. Inc. Personal Vote			.0009 (.0172)
Rep. Inc. Personal Vote			.0306 (.0242)
Constant	4.976 (.9725)***	5.348 (1.368)***	4.389 (2.878)
N	100	100	100
Adj. R^2	.94	.95	.95
Kentucky Senate			
Parent Base Vote	.9473 (.0372)***	.7323 (.0531)***	.7162 (.0550)***
In-party District		−11.40 (2.276)***	−7.34 (3.869)*
Competitive District		−8.72 (1.795)***	−7.67 (1.931)***
In-party * Competitive		11.88 (2.452)***	10.82 (2.528)***
District Intactness			−.020 (.0209)
Dem. Inc. Personal Vote			.0463 (.0276)
Rep. Inc. Personal Vote			.0039 (.0379)
Constant	1.770 (1.668)	20.23 (3.920)***	18.05 (4.658)***
N	38	38	38
Adj. R^2	.95	.97	.97
Ohio House			
Parent Base Vote	.9446 (.0231)***	.7248 (.0510)***	.7171 (.0581)***
In-party District		−10.2 (2.191)***	−11.00 (4.333)**
Competitive District		−6.80 (1.594)***	−6.67 (1.646)***
In-party * Competitive		9.332 (2.208)***	9.257 (2.255)***
District Intactness			.0017 (.0214)
Dem. Inc. Personal Vote			.0185 (.0443)
Rep. Inc. Personal Vote			.0297 (.0438)
Term Limited Parent District			.7338 (1.339)

(continued)

Table A1.2. (*continued*)

Independent Variables	*Model 1*	*Model 2*	*Model 3*
Constant	2.109 (1.209)*	19.65 (3.845)***	18.59 (4.736)***
N	99	99	99
Adj. R^2	.94	.95	.95
Ohio Senate			
Parent Base Vote	.9591 (.0356)***	.8158 (.0839)***	.7974 (.0905)***
In-party District		−5.90 (3.285)*	−11.38 (6.67)
Competitive District		−1.78 (2.154)	−3.09 (2.649)
In-party * Competitive		3.447 (3.072)	5.26 (3.621)
District Intactness			.064 (.0411)
Dem. Inc. Personal Vote			−.021 (.057)
Rep. Inc. Personal Vote			.026 (.0414)
Term Limited Parent District			−.664 (1.70)
Constant	1.096 (1.842)	11.76 (6.154)*	10.48 (8.287)
N	33	33	33
Adj. R^2	.96	.96	.96
Texas House			
Parent Base Vote	.9039 (.0255)***	.7067 (.0431)***	.7131 (.0459)***
In-party District		−12.10 (1.973)***	12.70 (4.408)**
Competitive District		−11.10 (1.338)***	−11.10 (1.364)***
In-party * Competitive		18.92 (2.469)***	18.90 (2.493)***
District Intactness			.0063 (.0190)
Dem. Inc. Personal Vote			−.013 (.0321)
Rep. Inc. Personal Vote			−.006 (.0329)
Constant	3.551 (1.168)**	21.33 (3.067)***	21.90 (4.105)***

N	150	150	150
Adj. R^2	.89	.93	.93
Texas Senate			
Parent Base Vote	.9087 (.0616)***	.8870 (.1317)***	.7602 (.1746)***
In-party District		−4.10 (5.824)	4.191 (9.402)
Competitive District		−6.05 (3.882)	−5.26 (3.820)
In-party * Competitive		(dropped)	(dropped)
District Intactness			.0542 (.0504)
Dem. Inc. Personal Vote			.1402 (.0888)
Rep. Inc. Personal Vote			.0096 (.0686)
Constant	2.415 (2.765)	7.863 (9.467)	−.740 (10.62)
N	31	31	31
Adj. R^2	.88	.89	.89
Idaho			
Parent Base Vote	.7484 (.0468)***	.8851 (.0711)***	.8517 (.0807)***
District Typology+			
Leaning Democratic		6.60 (2.97)**	4.89 (3.23)
Leaning Republican		4.07 (2.19)*	3.07 (2.32)
Republican		5.74 (2.21)**	3.49 (2.50)
Proportion Dem. Vote Added			.0062 (.0463)
District Intactness			.0217 (.0512)
Parent District Pop. Deviation			.0001 (.0000)**
Constant	7.136 (1.467)***	−1.83 (3.781)	−.708 (7.544)
N	35	35	35
Adj. R^2	.88	.90	.91

(continued)

Table A1.2. (*continued*)

Independent Variables	*Model 1*	*Model 2*	*Model 3*
Washington			
Parent Base Vote	.9672 (.0190)***	.9473 (.0304)***	.9867 (.0256)***
District Typology+			
Leaning Democratic		.074 (.839)	−.925 (.685)
Leaning Republican		−.673 (.843)	.297 (.714)
Republican		−.735 (.891)	−.832 (.702)
Proportion Dem. Vote Added			−.067 (.0692)
District Intactness			.0184 (.0649)
Parent District Pop. Deviation			.00001 (.00002)
Constant	1.143 (1.037)	2.554 (2.025)	.1547 (6.544)
N	49	49	49
Adj. R^2	.98	.98	.99

Notes: OLS
Standard Errors in parentheses
***$p < .01$, ** $p < .05$, * $p < .10$

Rep. Inc Personal Vote: percent vote the incumbent received in Republican controlled districts (all models except Georgia House, Idaho, and Washington)
MMD: 1 if the district is a MMD, 0 if not (Georgia House)
Pop. deviation: percent deviation of 2002 district from the ideal district size (Georgia House and Georgia Senate)
Term Limited Parent District: 1 if incumbent from parent district was termed out, 0 if not (Michigan House, Michigan Senate, Ohio House, and Ohio Senate)
Proportion Dem. Vote Added to District: Percent Democratic vote of those precincts from outside the parent district (Idaho and Washington)
Parent District Population Deviation: Population deviation of parent district from the 2002 ideal district size (Idaho and Washington)

Details on Modeling District Partisanship

The first model is the base model that only includes the parent district partisanship. I expect the partisanship of the parent district to be the best predictor of the new district partisanship. This makes sense given that a new district derives most of its constituents from its parent district. This serves as the base model and primary control variable in the other models. As such, it does not have specific expectations based on the type of gerrymander attempted. The other outcomes in the other models should vary depending on the type of gerrymander attempted. If these variables are significant and add to the model fit then this supports the argument for a particular type of gerrymander in a plan. If these variables do not matter, then either this may fit with the neutral plan expectations or show the remappers were unable to produce changes that followed a specific gerrymandering pattern.

In the second model, I include the competitiveness of the district and the district control. I also include an interaction term that incorporates the competitiveness of the parent district along with the partisan control of the district.[1] These variables account for the district typologies and provide much the same information as the scatter plots. In the third model, I consider other factors such as district intactness, under- or overpopulation of the parent district, demographics, and incumbency. In these models, I am looking for significant relationships for the main effects of competition and district control along with any other key variables found in each state.

Note

1. This interaction term is a multiplicative term between the two dummy variables (competitiveness of the district and party control of the district). Robert J. Friedrich, "In Defense of Multiplicative Terms in Multiple Regression Equations," *American Journal of Political Science* 26 (1982): 797–833 and Melissa A. Hardy, *Regression with Dummy Variables* (Newbury Park, Calif.: Sage Publications, 1993) provide details on the appropriateness and use of this type of interaction.

Appendix 2

Political Subdivisions and Split Counties

Notes on Measurement

When examining county splits in a redistricting plan, counties fall into one of two categories, those counties with a population below the ideal district size and those with a population that exceeds this ideal size. The ideal district size is simply the total population of a state divided by the number of districts. This provides the size at which all districts meet the equal population criteria. If the remappers adhere to this principle, then, under most circumstances, no county with a population below the ideal district size will be split into multiple districts as the population of an entire county can fit into one district.

For each plan, I determine whether a county is split into multiple districts, has a population above or below the ideal district size, and the number of districts that splits the county for both the old and new plans in a state. For each of the counties above the ideal district size, I determine the minimum number of splits by determining how much larger the county is than the ideal district size. For example, if the county is two times the ideal size then the minimum number of splits in that county is two. This is important as part of the overall analysis of gerrymandering in a state. If the remappers are gerrymandering then they may split certain areas into more districts than necessary. Democrats may

Table A2.1. Percentage of Split Counties below Ideal District Size

	1990		*2000*	
Chamber	*% Split*	*Total below Ideal Size*	*% Split*	*Total below Ideal Size*
Georgia House	12.61	119	36.07	122
Georgia Senate	11.33	150	49.33	150
Michigan House	9.68	62	11.29	62
Michigan Senate	3.95	76	2.63	76
Indiana House	60.29	68	66.18	68
Indiana Senate	52.44	82	41.46	82
Kentucky House	3.00	100	6.06	99
Kentucky Senate	1.71	117	0	117
Ohio House	18.18	66	22.73	66
Ohio Senate	7.41	81	9.88	81
Texas House	1.32	227	0.43	230
Texas Senate	10.53	247	4.05	247
Idaho	22.86	35	5.56	36
Washington	27.59	29	20.69	29

Notes: Total Counties:
Georgia: 159
Michigan: 83
Indiana: 92
Kentucky: 120
Ohio: 88
Texas: 254
Idaho: 44
Washington: 39

want to maximize the number of districts in urban areas with traditionally strong Democratic support while Republicans will want to minimize these districts and instead draw more districts in the stronger Republican suburbs. If the principle works then remappers should not split any counties unnecessarily.

Appendix 3

Election Day Outcomes

Predicting Election Outcomes

Notes on Model Specification

The model I use is a variant of the linear regression technique advocated by Andrew Gelman and Gary King and follows closely with J. Morgan Kousser's and Ronald Keith Gaddie and Charles S. Bullock's analysis of vote shares and seats gained.[1] Kousser argues for this model over more complicated Maximum Likelihood Estimation models and measures of partisan bias because, "the index of party strength presented here . . . offers strong insights into the intentions of the redistricters (as indicated by the partisan consequences of their plans) and into just how those intentions are put into effect. The test is not only more intuitively meaningful, less dependent on complex statistical theory, and therefore easier for political activists, reporters, judges, and other interested parties to use than sophisticated variants of seats-votes ratios."[2] In each case, the dependent variable is the proportion of the two-party vote a party received in the 2002 elections with the independent variables being important structural components of each chamber's redistricting. In most cases, this is the base partisanship of the district and incumbency factors and in others, demographic characteristics are also considered.

Table A3.1. Models of 2002 Election Outcomes

Chamber	*Base Vote*	*Dem. Inc*	*Rep. Inc*	*Constant*	*Adj. R^2*	*N*
Georgia House	.6729	16.88	−8.11	15.29	.78	179
	(.0528)***	(1.891)***	(2.192)***	(2.928)***		
Georgia Senate	.7488	12.30	−9.99	13.06	.87	56
	(.0770)***	(2.481)***	(3.067)**	(4.467)**		
Michigan House	.9926	8.125	−7.04	−2.07	.94	110
	(.0332)***	(1.336)***	(1.236)***	(1.936)		
Michigan Senate	1.098	1.343	−7.55	−7.17	.91	38
	(.0656)***	(3.414)	(2.613)**	(3.632)*		
Indiana House	.5673	16.34	−13.80	21.46	.83	100
	(.1003)***	(3.060)***	(3.127)***	(5.003)***		
Indiana Senate	.6564	23.68	−10.70	13.95	.73	25
	(.5169)	(8.522)**	(7.358)	(21.14)		
Kentucky House	.1885	21.09	−18.60	42.32	.85	100
	(.0800)**	(2.593)***	(2.723)***	(3.856)***		
Kentucky Senate	1.409	3.405	−16.60	−3.69	.79	19
	(.3704)**	(6.027)	(5.430)**	(15.64)		
Ohio House	.7816	6.777	−8.71	10.76	.88	99
	(.0601)***	(1.896)***	(1.793)***	(3.396)**		
Ohio Senate	1.063	3.494	−3.77	−3.44	.92	17
	(.1135)***	(3.704)	(3.867)	(6.755)		
Texas House	.6861	15.78	−8.74	16.01	.82	150
	(.0642)***	(2.277)***	(2.132)***	(3.087)***		
Texas Senate	.8087	12.31	−10.20	12.53	.86	31
	(.1824)***	(5.140)**	(4.606)**	(8.098)		

Idaho House	.7354	16.08	−1.16	16.08	.37	70
	(.1850)***	(4.766)***	(3.130)	(5.796)*		
Idaho Senate	.7039	9.839	−9.99	22.41	.43	35
	(.2161)**	(7.664)	(3.515)**	(6.909)**		
Washington House	1.006	6.693	−2.63	−4.95	.71	98
	(.0950)***	(2.557)**	(2.764)	(6.909)**		
Washington Senate	.8941	8.023	−5.13	1.556	.70	24
	(.2070)***	(6.043)	(6.166)	(12.07)		

Notes: OLS
Standard Errors in Parentheses
***$p < .001$
**$p < .01$
*$p < .05$
Only half the seats were up for election in the:
Ohio Senate
Washington Senate
Indiana Senate
Kentucky Senate

The base model is as follows:

% Democratic Vote = constant + (Base Vote + Incumbency) + μ

where:

% Democratic Vote = Democratic Percentage of vote for the district race

Base Vote = Democratic Presidential Vote Percentage in the district

Incumbency = Coded for whether or not each party ran an incumbent in a district

In these models, I am concerned with which party won in a district in a single election and not summaries of the electoral system (such as seats-votes curves, bias, and responsiveness). I include uncontested elections with an adjusted district vote total, as suggested by Gelman and King. In each case, I convert uncontested Democratic seats to a vote share of 75 percent of the Democratic vote and uncontested Republican votes to 25 percent of the Democratic vote. This avoids dropping large number of cases in several states and attempts to capture the effect on voters if they had a say in a district (see Gelman and King for an extensive discussion of this issue).

Seats-Votes Relationship

The hypothetical swing ratio takes the actual percentage of votes and seats and generates data points based on how many seats the party would have won if it had gained or lost votes uniformly across all districts. Despite the assumption of uniform vote gains or losses across districts and the arbitrariness of generating outcomes within a set "competitive" threshold (generally +/– 5 percent points of the actual outcomes), the hypothetical swing ratio is commonly used and seen as the appropriate method for generating responsiveness and partisan bias measures.[3] From this hypothetical swing ratio, bias is

Table A3.2. Hypothetical Seats-Votes Changes

Chamber	*−5%*	*−4%*	*−3%*	*−2%*	*−1%*	*2002 Vote*	*1%*	*2%*	*3%*	*4%*	*5%*	*Total Races*
Georgia House	100	100	103	103	105	106	107	107	108	109	109	180
Georgia Senate	28	29	29	29	29	30	32	33	34	35	36	56
Michigan House	42	43	43	44	46	47	47	49	49	50	50	110
Michigan Senate	16	16	16	16	16	16	16	17	18	18	18	38
Indiana House	45	46	47	48	49	51	51	52	52	52	52	100
Indiana Senate	9	9	9	9	10	10	10	10	10	10	10	25
Kentucky House	65	65	65	65	65	65	65	65	66	67	68	100
Kentucky Senate	6	6	6	6	6	6	6	7	7	7	7	19
Ohio House	37	37	37	37	37	37	37	37	37	37	37	99
Ohio Senate	7	8	8	8	8	8	9	9	9	9	9	17
Texas House	59	60	60	61	61	62	62	62	62	62	63	150
Texas Senate	12	12	12	12	12	12	12	12	12	12	12	31
Idaho House	12	13	13	13	13	16	16	19	19	19	19	70
Idaho Senate	6	6	6	6	7	7	7	7	7	7	8	35
Washington House	44	46	47	49	51	52	53	54	55	56	57	98
Washington Senate	12	12	12	12	12	12	13	13	14	16	16	24

Notes: Cell entries represent Democratic seats won
2002 Vote = seats won based on actual vote
Positive change are more Democratic, negative change more Republican

primarily measured as the difference in the percentage of seats parties receive when they are projected to have the same percentage of the vote and allows for a comparison of both parties in winning seats at any percentage of the vote. With this, I can look for evidence of gerrymandering based on the responsiveness of the plans. In a gerrymandered plan, I expect to find outcomes that do not exhibit responsiveness in terms of a corresponding shift between the votes a party won in an election and the seats won. Specifically, in a partisan gerrymander, I expect to find the controlling party won as many seats as possible with the fewest votes possible.

Notes

1. Andrew Gelman and Gary King, "A Unified Method of Evaluating Electoral Systems and Redistricting Plans," *American Journal of Political Science* 38 (1994): 514–54; Ronald Keith Gaddie and Charles S. Bullock III, "The Political Consequences of an Uncontrolled Redistricting" (paper presented at the annual meeting of the Southern Political Science Association, New Orleans, January 2005); and J. Morgan Kousser, "Estimating the Partisan Consequences of Redistricting Plans-Simply," *Legislative Studies Quarterly* 21 (1996): 521–41.

2. Kousser, "Estimating the Partisan Consequences," 522.

3. For more information, please see Gelman and King, "A Unified Method"; Richard Niemi and Patrick Fett, "The Swing Ratio: An Explanation and an Assessment," *Legislative Studies Quarterly* 11 (1986): 75–90; and Janet Campagna and Bernard Grofman, "Party Control and Partisan Bias in 1980s Congressional Redistricting," *Journal of Politics* 52 (1990): 1242–57.

Selected Bibliography

Adams, Bruce. *Toward a System of "Fair and Effective Representation": A Common Cause Report on State and Congressional Reapportionment*. Washington, D.C.: Common Cause, 1977.

Alm, Leslie R., Ross E. Burkhart, W. David Patton, and James B. Weatherby. "Intrastate Regional Differences in Political Culture: A Case Study of Idaho." *State and Local Government Review* 33, no. 2 (2001): 109–19.

Altman, Micah. "Districting Principles and Democratic Representation." Ph.D. diss., California Institute of Technology, 1998.

Baker, Gordon. *The Reapportionment Revolution*. New York: Random House, 1967.

Barber, Kathleen L. "Michigan." In *Reapportionment Politics: The History of Redistricting in the 50 States*, edited by Leroy Hardy, Alan Heslop, and Stuart Anderson. Beverly Hills, Calif.: Sage Publications, 1981.

———. "Ohio." In *Reapportionment Politics: The History of Redistricting in the 50 States*, edited by Leroy Hardy, Alan Heslop, and Stuart Anderson. Beverly Hills, Calif.: Sage Publications, 1981.

Basehart, Harry, and John Comer. "Partisan and Incumbent Effects in State Legislative Redistricting." *Legislative Studies Quarterly* 16, no. 1 (1991): 65–79.

Bensen, Clark. "Substantial Political Consequences, A Practitioner's Perspective on Redistricting." *Extensions* Fall (2004): 5–8.

Billingsley, Keith R. "Georgia." In *Reapportionment Politics: The History of Redistricting in the 50 States*, edited by Leroy Hardy, Alan Heslop, and Stuart Anderson. Beverly Hills, Calif.: Sage Publications, 1981.

Bone, Hugh A., and Richard Morrill. "Washington." In *Reapportionment Politics: The History of Redistricting in the 50 States*, edited by Leroy Hardy, Alan Heslop, and Stuart Anderson. Beverly Hills, Calif.: Sage Publications, 1981.

Born, Richard. "Partisan Intentions and Election Day Realities in the Congressional Redistricting Process." *American Political Science Review* 79, no. 2 (1985): 305–19.

Butler, David, and Bruce Cain. *Congressional Redistricting: Comparative and Theoretical Perspectives*. New York: MacMillan, 1992.

Cain, Bruce. "Assessing the Partisan Effects of Redistricting." *American Political Science Review* 79, no. 2 (1985): 320–33.

Cain, Bruce, and Janet Campagna. "Predicting Partisan Redistricting Disputes." *Legislative Studies Quarterly* 12, no. 2 (1987): 265–74.

Campagna, Janet, and Bernard Grofman. "Party Control and Partisan Bias in 1980s Congressional Redistricting." *Journal of Politics* 52, no. 4 (1990): 1242–57.

Chamberlin, John R. "The Republicans Take Control: The 2001 Redistricting in Michigan." In *Redistricting in the New Millennium*, edited by Peter F. Galderisi. Lanham, Md.: Lexington Books, 2005.

Claunch, Ronald G., Wesley S. Chumlea, and James G. Dickson Jr. "Texas." In *Reapportionment Politics: The History of Redistricting in the 50 States*, edited by Leroy Hardy, Alan Heslop, and Stuart Anderson. Beverly Hills, Calif.: Sage Publications, 1981.

Cox, Gary W., and Jonathan N. Katz. *Elbridge Gerry's Salamander: The Electoral Consequences of the Reapportionment Revolution*. Cambridge: Cambridge University Press, 2002.

Coyle, Marcia. "High Court Will Weigh U.S. House Remapping; Gerrymandering Might Have Limits." *National Law Journal*, December 8 (2003).

Cranor, John, Gary Crawley, and Raymond Scheele. "The Anatomy of a Gerrymander." *American Journal of Political Science* 33, no. 1 (1989): 222–39.

Desposato, Scott W., and John R. Petrocik. "The Variable Incumbency Advantage: New Voters, Redistricting, and the Personal Vote." *American Journal of Political Science* 47, no. 1 (2003): 18–32.

Duffy, Shannon P. "U.S. Supreme Court Rejects PA Democrats Redistricting Suit; Splintered Decision Leaves Small Opening for Future 'Partisan Gerrymandering' Lawsuits." *Pennsylvania Law Weekly* May 3 (2004).

Engstrom, Richard L. "Political Cartography in Kentucky: Legislative Redistricting, 1971." Ph.D. diss., University of Kentucky, 1971.

———. "The Post-2000 Round of Redistricting: An Entangled Thicket within the Federal System." *Publius: The Journal of Federalism* 32, no. 4 (2002): 51–70.

Engstrom, Richard N. "District Geography and Voters." In *Redistricting in the New Millennium*, edited by Peter F. Galderisi. Lanham, Md.: Lexington Books, 2005.

Epstein, David, and Sharyn O'Halloran. "Measuring the Electoral and Policy Impact of Majority-Minority Voting Districts: Candidates of Choice, Equal Opportunity, and Representation." *American Journal of Political Science* 43, no. 2 (1999): 367–95.

Erikson, Robert. "Malapportionment, Gerrymandering, and Party Fortunes." *American Political Science Review* 66, no. 4 (1972): 1234–45.

Farrand, Max. *The Records of the Federal Convention of 1787*. New Haven, Conn.: Yale University Press, 1966.

Ferejohn, John A. "On the Decline of Competition in Congressional Elections." *American Political Science Review* 71, no. 1 (1977): 166–76.

Friedrich, Robert J. "In Defense of Multiplicative Terms in Multiple Regression Equations." *American Journal of Political Science* 26, no. 4 (1982): 797–33.

Gaddie, Ronald Keith, and Charles S. Bullock III. *Elections to Open Seats in the U.S. House: Where the Action Is*. Lanham, Md.: Rowman and Littlefield, 2000.

———. "The Political Consequences of an Uncontrolled Redistricting." Paper presented at the annual meeting of the Southern Political Science Association, New Orleans, January 2005.

Gelman, Andrew, and Gary King. "Enhancing Democracy through Legislative Redistricting." *American Political Science Review* 88, no. 3 (1994): 541–59.

———. "A Unified Method of Evaluating Electoral Systems and Redistricting Plans." *American Journal of Political Science* 38, no. 2 (1994): 514–54.

Glazer, Amihai, Bernard Grofman, and Marc Robbins. "Partisan and Incumbency Effects of 1970s Congressional Redistricting." *American Journal of Political Science* 31, no. 3 (1987): 680–707.

Gopoian, J. David, and Darrell M. West. "Trading Security for Seats: Strategic Considerations in the Redistricting Process." *Journal of Politics* 46, no. 4 (1984): 1080–96.

Grofman, Bernard. "Criteria for Districting: A Social Science Perspective." *UCLA Law Review* 33, no. 1 (1985): 77–185.

———. "Would Vince Lombardi Have Been Right If He Had Said: 'When It Comes to Redistricting, Race, Isn't Everything, It's the Only Thing'?" *Cardozo Law Review* 14, no. 5 (1993): 1237–76.

Grofman, Bernard, and Lisa Handley. "Estimating the Impact of Voting-Rights-Act-Related Districting on Democratic Strength in the U.S. House of Representatives." In *Race and Redistricting in the 1990s*, edited by Bernard Grofman. New York: Agathon Press, 1988.

Gronke, Paul, and J. Matthew Wilson. "Competing Redistricting Plans as Evidence of Political Motives: The North Carolina Case." *American Politics Quarterly* 27 (1999): 147–76.

Hardy, Leroy, Alan Heslop, and Stuart Anderson, editors. *Reapportionment Politics: The History of Redistricting in the 50 States*. Beverly Hills, Calif.: Sage Publications, 1981.

Hardy, Melissa A. *Regression with Dummy Variables*. Newbury Park, Calif.: Sage Publications, 1993.

Jacobson, Gary. "The Marginals Never Vanished: Incumbency and Competition in Elections to the U.S. House of Representatives, 1952–1982." *American Journal of Political Science* 31, no. 1 (1987): 126–41.

Key, V. O. *Southern Politics in State and Nation*. New York: Vintage Books, 1949.

King, Gary. "Representation Through Legislative Redistricting: A Stochastic Model." *American Journal of Political Science* 33, no. 4 (1989): 787–824.

Kousser, J. Morgan. "Estimating the Partisan Consequences of Redistricting Plans-Simply." *Legislative Studies Quarterly* 21, no. 4 (1996): 521–41.

Kubin, Jeffrey C. "The Case for Redistricting Commissions." *Texas Law Review* 75, no. 4 (1997): 837–72.

Locke, John. *The Second Treatise of Government*, edited by Thomas P. Peardon. New York: Macmillan, [1960] 1952.

Lublin, David. *The Paradox of Representation*. Princeton, N.J.: Princeton University Press, 1997.

Lublin, David, and D. Stephen Voss. "Racial Redistricting and Realignment in Southern State Legislatures." *American Journal of Political Science* 44, no. 4 (2000): 792–810.

Mayhew, David. *Congress: The Electoral Connection*. New Haven, Conn.: Yale University Press, 1974.

McDonald, Michael P. "A Comparative Analysis of Redistricting Institutions in the United States, 2001–2002." *State Politics and Policy Quarterly* 4, no. 4 (2004): 371–95.

McDowell, James L. "Indiana." In *Reapportionment Politics: The History of Redistricting in the 50 States*, edited by Leroy Hardy, Alan Heslop, and Stuart Anderson. Beverly Hills, Calif.: Sage Publications, 1981.

McFeeley, Neil. D., and H. Sydney Duncombe. "Idaho." In *Reapportionment Politics: The History of Redistricting in the 50 States*, edited by Leroy Hardy, Alan Heslop, and Stuart Anderson. Beverly Hills, Calif.: Sage Publications, 1981.

McKee, Seth C., and Daron R. Shaw. "Redistricting in Texas: Institutionalizing Republican Ascendancy." In *Redistricting in the New Millennium*, edited by Peter F. Galderisi. Lanham, Md.: Lexington Books, 2005.

McKee, Seth C., Jeremy M. Teigen, and Mathieu Turgeon. "The Partisan Impact of Congressional Redistricting: The Case of Texas, 2001–2003." *Social Science Quarterly* 87, no. 2 (2006): 308–17.

Monmonier, Mark. *Bushmanders and Bullwinkles: How Politicians Manipulate Electronic Maps and Census Data to Win Elections*. Chicago: University of Chicago Press, 2001.

Morrill, Richard. *Political Redistricting and Geographic Theory*. Washington, D.C.: Association of American Geographers, 1981.

Niemi, Richard, and Patrick Fett. "The Swing Ratio: An Explanation and an Assessment." *Legislative Studies Quarterly* 11, no. 1 (1986): 75–90.

Niemi, Richard, and Simon Jackman. "Bias and Responsiveness in State Legislative Districting." *Legislative Studies Quarterly* 16, no. 2 (1991): 183–202.

Ostdick, Donald. "Congressional Redistricting and District Typologies." *Journal of Politics* 57, no. 2 (1995): 533–43.

Owen, Guillermo, and Bernard Grofman. "Optimal Partisan Gerrymandering." *Political Geography Quarterly* 7, no. 1 (1988): 5–22.

Persily, Nathaniel. "Forty Years in the Political Thicket: Judicial Review of the Redistricting Process since *Reynolds v. Sims*." In *Party Lines: Competition, Partisanship, and Congressional Redistricting*, edited by Thomas E. Mann and Bruce E. Cain. Washington, D.C.: Brookings Institution Press, 2005.

Petrocik, John R., and Scott W. Desposato. "The Partisan Effects of Majority Minority Districting, 1992–1994." *Journal of Politics*. 66, no. 3 (1998): 613–33.

Rush, Mark. *Does Redistricting Make a Difference: Partisan Representation and Electoral Behavior*. Lanham, Md.: Lexington Books, 2000.

Schaffner, Brian F. "House Members, Legislative Activities, and Local Coverage." Ph.D. diss., Indiana University, 2002.

Schaffner, Brian F., Michael W. Wagner, and Jonathan Winburn. "Incumbents Out, Party In? Term Limits and Partisan Redistricting in State Legislatures." *State Politics and Policy Quarterly* 4, no. 4 (2004): 396–414.

Singleton, J. Allen. "Kentucky." In *Reapportionment Politics: The History of Redistricting in the 50 States*, edited by Leroy Hardy, Alan Heslop, and Stuart Anderson. Beverly Hills, Calif.: Sage Publications, 1981.

Storey, Tim. "2002 State Legislative Elections." *Spectrum: The Journal of State Government* 76, no. 1 (2003): 7–11.

Swain, Carol. *Black Faces, Black Interests: The Representation of African-Americans in Congress*. Cambridge, Mass.: Harvard University Press, 1993.

Swain, John W., Stephen A. Borrelli, and Brian C. Reed. "Partisan Consequences of the Post-1990 Redistricting for the U.S. House of Representatives." *Political Research Quarterly* 51, no. 4 (1998): 945–67.

Thompson, Dennis. *Just Elections: Creating a Fair Electoral Process in the United States*. Chicago: University of Chicago Press, 2002.

Tufte, Edward. "The Relationship between Seats and Votes in Two-Party Systems." *American Political Science Review* 67, no. 3 (1973): 540–54.

Van Dunk, Emily, and Ronald E. Weber. "Constituency-Level Competition in the U.S. States, 1968–1988: A Pooled Analysis." *Legislative Studies Quarterly* 22, no. 2 (1997): 141–59.

Weber, Ronald. 2002. "Emerging Trends in State Legislative Redistricting." *Spectrum: The Journal of State Government* 75, no. 1 (2002): 13–15.

Wright, Gerald, Tracy Osborn, and Jon Winburn. "Parties and Representation in the American Legislatures." Paper presented at the annual meeting of the Midwest Political Science Association, Chicago, April 2004.

Wright, Gerald, and Jon Winburn. "The Effects of Size and Party on the Dimensionality of Roll Calls." Paper presented at the annual conference on State Politics and Policy, Tucson, Ariz., March 2003.

Index

About the Author

Jonathan Winburn is assistant professor of political science at the University of Mississippi.